ADDICT

A true life story by Stephen Smith

Drugs imprisoned me for twenty-six years of my life.
Towards the end of my addiction I lived in shop
doorways on the streets of London.

When all was lost a miracle came along which enabled
me to rejoin the human race. I know of nobody who
slipped so far down for so long and had the good
fortune to come back.

I hope this book serves as a lesson for others and helps
those less fortunate who are still in the clutches of
addiction.

http://www.addict.fm

First published 1997 © Stephen Smith
The right of Stephen Smith to be identified as Author of
this work has been asserted by him in accordance with
the Copyright, Designs and Patents Act 1988.

Published by Westworld International Limited,
London, England.
020 7222 4002
A CIP catalogue record for this book is available
from the British Library. ISBN 0-952-9215 0 2

Printed in the UK by CPI Bookmarque, Croydon, CR0 4TD

1st printing January 1997
2nd printing November 1997
3rd printing August 1998
4th printing March 1999
5th printing July 1999
6th printing October 1999
7th printing April 2000
8th printing December 2000
9th printing September 2001
10th printing March 2002
11th printing December 2002
12th printing January 2004
13th printing August 2005
14th printing April 2009

Westworld International Limited will donate 5% of the
purchase price of each book sold, (this being the
author's royalty) to helping homeless people either by
donations to registered charities or by giving directly to
those living in the streets.

We are born and we die. Those are your only two guarantees.

The rest your life is just a series of pages turning over till the end. Don't read anything twice. That won't change the words you've already read. Turn over and experience the next page.

Relax, go with the flow because you're not really writing your story. It's already been written.

CONTENTS

Introduction

Introduction

A CHILD ON ROUTE TO ADDICTION

At the age of fourteen I became addicted to amphetamine and for twenty-five years I took up to one hundred tablets a day. The drugs led me to a bizarre life of crime and lunacy. As the addiction took its toll I fell from being a playboy, owning expensive homes and horses, to live in Salvation Army hostels, ending up alone on the streets with the winos of skid row. Why did all this happen to me? Looking at young children today I wonder if some of them are just a few years away from a similar roller coaster hell-ride. Why are some youngsters destined for a life like mine with all the hallmarks of a horror movie? What distinguishes them from the others, the normal children? Maybe my story has the answers.

I grew up just after the war in a boring middle-class London suburb called Winchmore Hill where nothing ever happened. Every street looked alike with rows and rows of semi-detached houses.

Mum and Dad met on a bus and instantly fell in love. Their family backgrounds were totally different. He was Jewish and defied his orthodox parents by marrying mum, a Christian from a working class family. They had two weddings, the first for her family in church and a second the following day in a synagogue for his Jewish relatives. Neither family attended or even knew of the other side's celebration. To marry in a synagogue my mother had to actually change her religion to Jewish.

When I was born my parents were both thirty-four. I had a sister five years older than me called Annette, a pretty little girl with curly black hair who had just started school. In 1945 my father had opened a tailor shop which soon began to prosper. The war was over and the returning soldiers were all buying suits with their government clothes coupons. Dad made a lot of money then and we became by far the richest people in our street. Those were the days of ration books but there was always plenty of black market food on our table. We were the first in our street to own a car and all crammed into it every summer to go to the South of France where for two weeks my father gambled non-stop in the casinos, leaving us on the beach all day.

My mother was an extremely attractive woman, slim and blonde with Marilyn Monroe looks who, having grown up in poverty, relished in my father's new-found affluence. She was a poser who loved to be admired in her fancy clothes, especially by her working class sisters.

Father was a good-looking man. He wore his dark hair combed back in a central parting and I remember him always wearing suits, even at home. He chain smoked all day. Dad became very fat but being tall presented a commanding figure, not unlike the older Marlon Brando. He extended our house, adding a garage, two extra bedrooms and a large fitted kitchen, trying to turn our small semi into a mini mansion. A high brick wall surrounded our back garden and the front was completely paved over. This was totally different from the neighbours' gardens where roses and jasmine grew around their manicured lawns. With no flowers our garden knew no seasons, the concrete and weeds always looked the same. Like our garden as a family we were different, misfits in that street.

Dad never hit us but he was the boss in our house and my mother always had to make sure his three course dinner was ready and waiting. As a couple my parents never seemed very loving towards each other, their relationship was more like a business deal with mum cooking and dad financing the expensive lifestyle. As their wealth improved dad became a compulsive gambler but my mother was more than happy to be out with him in the posh club surroundings where she mixed and dined with the other gamblers' wives. Materialistically my sister and I never lacked for anything but in terms of love and affection we got nothing. I don't recall my parents ever reading us bedtime stories or playing with us. They were simply not there but always out socialising, leaving us to be brought up by a series of live-in nannies. The only evening they were in was Wednesdays which was card night at our house. A green baize table would especially come out along with expensive cakes for visiting players. We children were not allowed to touch, let alone eat one.

When I was born a new nanny had just started. Her name was Violet. She was a short, stocky woman of about sixty with grey hair and thick glasses. Violet never had the child she had so desperately wanted and showered all her locked-up affection on me. Her love, however, never extended to my sister who was a headstrong little girl and wouldn't be manipulated by the new nanny.

I became Violet's favourite. She talked and played with me all day, always calling me 'her Stephen'. She was cruel to Annette, often scolding her and so it is little surprising that my sister came to hate the nanny along with her spoilt little brother. I became emotionally dependent on Violet and on her days off would cry non-stop, making sure she came back early or cancelled her weekend off altogether. Violet represented my mummy to me.

When I was about four Violet started to read Robin Hood to me night after night. After a while I couldn't go to sleep without it. This outlaw who robbed the rich to help the poor totally fascinated me and on my insistence for the next four years she read the same story every day. Later in life I was to copy the robbing of the rich. The only difference between me and Robin was that I kept a rather higher percentage for my own running costs.

When I was five my twin brothers were born and I persuaded my mother to call them Peter and Paul after the 'Two little Dickie Birds' poem Violet had taught me. For the next two years Violet took complete control of me while my mother struggled with the twins. When the boys were two years old mum had the first of many nervous breakdowns. From then on mum was constantly in and out of hospital.

I was eight when my mother returned from a hospital following one of these breakdowns and suddenly sacked Violet without notice. Mum had become jealous of my affection for her and she was replaced with a French nanny whom I hated. Annette, of course, who was now learning French at school loved the new girl but to me she was just the strange woman from France. Alone now with nobody to read to me at night I cried myself to sleep and started to wet the bed, continuing to do so until I was twelve.

Sometimes at night when I was in bed the lights upstairs would suddenly go off and a monster appeared, shining a torch in my face. This was no dream. It was real. When the lights went on the monster vanished. I never forgot its face.

About this time I began having two recurring nightmares. I dreamt that my bedroom became detached from the house and was floating off to the sky. To calm me down the landing light was left on with my door open. My dream was so real I tied a piece of string to my bed, trailing it down the stairs and tying it to the bottom stair-rail. In the second nightmare I was tormented by two identical Violets who were fighting for my love, both saying, 'I'm your real Violet'. To solve this awful dilemma I had to stab the pretender with our family carving knife. As I plunged the knife into who I thought was the bad Violet blood squirted out and I always woke up screaming.

I became obsessed with my toys and other possessions which I jealously guarded. When Eric Shepherd, who lived opposite, came to play I threw his toys over into the cemetery behind our garden, thinking to myself, you have a dad who plays football with you, you don't need them. I warned Eric that if he ever tried to retrieve his games the dead would get him. When he went home I climbed over the big wall, adding his cowboy guns etc. to my hidden collection. All other visiting kids suffered the same fate.

I remember catching flies with a glass to burn their wings off one at a time, getting a great sense of power as they crawled about helpless. When our cat had kittens I separated and hid the young from the mother cat, reasoning that if I couldn't have my mum, why should the kittens have theirs?

One day I was looking through a drawer in my mother's bedroom where to my horror I found a mask. It was the monster's face. I cut it into pieces and threw it over to the dead people in the cemetery behind our house. The monster and his torch never came to scare me again.

Soon after that I discovered an abandoned nursery in our neighbourhood with derelict greenhouses and a wooden shed. There was a table with chairs inside and the door locked with a rusty key. It was the perfect headquarters for me and my gang of three younger boys whom I used as obedient slaves to boost my already shaky ego. Plotting our wild childhood schemes we looked like characters from the 'Just William' stories with grubby faces, grey short trousers and knitted jumpers. One day, out of the blue, disaster struck. Annette, my elder sister, was outside giggling at us with two of her big friends. I was devastated. Once again the bully had destroyed my world. Furious and not wanting her to get the shed I plotted revenge. Using oil found in discarded petrol cans I set fire to the entire nursery compound. Quickly it spread and I ran back to our house to watch the enormous blaze from my bedroom window. I felt proud as the flames leapt into the sky and crowds gathered to watch the fire brigade fight the blaze for hours. Walking amongst the ashes the following day I found the rusty key to my vanished empire. Well, no one has got the shed now ! I thought with satisfaction. That fire marked the beginning of a habit of a lifetime, 'Burn the lot - bury the ashes,' after each crime to ensure my past was always hidden with only God and myself left to testify.

I never liked school. Lessons bored me and I rebelled against the discipline. I stole books, taking them home to hide under my bed, telling myself that Violet would be back to read them to me one day. I was always bottom of the class in every subject up to the age of eleven when I had to take the compulsory eleven-plus exam. This test at the end of elementary school divided pupils between a grammar or secondary modern school education - doctors and stockbrokers to the right, factory and manual workers to the left. With six months to go my father sprang into action, realising I would never pass. For his Jewish son to go to a secondary modern school was out of the question so he paid to have me privately tutored every night to ensure success. In six short months I went from bottom to top, passing the exam with honours and qualified for Edmonton Grammar School which only accepted the highest of grades.

My sister Annette had just graduated from this school where she had been head girl and captain of the hockey team. Naturally she'd passed her exams with her usual bloody brilliance and was a hard act to follow. From the start I hated the uniform, especially the blue and yellow cap. I also felt self conscious and different in short trousers when every other boy was already wearing long ones. I begged my father for long trousers but he insisted I wore the short ones out first.

Initially I was proud of my eleven-plus results but soon reverted back to my accustomed position at the bottom of the class. Amongst the six hundred pupils in that school only two were Jewish. One was a boy with the tell-tale name of Levy and the biggest nose God had ever dished out. The other one was me. I knew Levy from Synagogue but avoided contact with him at school like the plague. At first no one knew I was Jewish and I intended to keep it that way because at Edmonton County anti-Semitism was rampant, I could tell from the jokes made about Jewish people. The only difference between the kids there and Hitler was that they didn't actually try to gas me. Every time my father forced me to take a day off school for Jewish holidays I

12

covered up by forging a parent's note saying I'd been ill. But one day the inevitable happened. I was caught out and in front of the entire class my teacher asked me the dreaded question, 'Are you Jewish?' 'No, not really,' I replied. 'Only sort-of.' From the reaction of my classmates you would have thought I had leprosy. That day at playtime I felt like an outcast, more isolated than ever before. All the other children talked about me. I was now one of those dirty Jew boys they always joked about. With no child wanting to sit next to the Jew, I was put at the front on my own.

The only thing I was good at was long distance running. My fantasy was to beat Roger Bannister's 1954 four minute mile. I practised most playtimes which saved me from mixing and being teased by the other kids. The teachers were furious when I arrived for their lessons panting, having run there directly from the race track.

My emotional support at home was nil. My eight-year-old twin brothers just represented two snotty-nosed pests and Annette at eighteen was out with her grown-up boyfriends. I was now nearly thirteen and felt more lost each day until a miracle happened. I met Raymond, a Jewish boy nine months older than me, at our Hebrew Sunday School. Ray became precious to me. He was bigger than me in size and more grown-up in every way. Every day after school we went over to the park on our bikes or to one of the new local coffee bars with their juke boxes. Ray had his own record player and we often listened to his 78" records one of which was by a young man from America singing, 'You ain't nothing but a hound dog.' Elvis had arrived and with him a new era was beginning. I was instantly mesmerised by Elvis who was so unlike Guy Mitchell and the other tame crooners my mum and dad liked. In a funny way Raymond and Elvis almost blended into one. I admired them both. Like Elvis, Ray combed his hair back for our weekly visits to a Jewish youth club. We danced to Bill Hayley's 'Rock Around the Clock' with girls wearing petticoats and lacquered hairstyles. A week after seeing Ray in his latest outfit, blue suede shoes and drainpipe trousers, I arrived in the same hip gear. He was a super jiver, never short of a girl and captivated them all with his smile. As his willing lieutenant I learnt fast and was soon drawing level.

Ray started to see a girl every Saturday and began boasting about his exploits. After their first date he told me how he had touched her tits, putting his hand on top of her jumper. The second week he had his hand inside her brassiere. By week three his hand was down her knickers and by week four she had his dick out - I couldn't wait for the news from week five. He was streets ahead of me where sexuality was concerned. I hadn't even kissed a girl, let alone touched one.

One day in the park Raymond explained the facts of life to me, having just been told by his father. I listened intently, thinking, why the fuck didn't my dad tell me all this? Ray finished his lesson with a demonstration on how to get your dick stiff and make the white stuff come out, masturbating in front of me. That night I began experimenting with my own dick but it frightened me and I stopped.

Over the fourteen months we knew each other we became inseparable, two teenagers growing up. I even went away with him and his parents for a week to Bournemouth at the seaside. Sometime later I kissed my first girl and afterwards remarked to Ray that I couldn't see what the big deal was with this tit business, they

14

just felt soft to me. He laughed and said, 'You'll soon get to like them.'

One day we followed two girls home and larked about with them outside their house, completely forgetting about the time. I never thought that this would lead to the first of two devastating events which were to change my entire life.

That fateful night Raymond's dad, who was very strict about the time his son came home, was furious. We were exactly thirty minutes late but he acted as if we had just committed a major crime and rang my parents there and then to inform them of his decision. He was banning us from seeing each other for six months. To a fourteen-year-old six months seemed a life-sentence. Not understanding what we had done so wrong I cycled home in tears. The next morning I woke up heartbroken, realising I had no Raymond anymore. I had nobody again.

I hated Ray's dad so much for what he did to me that for the next twenty years I made periodical midnight phone calls just to disturb this man's sleep. That Monday night was my last contact with Raymond for thirty-five years. When he told me all those years later that his father had died I was so delighted I celebrated with the best champagne.

Those fateful six months of the ban were to take me far away from Raymond into another world altogether.

I was now a very hurt fourteen-year-old when the following day at school the second blow hit me. Money had been reported missing from children's coat pockets and at morning assembly I was accused of stealing it in front of the entire school. Knowing I was innocent didn't save me from the overwhelming feelings of shame and humiliation. It was just too much for me to bear and I was unable to face going to school ever again. Pretending to my parents to carry on as normal I now headed for the park each day. I was caught truanting several times and taken back but refused to stay and just ran away at the first opportunity. I never attended school in my life again.

Chapter 1

MY FIRST CRIME

By banning me from seeing my best and only friend, Raymond's father destroyed my world. His action was the key that opened the door to a bizarre life of crime and drug addiction.

Early in 1958 I started venturing into rougher neighbourhoods and it was here I met Brian, who at sixteen was two years older than me. He was a tall boy and street wise way advanced on Raymond. He always wore a leather jacket and with his greased brown hair combed back in a DA (ducks arse) style was a typical fifties Teddy Boy. His elder brother Harry was a member of a feared motorbike gang and they both had lots of pocket money to spend. Brian was a confident boy, always laughing and sharing his sweets or Woodbine cigarettes with other kids in the park. Everyone seemed to know him. Getting bigger and wilder myself I began to treat Brian as an equal. I was growing up fast, too bloody fast. In the evenings we all hung round the bikers' cafe dressed in drain-pipe trousers, suede chucka boots and leather jackets looking like little Marlon Brandos. That February lots of boys in the cafe wore black arm bands. The whole nation was shocked following the plane crash in Munich which had killed many of "Busby's Babes", Manchester United Football team.

One evening when we were out together Brian was beaten up by a vicious bully. He put up a brave defence but finished up with a black eye and a swollen lip. After the bully left I, the brave one who hadn't even

17

dared to become involved in the argument, said to Brian, 'Don't worry, we'll pay the bastard back.' The following night the same nasty character found me alone and began to hassle me. He pushed me over and started kicking me but instead of fighting back as Brian had done I just lay on the ground covering my face, pleading for mercy. The guy, a fat boy with red curly hair, got annoyed. He stood over me and screamed, 'Get up and fight, you big softie !' But I was too scared even to move. A passer-by interrupted the kicking and the bully ran off, leaving me crying on the ground. Finally I picked myself up and went home quite badly beaten but even more ashamed of my cowardice.

That evening, for the first time in my life I helped myself to a bottle of wine from the family drinks cabinet - to 'steady my nerves'. This wine changed me instantly - from a timid fourteen-year-old coward afraid of physical fights into a wild tiger full of courage. After several more swigs I became a little monster and jumped on my bike, riding round to the bully's house which was in the roughest of areas called Barrowell Green. The small, scruffy looking terraced houses looked so different to the spacious semi-detached ones in my street. Standing in his front garden surrounded by rubbish I could hear the Lonnie Donnegan record 'My old Man's a Dustman' going full blast somewhere. Banging on the front door, screaming hysterically, I confronted my tormentor in front of his mother and older brothers. Shouting at the top of my voice, 'I want a fight ! I'll kill you ! I'll burn your bloody house down !' I made such a scene that people came to their doors to see who was challenging the infamous Sullivan brothers. The red haired bully and his bigger brothers stood there speechless as their mother, curlers in hair, called to a neighbour to get help. With me still screaming my threats the local policeman arrived and trying to calm down the whole scene made the bully boy apologise to me for my swollen lip. Satisfied with myself I finally rode off, shouting back to the crowd, 'Be careful next time !' That night I felt like Al Capone.

When I woke the next morning I went into a panic, horrified at the drunken threats I'd made the night before. I was so afraid I decided to call at the bully's house to apologise and was on my way there when I met him and his brothers in the street. Expecting the worst I came out in a cold sweat but to my amazement all three just smiled and shook my hand with respect. Later I met Brian who'd already heard about my threatening the Sullivans. I had become an instant hero. But at what cost ! This incident had taught me a fateful lesson which was to alter my entire life. I'd discovered bravery in a bottle, always available in a variety of flavours. With a bit of chemical assistance I had overcome my inhibitions and feelings of inadequacy, finding enough courage to bluff the bully and his family. Wine had given me back the confidence which the previous events of my life had so sadly knocked out of me.

Alcohol changed my personality and I became the leader in my relationship with Brian who now looked to me with stars in his eyes. Wine made me want to escape from the humdrum life of North London into a fantasy world like the one Robin Hood lived in. I was getting bored of hanging round the parks like all the other kids and looking for action said to Brian, 'Come on, we're not sissies, having army haircuts. It's Elvis who's joined the army, not us !' Soon afterwards I suggested we went out robbing people. We could swoop like highwaymen on our bikes and snatch women's handbags. That evening the two of us followed an old lady from the local train station into a quiet street. I was full of wine and on giving the signal we rode up either side of her as I snatched her bag. My heart was pounding as we raced away and with her screams fading in the distance I suddenly realised that Brian had gone, leaving me alone on my getaway bike. Clutching the handbag I cycled to some nearby fields where I emptied it to find twenty pounds, a great deal of money those days. Stuffing the cash into my pockets I hid the bag, pushing it to the bottom of a stream. Getting rid of all possible evidence with such precision and care was to become the hallmark of my illness cum profession for many years. I kept my gloves on, just in case, until I reached the safety of my bedroom. Later in life I would always wear gloves for a week before and after each robbery.

Why did I do it? With my parents indifference and Raymond gone, was this my first cry for help? Was I thinking, better to be punished than alone and ignored?

The next day I offered Brian ten pounds, his share of the robbery but he refused, saying he couldn't carry on and was afraid of being caught. 'Haven't your parents got any red wine?' I asked him with disgust. We parted with him wishing me luck. He looked quite relieved. He was going with his brother on the motorbike to Trafalgar Square to see the first 'Ban the Bomb' march arrive from Aldermaston.

Left to continue on my own I successfully relieved the rich of their surplus cash over the weeks to follow. When my parents wine started to run down I got bigger boys to buy me some and now kept my own bottle under the bed. As the wine intake increased so did my bravado and the daring of my robberies.

20

One summer evening I spotted a woman walking down a busy road flanked by two men. Of course it was suicidal to try but swallowing the last of the wine from my handlebar bottle I mounted the pavement and rode in between them like John Wayne. The woman hung on to her bag so tight I dragged her down the road before she let go. Now the chase was on with all three running and screaming after me. Trying to get off the main road I panicked, taking the first turning to the left. It turned out to be a dead-end street with no way out. With the three grown-ups in hot pursuit I was soon caught. For a fourteen-year-old I put up a good fight against two big men but they soon overpowered me and held me down while the woman called the police. I was panic-stricken. Oh my God, I thought, what have I done?

Chapter 2

MY FIRST DRUG

As the two men held me down the woman picked
up her bag and shouted, 'How would you like someone
to snatch your mother's bag?' A crowd of people came
out in their pyjamas to investigate the commotion to
find a fourteen-year old boy fighting with two grown
men. Finally the police arrived but I was in such a state
of shock that I only vaguely remember a round-faced
policeman sitting in the back of the car with me as I was
driven to the station. Those days handbag-snatching
was a rare and serious offence. Many of my crimes had
been reported over the previous months and now every
officer wanted to see the young highwayman who had
at last been caught. Heads kept popping round the door
of the detention room to have a look. The older
policeman questioning me looked puzzled when I told
him where I lived, a respectable street, the opposite of
the rough estates where most of the delinquents came
from.

Within the hour my parents arrived. My father
was shocked and started to question me but I just stared
back in silence. My mother said nothing, just burst into
tears. It was only when I was not allowed to go home
with them that the enormity of what I had done sunk in.
After my parents left I was put into a cell for the night.
The station police were listening to the radio report
about Brazil who'd beaten Sweden 5-2 in the World
Cup. Seventeen-year-old Pele had scored. It was June
1958. The cell was dark and falling into a pit of despair I
cried all night for Violet.

The following morning in court I was led up from the cells to find three magistrates sitting in front of a huge picture of the Queen. They remanded me in custody for four weeks to obtain further reports and I was taken away in a locked police van along with two other rough looking boys. The bigger one who seemed to be an old-timer asked the driver if we were going to 'St. Nicholas Boys' Home'. 'There are some hard cases in there,' he remarked, 'this happened to me last time,' pointing to his missing front teeth. It was a sunny day and I sat in silence as we drove through the countryside. Finally we arrived at the gates of a big building with security fencing all around where we were met by a fat woman wearing a red apron. 'Are these today's junior criminals?' she joked with the driver. 'We've got a little handbag-snatcher in here,' he replied. 'Thinks he's Robin Hood !' As I got out she smirked and pulled me by the collar, 'Well, welcome Robin. I'm Maid Marion !'

The three of us were taken to a large dining room where about fifty other boys were noisily eating their bangers and mash. As we entered someone called out in an east London accent, 'Look, Barry's back. Alright old son?' greeting the boy with the missing teeth. Here, wearing khaki uniform and all much older than me, were the up and coming criminals of tomorrow. Compared to them Raymond and Brian were like babies still in their prams. That night we were shown to our bunks in a large dormitory and as the lights went out the matron shouted, 'No masturbating, go to sleep, the lot of you !'

It was next morning after breakfast when I realised I was in at the deep end in a world of teenage crime. I was put to work with two others in the kitchen. They argued about whose father was the more famous gangster when suddenly one of them took the knife he was washing and stabbed the other in the arm. I was mortified as I watched the victim stagger out of the room, leaving a trail of blood. Immediately the bigger boy grabbed me and holding the bloodstained knife to my neck told me what would happen if I told on him. 'Now scoot !' he hissed and I ran out of the kitchen, up into the dormitory to hide under my bed. When I was questioned later I maintained that I had been on the toilet when the incident happened. Amongst those big boys I realised I wasn't Robin Hood, just a very junior Merry Man !

The next three weeks were frightening, like a bad dream. My parents visited each Sunday for an hour but they seemed so far away from this world of tough boys. One group was plotting a break-out following the example of their hero Alfred Hinds who'd escaped from Chelmsford prison a few weeks before. Towards the end of my stay I became a bit braver and began to imitate Elvis as I could imagine him in the film 'Jailhouse Rock'. One evening I wanted to play billiards during the recreation period but a Scottish boy who'd been playing for ages refused to move off the table and I got angry, challenging him. During the row he hit me with the billiard cue, busting open my lip. The fact that I did not retaliate, I was too shocked to, went well for me when I appeared in court a day or so later with my face covered in bandages.

At that hearing my father somehow convinced the magistrates that it was psychiatric treatment I needed, not imprisonment. He reasoned that it was better to have a sick son living with mentally disturbed people than a healthy son in prison. I was duly sentenced to become a live-in patient at the Friern Barnet Mental Institution. At the time it appeared better than three years in a young offenders prison but in view of what was about to happen there prison would have been far better. It might have saved me from a life-sentence on drugs.

I was taken to the asylum in a locked van and it was only after the police left I fully realised that this was not a boys' detention home. Instead of young criminals now I was surrounded by strange people roaming about in dressing gowns.

Friern Barnet was a huge gothic complex of buildings set in large grounds. It had the longest corridors in Europe and lock-up wards from which patients only emerged in coffins. Many inmates had been there since the turn of the century, having been admitted as teenagers and kept under sedation for forty years. Later it was revealed that experimental brain operations had been performed without seeking their relatives' permission. While other fourteen-year-olds were at school or the unruly ones perhaps in prison I was locked in the loony-bin with seriously deranged mental patients. I was not depressed, not suicidal, not anorexic, just a kid caught stealing. I could have coped with prison but this mental institution and its patients were very scary to me. I didn't really understand why I was there.

My unit, the Halliwick Ward, was full of strange freaks locked in a large common room all day. This room, about sixty feet long, had huge windows which overlooked the grounds. Occasionally a disorientated escaped patient from another ward roamed by. There were about ten round tables with lots of chairs and the floor looked like a giant chess board with its black and white lino squares.

For the next few months I lived alongside the other twenty or so nutcases in our ward, some of whom I remember very clearly. There was Alan, an artist, tall and slim with black curly hair and a long filthy beard. He always wore a black polo neck jumper, baggy trousers and sandals and sketched the other patients all day. He was forever sharpening his pencil or holding it up to measure as artists do. When each picture was finished he carefully put it into a grey folder. Alan never spoke or wanted anyone to see his work and I think he was in for acute depression.

Another man, Mr. Do Die, moved round the lounge all day muttering, 'Don't care if I do die,' laughing to himself as he repeated the same words. All day long he climbed out of the open window, did a curtsy on the grass and then came back in. Do Die was short, in his twenties and always wore a hospital dressing gown. He refused to wear shoes or socks and had a green beret pulled down over his ears.

The noisiest patient was Fatsoe, a woman of about fifty. She must have weighed twenty stone and had breasts like water melons. She wore no bra and her nipples, big as saucers, poked through her tight nylon jumper. Fatsoe chain-smoked Park Drive cigarettes all day, lighting each new fag with the last one. Ash always fell on her tits, dropping to the floor each time she crossed the room to drop another burning dog-end into the waste bin. As she walked her trousers slipped down, showing the crack in her bum. Often she crashed into Do Die, shouting at him, 'Fuck off,' to which he always said, 'don't care if I do die.' In reply she would bark, 'Die then,' as she sat back in her usual chair by the open window. Forever clutching several packets of fags her answer was always, 'Fuck off,' if new patients asked her for a cigarette. In fact, she never said anything else.

The guy who slept in my room was Roger. He was about forty and completely bald. Roger had been brought in wearing a postman's uniform by the police who'd found him aimlessly wandering the streets at two in the morning. He'd lost his memory and didn't know who he was. He sat doing nothing all day except for when a nurse or doctor came in. As soon as he saw them he would jump up insisting he was not a postman and his name wasn't Roger.

In one corner sat Doreen, a beautiful thirty-year-old woman with long blonde hair and blue eyes. She had a good figure and wore a body-hugging yellow jumper, showing the stitching in her bra. If I sat on one of the low chairs I could look up her skirt and see her white aertex knickers. When she opened her legs I saw her pubic hairs, she was genuine blonde. Doreen rarely spoke but on one occasion told me that she didn't want to have the frontal lobotomy scheduled for the following week. She was frightened of this brain operation and cried out, 'I don't want my head cut open !'

Amongst the Jesuses, Russian spies and a boy who washed his hands all day was another regular, Mr. Money as I called him. He was a wealthy button manufacturer only in hospital, I think, to avoid a fraud charge. A good-looking man he wore expensive suits and shiny shoes which made him look more like a doctor than a patient. Most of the day he read newspapers specially sent in for him. Occasionally he talked to Doreen and behind the nurses backs tried to touch her up. Always cheerful he shared his cigarettes with all who asked. The only time he developed a troubled look was when the nurses gave him a letter one day.

We all sat together in that room all day, every day, watching the hands go round on the big wall clock. In the evenings we listened to Radio Luxembourg playing the Everley Brothers or Tommy Steele who seemed to be on every night. Only meal times or the medicine trolley arriving broke the monotony. After two weeks like this I began to wonder what was happening when I was told that my treatment with a certain Dr. Newam would begin the next day.

It was eight the following evening with all the other staff off duty when Dr. Newam called for me. I had seen him in our ward before. He was a good-looking, slim Australian with very dark features. His enormous smile showed perfect white teeth. Every strand of his thick black hair was in place and he always wore pale blue suits and bright yellow ties. The doctor smiled as he introduced himself and asked me to follow him down a long quiet corridor, showing me into a therapy room which he locked from the inside. This room was empty apart from a high couch in the middle and a lamp suspended above it. It looked frightening, like an operating theatre. Pointing to the couch he asked me to lay down. From his black case he took a syringe and gave me an injection. Immediately this made me feel light headed, like I was floating. The room seemed to get larger and the doctor standing over me smaller. In a jovial manner Dr. Newam asked what had made me snatch handbags. I said that I didn't really know when I felt his hand rubbing my stomach as he told me to relax. I don't remember all his other questions but I do recall him saying, 'You will like this,' as he unzipped my trousers to give me oral sex. I became aroused and before I knew it had an orgasm. Licking the end of my dick dry he told me not to feel guilty but to enjoy it. It was my first ever real orgasm and it frightened me. I was confused and the next day complained to Dr. Barkin, the senior consultant, an older but, alas, homosexual man himself. He merely told me not to let my imagination run away with itself. When my parents visited I pleaded with them to let me leave but I was in that asylum on the order of the court and they could do nothing. Regardless of my pleas the sex sessions continued. After a while I began to enjoy the hazy feeling the injections gave me and with Dr. Newam making sure I felt no guilt the orgasms felt good as well.

How this doctor had the audacity to do what was to follow is unbelievable but somehow he arranged for me to meet him in Central London and stay overnight in his Kensington flat. My protests had long stopped by the time I was given the fare money to travel to London's West End and feeling very excited I took the crowded underground train to Piccadilly Circus.

Waiting for me outside a cinema under the flashing neon signs smiling from ear to ear was Dr. Newam with his latest cure for handbag-snatching. He took me to a nearby pub where, inspite of my age, we were served. Sitting in a quiet corner he said, 'I want you to really enjoy yourself tonight !' handing me a little yellow pill. 'This will make you feel better.'

Obediently I swallowed the tablet, not knowing that it was my introduction to the twilight zone of Dexedrine, a potent amphetamine drug. This drug became the biggest force in my life for the next twenty-five years.

Sitting in the bar I began to feel better by the minute. To be out at night in Piccadilly Circus would have been exciting for any fourteen-year-old but this tablet took me into a different world altogether. Within half an hour I was bursting with uncontrollable excitement, running all over the pub, talking to strangers as if I'd known them all my life. This mind-altering drug made me excited, talkative and extroverted as it took effect. We left the bar and walked through the red light district where all the flashing signs seemed to get brighter, as if they were lit just for me. My head was like a volcano exploding with happiness. Never had I felt like this before, so uncontrollably good ! I wanted to sing. As we passed the prostitutes in the streets they were smiling at us, beckoning us inside their dimly lit doors. We looked at the pictures of naked girls outside a strip club and were soon downstairs watching them take their clothes off. My heart started pounding and my dick got very stiff as I looked up through the smoke to see a woman completely naked for the first time. High on the drug and feeling no inhibitions I went to the toilet cubical and masturbated, thinking of the naked girl. Climaxing all over the floor this happy fourteen-year-old handbag-snatching patient was really on the mend. The after-hours therapy was definitely working ! Outside in the main toilet the doctor was waiting for me with his usual big smile.

Leaving the naked girls in their cellar we walked to a nearby Spanish Restaurant. It was packed but a table had been reserved for us near the piano. My head was spinning as I sat there listening to the music. Constant additional explosions of joy erupted as the full blast of the drug hit my bloodstream. Every mouthful of prawn cocktail, steak and strawberries went down with ecstasy. The cream in the coffee cup was still floating round in my mind as I drifted out through the front door and into a taxi on route to Newam's Kensington flat.

The next day I woke up alone in an enormous bed with my head sunk into a huge pillow. The starched pale blue sheets had not a crease in them, as if I had been put there by magic. I was naked and felt unable to move. What had happened? I could remember getting into the taxi but not a thing after that. I lay motionless for what seemed like hours, feeling sad for no reason, wondering where the magical happiness of the previous evening had gone. Why did I feel so fed up? I didn't feel ill, I had no headache, I just felt totally dejected. Sitting up in my bed I looked around. The high ceiling of this huge room was one big mirror. Everything was tidy like in a museum. Large photographs of naked boys in ornate gold frames hung everywhere like in an erotic art gallery. Shelves full of impeccably arranged leather-bound books completely filled one wall. The heavy blue curtains were half open, letting in the midday sun on this scene of splendour. Either side of the bed were giant gold lamps shaped like statues of naked men. Slowly I began to wake up but felt lower and lower. This was not a hangover. A black hopelessness engulfed me for no reason. I had always been a happy-go-lucky kid and never before had experienced such isolation and despair as on that morning.

Listlessly I got up. My feet sunk into the deep pile of the blue carpet as I crossed the room to open the smaller of two doors. It led to a huge bathroom with a bath big enough for ten people. The gold taps were the shape of nude men with water pouring from their penises. Every wall was a mirror with golden lights in each corner, it felt like being in an Egyptian Pharaoh's Palace. I opened a large bathroom cabinet to find rows of small bottles of pills, all neatly positioned the same distance apart. So many pills in all different shapes and colours, like a medical sweet shop stocked with mind altering candy ! I reached out to take some when suddenly Dr. Newam was standing behind me in the mirror. He was naked. 'Here, take this,' he said, handing me another yellow pill, the same as the previous evening. 'You will soon feel better.' I took the tablet and got into the warm bubbly bath he'd already poured. I still felt miserable and lifeless. A glass tray fitting across the tub appeared with breakfast fit for a king, consisting of boiled eggs, thickly buttered toast cut into fingers and boiling hot coffee in a giant blue cup. I began eating, dropping toast into the bath. Our doctor, sitting naked on a high chair by the bath, laughed, 'That's for the fishes !' After a few moments he almost danced out of the room, giggling.

Suddenly I started to feel great, no longer dreary but excited and wide awake. The happiness switch inside my head was on again. The feeling from the night before was back and bursting with joy I leapt out of the bath, spilling the last of the coffee. I'd just had my first speed breakfast - drugs on toast. Doctor Newam reappeared, dressed all in blue as usual and in his tight fitting clothes looked very handsome. 'Come on darling, wear some of my clothes today,' he suggested. I was shocked hearing him call me 'darling,' but felt so good, nothing mattered. Soon I was dressed all in blue and with my own dark hair now looked a clone of Newam.

In high spirits we left Newam's flat which was in an exclusive block near Marble Arch and crossed over to Hyde Park where we danced between the trees. The flowers looked good, the people looked good, everything looked good. I felt even more happy than I had done the previous evening. For lunch we went to an expensive hotel; where we were served by waiters dressed up like penguins. I could hardly eat, I was too high, too excited to concentrate on food. After our meal we took a cab to the Serpentine Lake in the middle of Hyde Park to hire a rowing boat. The lake was crowded on that windy day. The doctor took the oars and our boat floated off through the water like a magical swan. Gliding past the ducks and under the bridges we looked up at peoples smiling faces as if they were dropping happiness down to us.

But suddenly it started, slowly at first. Out of nowhere an invisible cloud crept over me and I started to feel low. Hoping it would pass I thought, how can I feel low when a moment ago I was so deliriously happy? After all, I am still in the same boat on the same lake ! But the sadness stayed. Everything started to look different. I now wanted out off this stupid boat and these ridiculous blue clothes. The people on the bridges were sneering at us. I wanted to get away from this pale blue monster sitting next to me. This dream was turning into a horror movie. Sensing my drug come-down Dr. Newam quickly returned the boat, hired a cab and took me back to his flat where I changed into my own clothes. I felt worse and worse as another taxi took me back to the hospital. On arrival I was taken to my room and given a sedative by the big male Irish nurse. Quickly I fell asleep.

The next morning I woke with the same unhappy feeling I had experienced in the doctor's huge bed. I just refused to get up and in the end the nurses had to force-dress me. When I asked for Dr. Newam I was told he wouldn't be on duty till midday. All morning I waited in the lounge like a zombie, not speaking to anyone. I had become the exact opposite of the chatty little Herbert that had arrived a month or so earlier. Later when I saw the doctor's car pull in I jumped up with excitement, feeling instantly better. My own reaction startled me. Why did I need him so much? Was I gay?

Was I in love with this man? Soon I realised that it was not the doctor I needed but the drugs in his black case. At fourteen I was now hooked on amphetamine, already an addict. Climbing through the open window I ran up to Dr. Newam, obviously embarrassing him. He sensed the state I was in and promised to see me immediately after his ward round with Dr. Barkin. I was taken back to the common room where I sat waiting, sharing the doom and gloom of my fellow patients. Doreen was in a corner, her head now covered in bandages like an Indian turban with her blond hair hanging out. She'd had her brain operation and sat there motionless.

After what seemed an eternity I got to see Dr. Newam in his room. From his black bag he produced another of the yellow pills. 'Please give me two!' I pleaded but he refused saying, 'I will be seeing you tonight after tea.' I put my arms round him and as I rubbed up against him I could feel him getting excited under his trousers. I had this gay man under my control. After climaxing he zipped up his trousers and looking flustered gave me my extra tablet. 'Don't take them both today,' he said. 'Save one for tomorrow when I'm off duty.' Having prostituted myself for tablets of instant karma I went straight to the toilet and took them both.

Back in the common room I came alive and couldn't stop moving round, talking to all the other weird characters. A happiness movie was running faster and faster inside my brain as the pills took over. However, the other freaks all stayed their same lifeless selves. They need a cure like me, I thought.

That night things in Dr. Newam's treatment room took a dramatic turn. The effect of the two pills taken earlier plus the injection made me want more drugs at any cost. I pulled the doctor onto the couch and unzipped his trousers. I had him going mad with excitement when I stopped for a commercial break. Two more pills before I finish. As he handed me the tablets the telephone rang. In a state of panic he pulled his trousers up and hurriedly left the room, locking me inside. Looking down on the floor I saw paradise staring me in the face. The black case full of pills was unlocked. I put two bottles down my socks and lay back on the couch. Soon he returned with his mind on the interrupted sex which we finished all over the marble floor. 'See you Friday,' he said as we left the room. 'Go and fuck yourself,' I thought, as I walked back to my bedroom. Roger wasn't there. I counted the pills, there were sixty in all. I was ecstatic, still high from the pills inside me but now I felt even better with a stock of happiness at my disposal.

That night, like every night, the Irish nurse came round with his squeaking trolley from which he dished out eggcups full of sleeping syrup. The rattle of the trolley caused one of two reactions - either the patients buzzed around it like bees round a honeypot if they liked the sleepy feeling or hid like frightened mice. As I took my dose he always shouted, 'Mouth open !' checking if I had swallowed it all. Back in my room I waited for the usual sleepy feeling to arrive but it didn't. I was wide awake with the high dose of Dexedrine overpowering the mild sedative. I lay on my bed until three o'clock when I finally gave up trying to sleep and took four of my stolen pills. Within an hour I was uncontrollably high. For the first time I experienced the cocaine-type rush mega-doses of speed give you. It felt better than slipping out of my mother's womb fourteen years before. Compared to this, the previous weekend with Newam seemed like a funeral procession. Roger was fast asleep so I tried to control my avalanche of joy which felt like a never ending orgasm. I could well have been in the Russian Sputnik orbiting the world above my head. After a while, unable to keep silent, I woke Roger and gave him a pill. With me whispering in his ear he listened to all my fourteen-years-worth of wisdom.

An hour or so later as dawn broke Roger and I took four more pills each and were soon out of our heads. During our bedside discussions we both reached a monumental decision - today we would tell them. On hearing the medicine trolley we walked out into the corridor in our pyjamas, holding hands. Roger was wearing his postman's hat. Going up to the Irish nurse he proudly announced, 'My name is Roger and I'm a postman from Lewisham.' The entire ward went silent, then all the nurses started clapping. I had treated and unconditionally cured my first patient without sucking his cock.

At breakfast I was no longer alone on my island of ecstasy. Roger, feeling so much better for admitting he was Roger, had become my assistant. Looking around the room I noticed the others, brain-dead zombies all of them ! Their daytime wake-me-up syrup was so cruelly diluted ! Feeling a rush of overwhelming love I decided that everybody must get the cure - move over Dr. Newam, you pale blue pansy.

By that time, as a trusted patient, I was allowed out to the local shops. That day I bought several large bottles of cola, cigarettes and chocolates. Then I returned to my office, a cubical in the toilet, where I prepared the cure for all ills. Crushing about twenty of the Dexedrine pills I mixed them up with the cola while

36

my assistant stood guard outside. Together we returned to the lounge - it was treatment time ! All these poor souls who'd shared the misery of my handbag-snatching disease were about to share something else !

Fatsoe was given two glasses of the slightly bitter tasting drink. Roger made sure she drunk it all by bribing her with a whole packet of fags. Alan, my depressed artist, was thirsty and drunk at least five glasses. After about half an hour he began to smoke for the first time in his life, setting fire to his beard in the process. We put him on chocolate after that to prevent a major fire. Looking round I shouted, 'Roger, give Do Die the cola ! Hold the bastard still ! Pour it down his throat !' Somehow Roger got him to drink several glasses. I took four more undiluted pills. After all, I was more ill than the others, I had pale-blue handbag-problems. All the patients, including the spies and Jesus', were cured. The whole room had come alive. Suddenly I realised I'd missed poor Doreen, still sitting in the corner motionless with a hole in her head where part of her brain used to be. I persuaded her to drink the last half bottle.

Fatsoe was now out of her chair giving away all her cigarettes. Do Die still wanted to die but was so much happier about it. He was talking to Fatsoe who taught him how to smoke. Roger got up behind them and started to squeeze Fatsoe's tits. Even Doreen was getting better. She looked good and sexy inspite of her bandages. I put my hand up her skirt. She liked it and her body began to move up and down as I poked about. Roger was now on the floor on top of Fatsoe who was into something she had long forgotten. She'd even stopped smoking for it. Do Die suddenly jumped up, climbed out of the window and ran out of sight. Someone turned the radio on full blast and out of our heads we all ran about the room dancing to 'Rock around the psychiatric clock.'

Suddenly the door opened and several nurses rushed in.

Chapter 3

GENTLEMAN GEORGE

Under a cloud of investigations I left Friern Barnet Hospital, never to see Dr. Newam again. The authorities wanted to hush the whole matter up and I was allowed home to live with my parents. Occasionally I had to report to a probation officer but he was very lax and accepted anything. As unbelievable as it seems, our local family doctor now gave me regular prescriptions for Dexedrine because in those days the medical profession was still oblivious to the dangers of amphetamine. My parents had given up asking me any questions and were satisfied if I came home now and then, just as long as the police were not ringing up.

High as a kite on drugs I was soon back to the flashing neon signs of Piccadilly Circus where I roamed the streets looking for action. It was there I was picked up by Jack Murray, a well known homosexual who owned the Alibi club in Berwick Street. Through him, at the age of fourteen, I got into the gay club scene at the deep end. In these drinking clubs I met lots of wealthy gays who spent freely on their young company. Drugs, too, were always available and throughout 1959 life became one round of wild nights.

By early 1960 I had become a right little Jack the Lad and like Elvis, who'd just come out of the army, I was also ready for the big time. One night I left an exclusive gay club and as I waited for a cab in the pouring rain a Rolls Royce pulled up. The chauffeur got out and asked me if I would like to join his master for a drink at the nearby Mayfair Hotel. Fascinated I got into the back of the car. As we arrived outside the hotel the driver took off his cap and started laughing. I now recognised this man, having often seen him looking at me in various clubs. 'Silly boy,' he said. 'Never accept lifts from strangers. You could be picked up by the wrong kind.' 'I trust my luck more than that,' I replied cockily. 'Come inside for a drink,' he said in a posh accent, introducing himself as George. Inside the Mayfair we sat down for drinks and I became quickly fascinated by this slim tall man whose curly brown hair hung over his forehead in a fringe. To read the drinks list he put on gold-rimmed glasses which made him look like something out of a 'Dickens' novel. Impeccably dressed there was such an air of elegance about him I expected the Queen of England to join us at any moment. He asked why I was out so late on my own and where I lived but I wouldn't tell him. He seemed a bit too concerned, just like a parent would be.

It was getting late. George kept looking at his pocket watch and after a few drinks invited me to spend the night at his hotel. 'You will have your own bed,' he promised, 'I'm not after sex !' He took me to a private hotel near Hyde Park where his small room was at the very top. That night, to my amazement, he gave me his bed and slept on the floor himself. He really was a gentleman. He never touched me except for kissing me on the forehead saying, 'You are truly beautiful.' His room was packed with furniture which looked like the last possessions from a lost stately home.

I began to visit George regularly and watched as he read the racing papers each day. He studied dozens of books with details on every race horse and often discussed how the horse had been training with various characters over the phone. He placed bets which were astronomical, two thousand pounds to win, which is worth twenty times that today. Still ignorant as to what George actually did I thought he perhaps came from an aristocratic family and had just sold his country house.

One day he took me for a ride out past Hendon in his Rolls Royce. I remember passing my uncle's house near Edgware. First we drove round what looked like a big country estate then George took me to a restaurant somewhere nearby. He ordered me a meal and giving me money to pay the bill left, saying he would be back soon. Strange, I thought, bringing me all this way just for a meal. My head was spinning round as usual with the drugs. Beginning to feel bored I paid and started to roam round outside when he reappeared, practically pulling me in the car. There was another man I didn't know in the front seat who seemed annoyed I was there. I could sense something was going on and kept quiet until they dropped me off.

I didn't see George on Sunday but when I visited him on Monday I found him laying on the bed with a glass of champagne. There was jewellery all over the floor. Newspapers were everywhere. The headlines read, 'Sophia Loren robbed in Elstree.' The TV set was on and just then I heard the commentator say that the robbery had been the work of a top professional, a 'Modern Day Raffles'. They showed the barn and the grounds where the robbery had taken place. I was stunned. It was where George and I had cruised round on Saturday. I was looking at the culprit ! Grinning at me was a top jewel thief, the best in his day, 'Gentleman George'. 'This was you !' I blurted out. He just laughed, saying, 'Not me. Prove it, my beautiful boy. This lot was stolen from somewhere else.' He then got up, scooped up the jewellery and kissing me on the forehead said, 'Let's celebrate.' We ate an expensive meal but I was so nervous I couldn't hold my knife and fork properly and just wanted to go back home to my parents. On Tuesday I was shocked to read that there was a twenty thousand pound reward out for the thieves. This really frightened me and I expected the police to call and arrest me at any moment. I was so scared I even considered volunteering to go back to school. I didn't go out all day and that evening watched more Sopia Loren news on television. My heart was pounding as my father joked, 'Wasn't you, I hope.' The name of the detective in charge of the investigation was Eric Shepherd, the namesake of my childhood friend still living across the street. Amused I thought, well he never got his toys back from the dead people so I doubt if his double will find the jewels.

The following day, with my pills reinstating my courage, George took me to Epsom to watch the derby. He put a fortune on a horse with the name of Angers which sounded a bit like angry. This is exactly what George was when it lost to Lester Piggott on St. Paddy. The whole scene with George seemed like a dream and the drugs swimming round inside me made it even more unreal. Over the next few days George told me all about himself. He hated the rich upper-class although he himself was one of them. He once had attended a top public school where he became close to a gay boy called Alistair who introduced him to London's gay scene. Alistair often boasted about an aristocrat who paid the rent for his London flat for him and visited him there every Sunday for sex. This mystery gentleman was married but secretly preferred sex with young men. Alistair had given George a spare key and one Sunday afternoon, unable to control his curiosity, George decided to spy on his friend. Quietly opening the front door he let himself in and heard voices coming from the bedroom. Through the gap in the door which was ajar he saw Alistair in bed with the mystery man. Suddenly George froze in shock. The man was his own father.

George never spoke to him again in his life. He went to live abroad, serving in the army for many years and returned to rob the wealthy he now so despised.

George's gambling was monstrous and only could continue thanks to his thieving. One evening, about two months after the Sophia Loren robbery, he kissed me on the forehead and said, 'Its time for you to learn the tricks of the trade.' George was in love with me but it never got physical.

He was the ultimate professional thief, planning in every detail way in advance who he was going to rob, when, and what of. He studied society magazines to find out who would be attending what function and even seemed to know what jewellery people would be wearing. Much meticulous research went into all his work and for the forthcoming job he bought me a pair of white gloves which fitted like surgeon's.

Our first trip was to a penthouse off Eton Square. I was very scared and took more drugs than usual for extra courage. This was a different league to handbag-snatching. Arriving at a block of flats we went to a top floor apartment for which George had a key and once inside we locked the door behind us. A bag had been left in the hall with grappling irons, ropes, etc. in it. Pinned to it was a note which George read and with a smile put it in his pocket. We then climbed up through a fanlight window and crawled across a flat roof. 'That's our place,' said George, pointing to a building about twenty feet across a dark mews street. I was by now in a dreamlike state induced by a combination of drugs and fear. After two attempts George managed to hook a rope across and soon had constructed a pulley system.

'Ssssh, be quiet,' George said, grabbing my arm as a laughing couple left a house in the mews below. Now it was my time to cross. I was petrified. Harnessing me to the rope he said, 'Hold tight, angel,' and pushed me off.

Five storeys high I was sliding across to the balcony of the flat opposite like Tarzan. Next a bag of tools was sent over, followed by a smiling George who pulled something which made the entire pulley system come over to our side. It was as if we had flown over like birds. George now put a black treacly fluid all over a small window pane, covered it with paper and broke the glass without noise. Before I realised it he had pushed me through. With the drugs hitting my bloodstream my heart was racing. Quickly I opened the balcony door to let George in. Kissing my forehead he gave me a sweet from his pocket and took off his overcoat as if he was at home, hanging it neatly over the back of a chair. We crossed the lavishly furnished sitting room and went out into a long hall. He knew exactly where to find the master bedroom. This, too, was a beautiful room with a four-poster-bed and oil paintings on each wall. 'That's the one,' he said, pointing to a smaller picture. Behind it was a wall safe with many dials on it which George began to turn. For a while nothing happened and I could see his face changing, he looked tense. This was the first time he ever looked troubled. Suddenly there was a loud click and the safe opened. Inside was a red jewellery box. George calmly emptied its contents into his pockets, carefully closing the safe and putting back the picture. We left, closing the bedroom door behind us to return to the lounge. George now went straight to the writing desk, opened the top left hand drawer and took out a set of keys. There was cash in that drawer, too, and I

44

reached out to take it but George interrupted, 'Leave it. It's not ours, not insured.'

The keys were obviously to the front door and I urged him to leave. I was scared stiff. George, instead, calmly sat down on the sofa as if he was the owner and pointed towards the kitchen, saying, 'Put the kettle on Stephen.' He then turned the TV on to watch the news. He knew that the owner would be at the theatre until at least 10.30. Smooth, that was his style but I was panicking and nagged George to go now to which he calmly replied, 'Either make the tea or go home on your own.' In the kitchen I took more pills, trying to calm down. After we had our tea and chocolate biscuits he made me wash up, telling me to show respect for other peoples homes. It seemed like hours before he got up and put on his coat.

Adjusting something in a box near the door we left the flat with our bag of ropes and took the lift to the ground floor. There were two policemen standing outside the front door. George walked out unperturbed and before they could say a word asked them sharply in his posh Eton accent, 'What rank are you?' 'Sergeant,' one of them replied, looking quite shocked. 'I never speak to anyone below the rank of a Chief Inspector. Do you know who I am?' George sternly continued. Frozen to the spot the policemen looked on bewildered as we hailed a black cab. I was frantic but too shocked to show any nerves and heaved a sigh of relief as we pulled away.

Soon we were leaving the wealthy, well-lit streets behind us and headed for a much poorer part of London behind Kings Cross railway station. 'Drop us here,' George instructed the driver as we reached the corner of a dimly-lit street. Waiting until the cab was out of sight we walked the last hundred yards. 'Can't be too careful,' George smiled. We climbed up a concrete staircase to a flat on the third floor of a very scruffy block. The door opened. 'Allo, come in,' said a large scar-faced man. 'Who's this?' he pointed at me. 'That's my new assistant,' George joked. In his lounge the man started to examine the jewellery George had taken from his pockets. 'We'll have to break this one up,' he remarked, looking at a stunning ruby and diamond necklace. They had obviously traded with each other before. 'Tea?' the man asked after a while, leading George into the kitchen where out of my earshot a price was agreed. When they came back the man handed me a giant tin of biscuits saying, 'The chocolate ones are at the bottom, hidden from George.' Then, looking at George he continued, 'Take me a week or so to get the cash. Do you want something on account?' George nodded and was handed the biggest wad of banknotes I had ever seen. It filled both his overcoat pockets.

The following evening George counted out one thousand pounds for me, worth twenty thousand in 1996 and said, it's your pocket money, angel, better than drinking with lecherous old gays, eh?' He looked very pleased with himself. His feelings were a bit mixed up. He couldn't reconcile his own homosexual wants with his desire to save vulnerable young boys like me from being exploited by old gays. He obviously also saw me as an apprentice, someone he considered worthy enough to teach the finer points of the burglary trade.

After tea with the usual chocolate digestive biscuits George suggested we went out to have a 'flutter' and took me to a basement club which looked like a film set from a Chicago gangster movie. The dimly lit cellar was filled with smoke. Ten tough-looking men in dark suits, typical gangsters, were standing around a billiard table playing dice. As we entered they all nodded and one called out, 'Had an earner then, George? I saw it on the news.' 'No, not me !' smiled George, putting his arm around me. 'We were at the pictures seeing Ben Hur, good film.' He pulled out two used tickets. The men returned to their game. Taking out a wad of cash George joined in. He lost. 'Your turn, precious,' he said, handing me the dice. I didn't know how to play but threw a seven and we won. After that I won three more times, doubling our money each time. On my next throw the dice hit the hand of a dark, sultry looking man in his mid twenties and I lost. 'You bloody idiot !' I shouted, getting really annoyed. Everybody started laughing but the man just stared at me with a cold smile. My drugs and all the laughing made me feel brave and I shouted again, 'You stupid idiot !' Suddenly the laughing stopped. The smile had left his face and he now looked at me like a wild dog with rabies about to attack. I glanced at George. He had gone white. Turning towards the man he said, 'Forget it, he's just a kid,' and dragged me up the stairs, leaving all our betting money on the table. Outside he hastily stopped a cab. I didn't understand the rush. 'Why are we running? We were winning !' I shouted at George. 'Do you know who you were threatening? That was Ronnie Kray, one of London's worst gangsters !' 'Ronnie Who?' I asked. I'd never heard of him. 'You are lucky he didn't cut you to pieces,' George shouted. Cut me to pieces? It all seemed so far out.

A few years later I learnt that the insane mind of Ronnie Kray worked like this - once his psychopathic anger exploded, his victim was always doomed and either got killed or mutilated. This man and his twin brother Reggie were already on their way to become London's most feared crime bosses. Their dark shadows would fall over my own life a few years later.

George got out near his hotel and leaving me in the cab said, 'Go home now and behave yourself. Next week I'll take you on something really big in Ireland.'

Back at my quiet suburban family home everybody was fast asleep. I crept into the kitchen and piled up all the cash on the table after which I lay a money trail down the hall and up the stairs to my parents bedroom door. Feeling very smug I went to bed and soon was fast asleep. The next morning I heard my parents scream, 'What's all this money? Where did it come from?' 'Oh, just an earner,' I replied coolly, swallowing my morning drugs. They were shocked but said no more, having long given up hope of ever controlling me again. A week later I was off again, leaving home for an appointment I'd made, meeting a man from the burglary trade. The note by the door read, 'Gone to Ireland on business. Stephen.'

At that time I was buying most of my drugs on the black market and took a large supply with me, not knowing where we were going or how long I would be away for. My money from the Eaton Square robbery was safely hidden in the roof of my parent's home.

Over the next few years I was to hide so much cash there it became Fort Knox of North London and some money probably remains hidden there to this day.

After meeting George at Euston we took a train to catch the ferry over to Ireland. Boarding the boat I was overcome by it all, any fifteen-year-old would have been excited but drugs and the nature of our trip added to my thrill. However, to the other passengers we must have looked just like father and son. The night crossing was very rough with the boat rolling from side to side and I couldn't sleep. I was restless and leaving George snoring in our cabin went on deck to watch the hilly coast of Ireland come into view at dawn.

On our arrival we booked into a small hotel in Cork. The owner obviously knew and expected George and they spoke privately in a room behind the reception. Through the door I saw them looking at a large map, discussing something. When they came out the man showed us up to our bedroom. George told me he was going out with the owner to get a car, asking me to wait there. This was fine with me because by now I was tired and soon fell asleep.

Many hours later George woke me, saying it was time to go to work. In the bathroom I took more drugs than ever before, unable to face the robbery without them. It was around midnight when we got to an area near Blackrock. Passing various large houses George slowed down, pointing to a mansion which looked bigger than Buckingham Palace ! It was three floors high and the front was covered with large painted windows like a church. There were two white pillars and steps that led up to huge black doors with statues of lions on either side. As we drove round we could see the depth of this huge building, enclosing an inner courtyard. There were no garden walls just extensive lawns down to the road. Two blocks away we parked the car and like Fagin and Oliver Twist walked back. The plan was to climb up to the roof from the side of the building which was concealed by large oak trees. We would then cross the roof to the inner yard and lower ourselves onto a back balcony from where we would gain access. I was now too drugged to be afraid, not even fully aware of what I was doing. Crawling along a narrow ledge three stories up some tiles broke lose and fell into the courtyard. I looked down and saw it was full of white stone statues lit up by the moon. George stared at me and whispered, 'Don't be afraid. It's fear that makes people lose and get caught.'

The balcony below us turned out to be one floor lower than expected and it was impossible to jump to it. When George told me he was going to lower me by rope I panicked. There I was, a young schoolboy way out of his league high on a roof in Ireland. I didn't want to go on with it. I wanted to go home to my parents. Sensing trouble George suddenly changed. 'Do as you're told !' he whispered sharply, gripping my arm. He looked different now, stern, his eyes were piercing. Frightened I obeyed. Hanging in mid-air I thought the rope would break any moment and I'd fall to my death but miraculously my feet reached the balcony. Still trembling I set to work, covering a small window with treacle and paper. When I broke the glass it fell inside and a dog began to bark somewhere. I froze with fear. This was heavy going compared to handbag-snatching. When no more noises followed George, looking down from above, instructed me to go in. I squeezed through the window and out of George's view took more pills. They were my constant companion, bravery in my pocket. Now I had to let George in from the ground floor. Creeping down the main staircase I got a terrible fright as I passed the suits of armour, thinking they were real people. I was petrified and began to sob but as I reached the bottom I heard George already tapping on the glass. Quickly I wiped my tears so he wouldn't notice and opened the large bolts on a huge window. 'You are beautiful,' said George, as he climbed inside. We went back up the main staircase and down a long corridor to the opposite wing. Quietly George opened a door and we entered an enormous bedroom. The four-poster-bed seemed to be miles away on the other side of the room. Then, suddenly, all hell broke lose. A man sat up in bed, shouting, 'What the dickens is going on?'

Slamming the door behind us we heard the barking again. It came closer and I ran so fast, my feet hardly touched the ground. Rushing down the main stairs I hit a suit of armour which fell down with us. It was sheer bedlam. With shouts at the top of the stairs and a huge dog rushing down after us we crashed to the floor amongst the rattle of armour. In my confusion I started to run to the wrong side of the hall but George grabbed me and practically threw me out of the open window. A shotgun went off as we vanished into the dark gardens behind the oak trees. 'He wasn't too pleased,' George laughed as we reached our car.

Back in the safety of our hotel George sat on his bed and bandaged his arm where the dog had bitten him. Smiling he said, 'Sorry old chap, information cock-up,' handing me a drink of whisky from his hip flask. I was in a state of shock but very impressed with smooth George who, inspite of everything, still had his hair in place. 'I'll take you to Dublin tomorrow to make up for this,' George promised as he fell asleep. He always lectured me that stealing was better than going with old queers for money. It was as if he wanted to save me from a life morally worse than his, like a sort of a gay Robin Hood. I can't say whether he knew I took drugs, at least he never mentioned it.

The next morning on the quiet country roads on route to Dublin George taught me to drive. I was thrilled to bits. We were doings things father and son would do, things my own father was always too busy for. George accepted me for what I was and always showed interest in me. He found me worthwhile, something my own father never had done.

On arrival we booked into Dublin's finest hotel, the 'Gresham' in the centre of town. Staying there was George's idea of a treat. The foyer was vast with porters rushing around helping the wealthy guests. We went up in a huge lift to be shown to a suite of rooms consisting of bedroom, bathroom and a separate sitting room. There was a TV, plush armchairs and a writing desk complete with hotel note paper. The bath towels were bigger than curtains, there was shampoo, aftershave, everything.

That evening George took me out to play roulette and he soon became totally engrossed with his bets. I was getting bored with the gambling when I noticed a boy of about my age. It was strange to see another kid out so late and intrigued I approached him. His name was Sean and like me was a lively boy looking for more excitement than a bedtime story. I instantly took a liking to Sean with his round freckled face, blonde hair and bright brown eyes. George, who was winning, gave us some money to enjoy Dublin while he played on. As we left he told me rather strictly, 'Make sure you are back at the hotel by midnight. Our plane leaves first thing tomorrow morning.' Who does he think I am? I thought. Bloody Cinderella?

Out in the street I offered Sean some of my pills. Soon we were both high as kites. It turned out that Sean was the son of the manager of a big bank near Grafton Street. I told him all about the free and easy criminal life I was leading in London when suddenly I had another of my brilliant ideas. 'Why don't you steal your father's bank keys?' I asked. 'With George's help we can rob the bank this coming weekend.' I told Sean that he could run away with me to London where we would live together like lords in our own posh flat. We'd have our own big car and a chauffeur till we were old enough to drive. Stoned and excited Sean agreed to my plan. We elaborated the details in an expensive restaurant over strawberries with ice cream and feeling like princes toasted the robbery with lemonade because the stupid waiters refused to serve us wine. It got later and later, way past midnight, but who cared ! We were far too stoned to go to bed ! At around three in the morning we took a further look at his father's bank. It was truly an enormous building. Stopping outside one of the expensive jewellers in the same street I suggested that before leaving for London Sean should buy his parents a gold watch each. 'They deserve a going away present,' I said. 'Especially your dad. After all its his bank getting robbed.' Finally we parted, arranging to meet the next day outside his school at 4 pm.

When I arrived back at the Gresham Hotel I found George in the foyer. He was furious. After taking me up to our suite he went berserk. 'It's three thirty ! Where have you been?' It all reminded me of Raymonds father and his screaming. Still bubbling over with excitement I told him all about my amazing plan to rob Sean's father's bank, fully expecting him to be enthusiastic. Instead George got angry. 'Are you out of your mind?' he replied. 'This is out of the question ! We are in this hotel under our real names and besides, the boy will crack ! Rob that bank and you will be caught before you leave Dublin !' Trying to calm down he continued, 'You are just a kid. Go to bed. We're flying back to London in a few hours.'

He sat down looking exhausted. But I wouldn't listen. My hero George was now treating me like some naughty kid. 'Never !' I screamed. 'You go back alone.

53

This is my chance to show them all !' George looked shocked and very upset. His obedient Oliver Twist had turned into a rebel. He stared at me with the same piercing eyes like on the roof the night before and shaking me by my shoulders said, 'You will fly back with me !' Defiantly I struggled free and ran out into the streets of Dublin.

Annoyed and very drugged I walked around for hours refusing to let myself go back to talk with George. He was just like any other bossy grown up ! Convinced I had found my chance of glory by robbing that bank nobody was going to stop me now !

Much later that morning I finally decided to return to George and was shocked to find he had already left. Suddenly I became very frightened, like a child abandoned in a strange city, which is exactly what I was. I couldn't think what to do so I took more pills and waited in my room for them to take effect. Later, with new-found bravado, I went out and roamed around all day until I met Sean outside his school at four. Walking back to my hotel I told him what I thought of school and that he soon could give it up. Unlike yesterday he was very quiet and somehow looked troubled but I thought it was just pre-robbery nerves. Up in my suite I ordered ice-cream and just before it arrived Sean broke down and started crying. 'I can't go through with it. I'm too scared, I just can't !' he sobbed. Just then the ice-cream was wheeled in but I pushed it away, screaming hysterically, 'You coward ! You've ruined our chance of glory. It's all your fault that George left me ! Get out of here, you big baby !' After Sean had gone I threw myself on the bed and cried into my pillow. The bubble had burst.

Later that day I realised I couldn't pay my extra hotel bill or get back to London. I had brought no money to Ireland. In a panic I rang the reception, saying I was in bed with flu and wanted to take all my meals in the room. For two days I stayed locked in there until I ran out of both drugs and courage, reverting back to a scared young teenager. A cleaner heard me crying and reported it to the management who came up to investigate. I confessed that I was alone in Dublin, saying that George was my uncle. The manager rang my shocked parents who bailed me out, paying the hotel bill as well as a one way plane ticket back to London. To make sure I actually got on the plane the manager sent his assistant to the airport with me.

Unwilling and unable to handle any more of my escapades my parents had already arranged for me to live with my uncle and aunt from now on and it was uncle Mick who met me at Heathrow airport, looking rather amused.

A few days later I collected the stolen money and the rest of my hidden drugs from the loft of my parents home. I rang Gentleman George but he had left his hotel with no forwarding address.

Years later I heard that George in his old age had tried to settle down and retired as a live-in butler to a very upmarket family close to the Queen. One day, as he was greeting the guests for the annual hunt ball, he saw Lady So and So arrive, wearing a priceless diamond necklace. A leopard never changes his spots unable to control himself George snatched it. He was never seen again.

Keep well George. He who rides the tiger never, ever stops. Perhaps we both never did.

Chapter 4

FUCKING, WHIPPING AND THE SHITS.

I now lived with my wealthy uncle Mick in his
Central London flat which kept my probation officer
happy. For work I managed one of his smaller shops. I
didn't like or want the job but it satisfied the authorities
I was actually working. Uncle Mick often joked, saying,
'You are the youngest manager in town. You'll be
president next !' Kennedy had just been elected in
America. This small, quiet shop was a hundred yards
from my uncle's main store and in the mornings he
gave me a lift to work. In the evenings, however, it was
different - I went off alone around the clubs of London.
My uncle and aunt allowed me to come home as late as
I pleased just as long as I was quiet when I did come in.
They asked no questions.

I had practically nothing to do in the shop all day
except take pills or read the papers. One morning I read
that Sammy Davis, who had just married Britt Ekland,
was staying in London. Watch your jewels, I laughed to
myself, wondering whether Gentleman George would
rob them now !

Above my shop lived an old lady, a tiny woman
with silvery grey hair who always looked sad and lost.
Despite her eighty years she seemed in good physical
shape but rarely ventured out of her two little rooms.
Her eyes had a glazed look, like death. With so few
customers and always stoned out of my mind I often
went upstairs to talk with her. She told me about her
granddaughter, a young girl of my age, whom she
hardly ever saw because her own son never brought the

child to see her. 'Only this little girl cares for me,' she would say. 'My son just wants me out of the way in an old peoples home.' Starting to cry she showed me a photo of a young girl with long blond hair. On the back was written, 'I love you, grandma.' I sympathised, explaining how my own parents had put me in a home when I was four while they took my older sister on holiday to France. 'We are all nuisances,' she said, 'either when we're young or very old.' A few weeks before Christmas I asked her where she was going over the holidays. 'Nowhere,' she replied, 'I will be here, alone as usual.' 'Don't worry, I'll make you cheerful,' I said, giving her ten of my pills. 'You're very old, so be careful and only take one each day,' I warned her. 'These pills will make you happy.' 'You're so kind,' she said, kissing my cheek. Her face felt cold, like a ghost's. Promising to take her happy pill later she remarked with a defiant look, 'Nobody will get us into a home, I'll see to that!' The bell went and I left her to go back down to serve a customer in the shop. Later I closed up and went off for yet another late night-club session, forgetting all about the old lady.

When I opened up the following morning I was hit by a strong smell. The entire shop smelt of gas. A terrible thing dawned on me! I rushed upstairs to find the old lady with her head on a small cushion inside the oven. Putting off the gas I smashed the windows for air and threw water over her face, but she was already dead. She looked peaceful with a slight smile on her face. Kneeling down I found two letters in her hand. One was addressed to her granddaughter, the other to me. Putting mine in my pocket I looked at her, wondering what had gone wrong with her happy pills.

The ambulance men taking her body away praised me for my bravery and after they'd gone I locked up the shop to calm down. I walked for miles, ending up in an old cemetery where I sat down on a bench amongst the battered gravestones. Still very upset I couldn't stop myself crying. It started raining but I didn't care as I opened the old lady's letter. It read, 'You need the happiness more than me. Goodbye, my jolly little friend. No homes for us !' The letter was impeccably written in ink and as the rain ran down the page it washed away the words, just like the old lady's life. The ten pills I had given her were still untouched inside the envelope.

At the coroner's court two weeks later I was praised and photographed by the local paper. As I was leaving a beautiful girl with long blond hair crossed the courtroom and put her arms round me. 'Thank you for what you did for my grandma,' she said. We both hugged each other before she walked back to join her parents who didn't even look my way. Fuck this life, I thought, walking from the court, swallowing more pills.

In the months that followed I began to play the part of a Chicago gangster. Deep down I was still Robin Hood but it was impossible to ponce about in Sherwood Green all day. Wearing my new camel overcoat and travelling about in black taxis I discovered the 'Cafe de Paris', a fashionable dance club. It was always packed with girls, many of them foreign au-pairs working for wealthy families. After dancing all night with one girl and taking her home afterwards I was amazed to find she lived in a enormous house. Seeing her unlock the front door with her own keys inspired my latest handbag scheme. No more snatching, my crimes had more finesse these days. At the 'Cafe de Paris' the girls would usually deposit their bags for safety to be given a cloakroom ticket. Their handbags contained, amongst other things, front door keys.

I began to chat up the au-pairs in the coffee bars of Hampstead and other wealthy areas. Any girl would do, however ugly, just as long as she was an au-pair. Politely I would escort her home. If she lived in a small house it spelt the end of our friendship but if she lived in the mansion-type property our love-affair continued. Without trying to kiss her I shook her hand, inviting her out to the 'Cafe de Paris' on her next night off.

What a nice polite boy, they must have all thought on our first date, he even looks after my handbag ticket ! While we danced I slipped the ticket to Bert, my accomplice. I'd met him some time earlier in an amusement arcade near Leicester Square, another young villain in the making. To look like he was on a date Bert was accompanied by his sister Nell who collected the bags with no queries in this crowded club. While I danced the 'twist', America's latest dance craze with my date, they would take the bag around the corner where a dubious character cut keys with no questions asked. Nell then re-deposited the bag and her brother slipped me the new ticket as I twisted the night away with the unsuspecting girl. At the end of the evening the romance ended. Bert and I always waited a couple of months before utilising the keys to rob the best properties in London. The takings were unbelievable, fur coats, jewellery, cash...... it all flowed in and back out again, financing my increasing drug habit and crazy life style.

One night we arrived to rob a monster of a mansion in The Bishops Avenue. The house lay in complete darkness as we let ourselves in and crept upstairs. A dim red light came out of a door at the end of a corridor. We sneaked up and peeked inside. Here was the owner of the house lying naked on his belly, chained to the bedposts by his arms and legs. He was gagged and made noises of pleasure as the au-pair I'd once danced with whipped him. She, too, was naked, wearing only a soldier's hat and black boots. The man saw us first but still gagged could only groan as she continued to thrash him. After a while, turning round, she noticed us and screamed with shock when she recognised me. High on drugs Bert and I both rolled around on the floor, laughing. Suddenly the man's gag came off and he started shouting at us. Still giggling we ran off.

On one of these escapades I met the au-pair of a top Hatton Garden jeweller. The usual routine of bag, keys, etc. followed but when I took her home to Hoop Lane in Hampstead I ran into a problem - I was falling in love. This twenty-two-year-old German girl with her curvy body completely captivated the heart of our sixteen-year-old apprentice villain. I wanted to see her again and couldn't say goodbye as usual, completely losing interest in Bert and all my robbing work. Her name was Gerda and with her long blonde hair she looked like Brigitte Bardot. Within days I was madly in love and started to meet her every night. Nothing else mattered anymore, apart from my drugs. Pretending to be twenty-four I made up many stories to look big. One night, trying to be romantic, I looked up at the sky and said, 'I'll get you the moon and stars !' 'Who's going to bring them down, Yuri Gagarin?' she joked. 'Can you phone him up there?' Gerda was genuinely interested in me and always told me how much she loved me. At the end of each evening after taking a taxi to her home we stood outside the house kissing and cuddling for hours, her hand down my trousers. Every night I went home to my uncle's with a wet patch in my pants.

Underneath Gerda's outward display of self-confidence was a nervous girl who, away from her mother's strict supervision, was free for the first time. I was the perfect find for her, a young boy who was obviously very naive sex-wise himself. Gerda, a bit scared of men, felt safe with a boy who wouldn't break her virginity with violence. With me she didn't feel stupid about her own lack of experience but could actually take the lead. Being in love with this girl was giving me something I had never experienced before. It made me feel secure and no longer alone. I began to take less drugs now and we made plans to be together forever. We wanted to get married and Gerda even arranged for me to visit her mother in Germany.

A few weeks before our planned trip my sister was holding her birthday party. Annette's boyfriends with their flashy sports cars had always treated me as the idiot kid brother, but now, with a curvy twenty-two-year-old beauty on my arm, it was my turn to shine. For this party I bought Gerda a low-cut, skin-tight dress which showed every bump in her body and wearing no bra she looked like a sex Goddess. My sister, herself a Liz Taylor-type beauty, had always been queen of the ball but that night it was to be all so very different ! As I entered in my red sports jacket with Gerda at my side I got the desired effect. Annette's male admirers' eyes popped out and they buzzed round Gerda all night. My sister, however, was very peeved finding herself being pushed into second place. Throughout the evening I stuck like glue to Gerda, making sure nobody spoke to her alone in case they divulged my true age.

A little while later Gerda's employers went away for the weekend and she invited me to spend the night with her. I was nervous. What was expected of me sex-wise? All I'd experienced up to now was gay oral sex or her hand down my pants and I had no idea about the female anatomy. I was embarking on a trip to unknown territory. That night as we were sitting on her bed having a couple of drinks to losen up Gerda undressed completely. She looked stunning. Apart from the stripper in the club with Dr. Newam I'd never seen a naked woman before. 'Now it's my turn for some satisfaction,' she said, taking my clothes off. We started to kiss and touch each other with me trying my best to make love to her. I was excited, my dick was stiff and I fumbled about pushing it everywhere but it wouldn't go in. Gerda didn't help and we both became more and more distressed. 'Why can't you make love to me?' she sobbed. Feeling ashamed I said nothing and went downstairs. After a while she followed with a blanket wrapped round her. 'Don't you like me anymore?' she asked. 'Do you find me ugly?' 'No, no,' I said. 'You look lovely. Let's go back upstairs. I'm okay now.' I took four more pills in the toilet, hoping they would help me find the right hole and returned for sex-attempt number two. I tried and tried, praying I would get my dick in but met with the same failure. Gerda, a virgin, was probably as frightened as me. Feeling a complete berk I got drunk and we had a row after which I left in a cab.

The next morning Gerda rang my sister who told her all sorts of undesirable things about me, including my true age. A day later when I rang Gerda her employer's told me that she had packed her bags without notice and left early that morning to return to Germany. I never saw her again.

I was heartbroken and in a hysterical drunken mood took all my hidden drugs and threw them into the river. 'Fuck these happy pills ! How can I be happy now Gerda's gone !' I screamed. Very drunk I returned to my uncle's where I carried on drinking all day locked in my bedroom, refusing to come out. After a couple of days like this uncle Mick decided he could no longer cope and phoned my father, asking him to collect me. By the time my dad arrived I had already left. Devastated I went to see my old nanny Violet, the only woman I trusted.

She was living in a small flat with her own ninety-five-year-old mother and shocked to see the state I was in invited me to stay. These two women lived in a weird world of the past. The old bedridden mother was treating Violet like a child and constantly demanded her attention. Pictures of Violet's father in a soldier's uniform from the first world war were everywhere. For the next few months I lived with these women in a permanent drunken stupor, trying to forget Gerda. One day, drunk and deranged, I went out and bought new Robin Hood books. 'You're too grown-up for them now, Stephen,' Violet said, 'I'll read you the news. Look, they are building a wall across Berlin in Germany !' 'I'm not interested in peoples fucking garden walls,' I screamed. 'I want my Robin.' Quite intimidated Violet had no choice and began to read Robin to me every night while I drunk myself into oblivion. 'Violet's with you. Go to sleep,' she would say. One night, close to alcoholic poisoning, I saw a carving knife on her kitchen table. My childhood nightmare of having to kill the false Violet became instant reality. Picking up the knife I went to her room. She was sitting up in bed and went white when she saw me brandishing the knife, screaming, 'I killed the wrong Violet and now it's your turn to die ! If I'd killed the right one Gerda would still be with me !' Suddenly I started to shake and broke down on the floor, sobbing. A petrified neighbour who'd heard the racket through the thin walls knocked on the door threatening to call the police. Scared I ran off and later passed out somewhere in the red light district of London.

After a few weeks of sleeping here there and everywhere I went back to my parents. What I mean is I started sleeping there. It felt strange. Off speed drugs it all seemed slower. The storm between my ears was subsiding and my parents appeared a lot less threatening now.

A little while later I met a new girl and with her learnt all the rules of the sex game. She was sixteen years old, beautiful with short black hair and legs that went on forever. She always wore short skirts which just pulled up around her waist when we made love. Like all game young girls those days she was on the new anti-baby pill. Sex was great and I had no problems getting my dick in.

In no time at all this girl's parents became concerned about their daughter's wayward new boyfriend and trying to split us up sent her to live in Brussels as a mothers-help. But this didn't stop me. I knew a Belgian politician whom I'd met recently in London's gay clubs. I rang the man, asking if I could stay with him for a while. He was delighted and I figured this way my romance could continue. I took the boat to Ostend from where I caught the train to the man's house near Liege. It was an enormous mansion and he had about ten live-in servants. There was a cook, a butler, four maids, a gardener, a chauffeur and several more. As I arrived they were all lined up to greet me by the front door like in a scene from a forties movie.

This politician was incredibly rich and paid me generously to act out his bizarre sex fantasies. Dressed up as a policeman I would tie him up, pretending he had been caught speeding, forcing him to confess how fast he had been driving while his large dog, a Great Dane, licked him. Then I gave him one stroke of the whip for each kilometre over the allowed speed limit. One day, at the end of a session, he confessed he'd lied and had really driven much faster. Drunk and bored by it all I screamed, 'You lying cunt No car goes that fast !' This man never touched me but one night the dog went berserk and bit me as I administered the punishment.

After a few days at the politician's mansion I took the train to visit my sixteen-year-old lover in Brussels. It turned into a very shitty day, to say the least. Due to my continual drinking I'd developed bad diarrhoea which made me visit the toilet every half hour. On seeing my girlfriend I started to wave excitedly and as she got closer I thought I was going to pass wind but, alas, instead of the expected fart I was shitting. I could feel it dripping down my leg. In sheer panic I ran into a lady's hairdressing salon, pushing past everyone and locked myself in the toilet. With a woman shouting in French and banging on the lavatory door I took my trousers off. I was covered in shit. Suddenly another smelly avalanche came out of my bum, going all over the floor, leaving me now standing in a puddle of it. I wiped off what I could and putting on my smelly trousers ran past the very shocked hairdresser to greet my girl still waiting in the street. In the cold Belgian air the smell was not so bad but when we went into a bar later the stink hit us both. We spent the rest of our date walking in the freezing cold with me forever running in and out of toilets. There was no sex and my lover went home early. We never saw each other again.

When I returned to London all hell broke lose. A new probation officer had been assigned to my case. I still had a few months probation left following my handbag-snatching crime. The new man was very strict and wanted to know why I had gone abroad without permission. He set me an ultimatum. Get a job within seven days or risk going to prison. I had to move quickly. That same day I attended a job interview after answering an advert which read, 'Exciting work, very high pay !' The job turned out to be a commission-only sales job, selling heating systems for a small and rather dubious firm. Waiting with me that first day in the reception were two people who were to change the course of my entire life.

The first was a flashy Jewish man who had just been released from prison. His name was Terry Marvin.

The second was a stunning Maltese girl, the most beautiful woman I had ever seen. Her name was Camilla.

We were three strangers, not knowing that fate, which was about to intertwine their lives, was already spinning it's web.

Chapter 5

LOVE AND A BROKEN HEART

The three loves in my life so far had been a Robin-Hood-reading Violet, a jewel-thieving George followed by runaway Gerda and with this confused emotional background I met Camilla. She was just seventeen with long black hair and big brown eyes. Cars literally stopped in the street as she walked by. Camilla dressed very conservatively in Chanel-type suits and reminded me of a nun who you could dream about but never hope to touch. She was unbelievably good-looking and knew it, always posing with an expression which said, go on, drool over me ! I know I'm God's gift to men !

The fact that Camilla wasn't interested in me in no way dampened my feelings for her. From the moment I first set eyes on her I was addicted and had to have her. I couldn't believe my luck when she was assigned to work in my team as an interviewer. Every day I took her and others to various locations outside London where they worked for a few hours. I used every opportunity to chat her up but as much as I tried she always rejected me with an air of total indifference. Sometimes I heard her talk to the other girls about her boyfriend, an Italian waiter who was apparently quite a bit older than me. To think that this greasy little bugger was touching her made me cringe with jealousy.

Each night taking her home after work I put my arm round her but she just pushed me away, saying, 'Don't keep pestering me.' Despite her rejections I had the feeling that she enjoyed knowing how much I wanted her and relished in the power it gave her over me. She only had to flash her eyes to finish work early or get a lift to the shops. At the weekends I thought about nothing else but her, pining for Monday to come so I could resume my fantasy love affair. Camilla was the only reason I stayed with this job after my probation was up.

Many days we worked alongside Terry Marvin, the Jewish man whom I'd met on the first day and I spent most afternoons with him while our interviewers canvassed. We went to various towns outside London and were actually in Bedford the day James Hanratty was hanged there. There were crowds protesting outside the prison. 'Poor bastard,' Terry said. 'Having to finish his days in a place like that.' Terry, a slim and dapper looking gent of about forty had himself just come out of prison and worked just to keep his own parole officer happy. We were paid on results only but without any real effort made a considerable amount of money. Tel, who impressed me with his spivvy street-wise ways already planned to open his own firm and invited me to become his partner. He obviously saw a talent in me that I didn't. 'We'll make a fortune,' he continually said. When I talked about Camilla Terry always laughed, 'Buy her flowers, that's the way to a woman's heart !' He became another father-figure to me and I looked to him for advice. Some days he met tough-looking characters and when I asked him who they were he replied, 'The heavy mob, Stevie Boy.' Wanting to emulate his worldly ways I began to copy him, even talk like him.

For the next few months all I did was try to get off with Camilla. Every night, following the usual cold rejection and her famous words, 'Leave me alone,' I went to the clubs and drunk myself into oblivion. One weekend I went alone and drunk to the cinema to watch 'Cleopatra' and finished up thinking Liz Taylor was Camilla.

Suddenly one night everything changed. My arm, which was by then on automatic pilot, went round Camilla as usual but she didn't push it away ! I was puzzled. She was letting me kiss her ! My heart was pounding. She kissed me back ! Soon we were in the back of the car making love. I was in heaven ! The forbidden fruit I'd chased for so many months was finally mine. It was so sudden I couldn't believe what was happening and afterwards asked Camilla if it would still be the same tomorrow.

Later I wondered why she suddenly had sex with me? Was she more in love with me than with the waiter or had he left her? Not wanting to burst my bubble of joy I stopped wondering and bought her the latest Cliff Richard love song. Overnight Camilla had become my own 'Living Doll'.

The next day Camilla still kissed me and I continued to float on cloud nine. We began going out together for meals and to the pictures. I was so proud being seen with this film star on my arm, she made me feel better about myself. It was as if people were now looking at me thinking, he must be an okay guy to have such an attractive girl.

Soon we began to spend every night together in a small hotel. I just couldn't let her out my sight and for the first time ever I was sleeping with the lights out. The monsters had gone. Having sex with Camilla convinced me I'd found true love, whatever that was.

Camilla herself lived in a small room in a poor part of London. Her father had died a year or so earlier and her mother and four younger sisters lived in Malta. Some months before she'd come to England to train as a nurse but never started. Life in England must have been very difficult for Camilla. In Malta she had many relatives whereas in London she had nobody.

Brought up a strict Roman Catholic she went to church every Sunday and, blindly in love, I soon found myself sitting alongside her. The church service was strange for a Jewish boy. They were forever standing up and sitting down. Why don't they make up their minds? I thought. Often she received Holy Communion which, considering we were living together unmarried, meant God was super understanding.

After a while she gave up her room and we took a small flat. The apartment, a large bed-sitting room and kitchenette, was very modest but I felt proud of it. The nicest thing about this second floor flatlet were its large bay windows and the pretty view. I was so happy and bought a blue tea pot which was proudly displayed on a shelf to celebrate our first home.

Relieved I didn't need to work anymore just to see Camilla I gave up the job to become involved in various crimes again. Camilla never asked me where I was going or what I was doing and was happy as long as money was coming in. At first life with her seemed perfect but soon the dream romance began sailing into stormy waters. We began to have rows every night and I discovered that she had an uncontrollable temper. Arguments always finished up with her screaming and hitting me. I shouted, too, but never hit her back, instead I would hold her down like a wrestler to protect myself. I really hated it especially when she scratched me and spat in my face. Often I wanted to leave her but I just couldn't, I loved her too much, I was addicted. For

Camilla with her Mediterranean upbringing the screaming was probably quite normal but I found it unbearable.

As time went on I started to wonder why Camilla never put her arms round me or said she loved me even when we weren't rowing. I began to think that she merely saw me as her way out of the bed-sit poverty zone. She had her own formula and with me it worked - the louder she shouted the more she got. I couldn't bear to think she was just using me and as the tragic truth of her feelings towards me started to show my drinking increased. True to my addictive make-up I stayed for more punishment like a trapped animal. One night I even contemplated suicide, thinking of Marilyn Monroe who'd killed herself a month or so before.

It will get better once we're married, I reasoned against all odds. In a rare moment of peace I proposed to her and for some reason she said yes. If she's going to marry me she must really love me I now made myself believe.

Early the following morning I went to see my father because in those days everyone under the age of twenty-one needed their parent's written permission to get married. He was still in bed when I arrived. Sitting at my mother's dressing table I proudly announced my wedding plans, expecting him to congratulate me. My parents had met Camilla a couple of times but had showed no interest in her, expecting this romance to be another flash in the pan. Instead of being happy for me my father sat up in bed and said very matter-of-factly, 'No son of mine is marrying a shicksa in a church ! And besides, you're too young.' Throughout my handbag-snatching and jewel-thieving days I'd done exactly as I pleased but now my father was having his hour of power. Without his signature there would be no wedding. I pleaded with him saying, 'You married mum in a church yourself. How can you be such a hypocrite?' But he was adamant. The answer was no and angrily I stormed out of the house.

I returned to Camilla but told her nothing of my father's refusal. I already had a plan to force his hand - get Camilla pregnant. Two months later she was expecting a child. Smugly I returned to my father holding what I thought was all the aces. On hearing the latest news he just said, 'Well, she'll have to get an abortion.' I was so shocked I swore never to speak with him again. How could I tell Camilla? She was eager now to marry quickly and had already booked a Catholic church for the wedding.

The following week, just before Christmas, we flew to Malta so I could meet Camilla's mother. Lucca airport was very small with only a few flights a day landing on the single air-strip and a terminal not much bigger than a shed. Malta, a small island south of Sicily was still a British Colony and in those days the tourist trade was non-existent. Only four hotels existed on the whole island and Valletta, the only town, had just one shopping street. Malta is so small you can drive round the entire island in an hour. This hot, barren island with its little villages surrounded by palm trees was so very different to London.

From the airport the taxi took us across the island to St. Paul's Bay, a small fishing village which lay in darkness. We stopped in a street so narrow the cab only just fitted between the flat roofed buildings either side. Leaving the suitcases in the street I followed Camilla who ran ahead up a flight of stone stairs. Waiting to greet us in their one-room home was Isabella, Camilla's mother and her four small daughters. This was where Camilla had come from ! A twelve foot square room with a small toilet on the landing. A single staircase lead further up to the flat roof. Camilla's mother, a woman of about forty, broke down when she saw us and started sobbing uncontrollably. She was apologising she had so little to offer explaining that following her husband's sudden death there was nothing left. 'He was a wonderful man. I loved him !' she cried hysterically, throwing her hands up in the air. Everywhere in the room were framed photographs of the dead man. The youngest of the children picked one up and shouted, 'Daddy, this is daddy !' 'Lives in heaven,' said the oldest child. Isabella, who was dressed all in black, cried bitterly and kissed the photograph before clutching it to her chest. She called out, 'George, my George,' as the four young girls hugged her. This woman had not just loved her man, she had worshipped the ground he'd walked on. Up to then I thought this kind of love existed only in movie scripts.

Eventually Isabella calmed down enough to greet Camilla properly and we all sat down. With the many presents I'd brought the small room burst alive with excitement as the children jumped up and down, guessing what could be inside each parcel. On their mother's suggestion they put the gifts in a corner to open them on Christmas morning. Camilla, who'd been distressed when we first arrived to see her mother in such a state, now relaxed and became the returning hero. She loved her family but had found the responsibility following her father's death too much. Her mother opened a bottle of red wine she'd kept for years and we all drank a glass. After that I continued drinking the brandy I'd bought on the plane. One by one the girls fell asleep on a large mattress on the floor.

Camilla and her mother talked about family news, often lapsing into Maltese. I found this family clinging to each other with so much love very moving. Love was all Isabella had to offer these kids but she had plenty to give. Soon I was asleep in my own make-shift bed on the floor.

The next morning I woke up to find four excited girls waiting for Camilla to return from the shops. They were all beautiful, dark-haired children wearing simple patterned dresses and open sandals. Roseanna, the oldest, was thirteen, then came Josephina, aged eight, followed by Louisa and Laura, aged seven and five. When Camilla returned the kids went mad, looking into her bags, shouting, 'Here's bacon ! Look, eggs in a box.' They hadn't seen so much food for ages. Isabella cautiously took it off them and put it on a shelf out of reach. Having so little money their usual diet was basic, mostly pasta, bread and olive oil.

In the early evenings with the room so crowded I began to sit alone on the flat roof. The unrestricted view over the harbour full of small fishing boats was amazing. Isabella kept two chickens up there for their eggs, a luxury for her poor family. She herself never ate eggs, they were for her girls only who shared them on a rota system. Having grown up in a town I regarded these chickens as pets and became very fond of them, calling one Charlie and the other one Fred. Night after night I got drunk and chased them round the roof. Charlie was my favourite, he ran faster but laid less eggs.

On Christmas eve I became very emotional, wanting to give these poor kids a surprise they'd remember all their lives, Christmas in wonderland. I went to the local shop and bought thirty pounds worth of sweets, filling four large carrier bags. The old lady shopkeeper was stunned as I cleared her entire stock. That night as the girls slept I covered the floor one inch thick with sweets. As they woke up in the morning their faces were beaming from ear to ear when I told them it had rained sweets in the night. Isabella was smiling as they jumped all over me covering me with kisses.

I'd found my own formula - buy people enough and you get instant love in return. This would become my mainstay for many years to follow. With enough money I would be able to buy all the love I wanted. I was a good thief so I need never go short on love again. Why hadn't I thought of this years ago !

As Camilla and her mother began to prepare the Christmas dinner I went off to the bar at the end of the street. Many brandies later all four little girls appeared at the door calling out, 'Dinner's ready !' Back in the room I found Isabella in the middle of what seemed like hundreds of boiling pots. We all squashed round the small table when I suddenly realised what we were eating 'Oh Fuck no !' I cried, rushing up to the roof. 'We are eating Charlie !' I was already very drunk and burst into tears. Isabella followed me and asked what was wrong. Sobbing I explained, 'I loved Charlie, we can't eat him.' 'I loved my husband, too,' she said. 'But you didn't eat him,' I cried. 'You're a good man,' she said, calming me down. 'You gave the children so much ! Nobody else ever did anything for them and I just wanted to give you the Christmas dinner you deserved !' Overcome by Isabella's warmth towards me I put my arms round her and sobbed, 'I'll get you a flat, a television, a fridge, a phone, everything.' She hugged me, saying, 'I love you,' and led me back down to the children who were happily tucking into their Christmas dinner with grease all over their faces. At least Charlie hadn't died in vain !

Over the following evenings I often lay down on the floor with the little girls telling them drunken fairy stories. They idolised me and this made me feel good, as if I belonged to a family for the first time in my life. Each night after the kids had gone to sleep I hit the bars, never returning until the early hours to always find Isabella waiting for me with hot soup. I couldn't believe how much this woman cared for me.

As her Christmas treat I took Isabella to the cinema to see Cliff Richard in 'Summer Holiday'. Wearing her curly black hair up and smiling with the small gap in her front teeth she looked both beautiful and sweet. Laura, the youngest child, cried so much we took her with us. I wanted to take a taxi but Isabella refused, saying it was too expensive so we went by bus. Riding up the winding coast road to Valletta Isabella pointed out various places - where she had met her late husband, where they had danced, where they had sat. This was the story of her life. It had revolved totally around the only man she'd ever loved.

On the day we had to go back to England everybody started crying. I turned to Isabella and said, 'You showed me love, you even killed Charlie for me. You will soon have a flat in Sliema. Your days in St. Paul's Bay are over.' Not so long after they got their new home, guaranteeing me their love. The formula was working.

Back in England my father still refused to consent to our wedding. 'Marry a Jewish girl when you're older,' he would repeat like a tape recorder. I was up against a brick wall and the following week, out of desperation, I forged his signature. Shortly after in May

1963 in an empty church in Tottenham with just the priest present we got married. Looking at the rows of empty seats made me sad. Once more my parents had deserted me. Afterwards the priest wished us luck. We need more than that. It's going to take plenty of money to keep this marriage alive I thought as we left the church. We celebrated our wedding alone with a meal, followed by the usual row. Afterwards I drunk myself to sleep with the lights back on.

We were married now but life became even more explosive than ever before. Our fights got worse. After each row Camilla sobbed her heart out, I consoled her, cuddled her, then often we made love. It was strange - it always took a fight to bring us physically together. In August, with the baby due any day, news about the Great Train Robbery hit England like a bombshell. Two and a half million pounds had been stolen in cash. That will buy plenty of love, I smiled to myself. A week or so later I got home to find Camilla had been rushed into Hackney Mother's Hospital. Like a lunatic I drove there and rushed into the ward. She had just given birth. Tessa Maria, our daughter, had come into the world. The baby girl was beautiful, a miniature version of her mother even at that age. I picked up the baby and looking into her eyes knew here was a person who would love me for life. I was the only dad she would ever have.

Not long after Camilla brought our daughter home everything exploded once again. As the Beatles sung their latest hit 'She loves you' I searched my soul, wondering if my wife ever had. Life became a war-zone without cease-fires. Camilla and I just couldn't be together without rowing - even at three in the morning when the baby was fed. There was only peace when we were both asleep. Unable to cope with it any longer I suggested Camilla took a six month holiday in Malta. It was the only way to stay married and not go potty altogether.

On the way to the airport Camilla became hysterical again, screaming that our flat was too small to bring up a child. She wanted a luxury home or she wouldn't come back to me. I promised to get one. Whatever it cost to keep her I would find it, steal it, whatever. I was addicted to that woman and now I had a baby daughter to love as well.

It will take ten Train Robberies to keep this woman happy, I thought with despair.

I cried as I watched the plane take off, swallowing the first of many drinks. Listening to my radio as I drove back I heard the news that Kennedy had just been shot in Dallas and wondered if I wouldn't be better off dead as well.

With Camilla away my alcohol intake spiralled out of control.

Especially at night drink was my friend, it held my hand.

Chapter 6

ALEN

It was a cold winter and the papers were full of news about Roy James, the train robber, being arrested and Christine Keeler going to prison. With Camilla and our baby now in Malta I should have felt more at ease but instead I got more depressed and up went my drinking. After Christmas I felt so very alone, desperately needing some understanding and a bit of kindness.

It was uncanny but as if I knew what was about to happen I went back to the bright lights of Piccadilly Circus. That evening the rain began falling heavy just like on the night I'd met Gentleman George. I dived for shelter in the doorway of a jeweller's shop and seconds later an elegant elder gentleman rushed in next to me. He was wearing a dark tailored overcoat with a bowler hat and for a few moments said nothing but kept looking at me. At last he spoke, 'Things are a bit expensive here, aren't they?' 'They sure are,' I agreed. 'Money gets you almost everything,' he said. 'If you've got enough of it,' I added. 'Why? Haven't you enough money?' he laughed. Thinking of Camilla I replied, 'I'll never have enough for what I want.' 'Well, let's see if we can put that right. Let's have a drink.'

He led me to an exclusive cocktail bar where inside, out of the evening rain, he suggested a brandy to warm us both up. Returning with two large glasses he announced, 'Cheers, my young friend. Come on, smile. I'm going to give you a thousand pounds !' (Today worth twenty thousand). I was speechless. 'Will that solve your problems?' he asked with a smile. I sat there dumbfounded. 'Sorry, I haven't got all the money on me tonight but I'll give you one hundred pounds now and the rest tomorrow,' he continued. Pulling out his wallet he counted out one hundred pounds. As he handed me the cash I thought, this must be some kind of television prank show, waiting for people to jump up saying, 'We fooled you !' Then the city gent stood up. 'I must fly. Let's meet in here at the same time tomorrow !' I nodded. Putting on his overcoat he introduced himself. 'My name's Alen. What's yours?' 'Stephen,' I replied. 'How nice,' he said, running out of the door into the night. I'd known him for ten minutes and here I was with one hundred pounds in my hand. Coming to my senses I rushed after this elegant stranger but he'd already vanished down the hole of the nearby underground station like the rabbit in 'Alice in Wonderland'.

The following evening I went to the bar as arranged but to my disappointment he wasn't there. He must have been drunk, I thought. People don't stop you in the street to give you a thousand pounds, not in real life. Thirty minutes after our arranged meeting I stood up to leave when a flustered Alen rushed in. 'I'm so sorry, Stephen,' he said panting, 'Forgive me, I'm in the middle of a business meeting and I must return !' He handed me an envelope and added, 'Here's the money I promised. Let's meet for dinner on Friday? Please say yes.' 'Okay,' I said. 'Seven in here then?' he smiled and like a puff of smoke was gone again. I sat back bewildered and opened the envelope which contained nine hundred pounds and a card which read, 'Beauty like your's cannot go unrewarded ! Love Alen.' This only happens in films, I thought ! Who'd sent me this strange benefactor? Why had he given me so much money? What did he want from me? All I knew was that his name was Alen and he had access to a lot of new bank notes. Wondering whether it was real money I spent one of the notes at the bar. It was real all right, very real.

That Friday we met as arranged. I turned up looking like something out of a fashion magazine in a new blue suit, yellow shirt and a bright red tie, bursting to learn more about my mystery friend. Alen was a tall, slim man with a round and friendly face. He had wavy grey hair and crooked white teeth. His eyes were alive, lighting up when he smiled. 'You look wonderful,' he said greeting me. 'I wanted to look nice for you,' I replied, feeling flattered. 'You're a funny boy,' he mused. Boy? I was nineteen years old. But of course I was a boy to this old man. We took a taxi to the Great Western Hotel where we were escorted by the head waiter to our booked table. I was handed the wine list but sensing my ignorance Alen suggested, '59 was a good year.' '64 is a better year,' I joked. 'Why's that?' Alen asked. 'Because that's the year I met you !' 'Yes, it's a wonderful year for us both,' he replied.

When someone loves you, you instinctively feel it. It's not what they say or do, you just know it and I knew this man called Alen had fallen in love with me. If I had to suffer through being in love with Camilla, Alen was about to suffer the same through me. In the middle of our meal he handed me a small red box. Excitedly I opened it to find a gold watch ! 'Turn it over,' he said. The inscription read, 'I love you. Alen.' I stared at him. 'I really do,' he said, 'I know it's a bit quick, but I do. I can't help it.' He held my hand. Looking in his eyes I saw the love I had searched for all my life. We talked on but now he kept things light-hearted. After our meal he beckoned the head waiter over to call me a cab.

'Tomorrow night, same time, same place !' he called out, waving goodbye.

At home that night I found a letter from Camilla in which she repeated that she would never return to our small flat. It read like a final notice, threatening love supply disconnection. Immediately I wrote back lying, telling her I'd already found a luxury flat but we couldn't move in till August. I hadn't even started looking but August seemed a lifetime away to someone with his head in the sand.

My mind was in permanent turmoil over anything to do with Camilla so my dates with Alen were my escape from reality. Apart from the financial rewards his adulation was the exact opposite to Camilla's demands and ultimatums. Where she found fault he found beauty. Alen and I soon began to meet regularly and during these romantic dinner-dates he always told me how much he loved me. Sometimes, a little drunk, I closed my eyes and pretended it was Camilla speaking. The evening after Cassius Clay beat Sonny Liston to become Heavyweight Boxing Champion of the World I joked with Alen, sparring, saying I could beat anybody. He put his arm round me and replied, 'Your face is too precious to be hit !'

Over the next few months Alen took me to the most exciting locations in town. It wasn't just the money now - I never needed it in the first place. His love meant just as much to me. With Alen I was in a fantasy world with no responsibility and no flats to find. I was being looked after and cared for. Alen never asked me about my background, my parents or where I had come from. For him I had been born outside the Jeweller's shop in Piccadilly Circus. This way I remained the perfect boy of his illusion. Of course I never mentioned that I was married, I don't think it would have enhanced our 'romance'. I began to wonder where it all was leading to. What did Alen really want from me? So far, nothing at all ! I had only to turn up for our dates, look nice, eat an expensive meal, accept another gift and get a cab home. I couldn't understand his kindness. As much as I enjoyed my new life with Alen I missed Camilla more and more. On the night I read Liz Taylor had married Richard Burton I thought of Camilla and almost flew over to Malta.

One night Alen asked me if I would mind having dinner at his home on our next date. At last, I thought, here comes the homosexual sex. Time to pay. Now I will have to prostitute myself for all the money and gifts. I was appalled but relieved at the same time. I couldn't cope with any more kindness. Love that asked for nothing in return was alien to me. Now we were getting down to basics - sex for money. I understood this one. It's got to be suitcases of money, not envelopes anymore, I laughed to myself. The following Friday I went to his address near Gloucester Road. Alen's spacious flat was on the ground floor of a six storey Georgian town house in very fashionable road opposite private gardens. That spring afternoon I was greeted by a smiling Alen. 'Come in, darling boy. We have company for dinner.' 'Oh, oh !' I thought, here we go ! Group sex ! Some homosexual queen to photograph the whipping sessions. This will cost you both a fortune.

Alen led me into an elegantly furnished lounge. The grand piano and oil paintings on the walls were just part of the immense wealth on display. I looked round for our perverted dining partner but what I'd imagined could not have been further from the truth. In the corner sat a sweet old lady, a slender woman with silvery hair which she wore in a bun. This elegant woman dressed in dark blue was Alen's old mum. Smiling at me she said, 'Hello Stephen, sit down here. Let me have a look at you ! I've heard so much about you !' Now this is really turning into a movie script, I thought. 'Isn't he beautiful, just like I told you Mummy?' Alen asked proudly. 'Yes Darling, he really is a beautiful boy,' the old woman replied. Oh fuck, I thought, this is his idea of group sex ! More kindness and compliments. 'Have a drink and a chat with mother. Do you know she's one hundred years old?' Alen said proudly. 'I'll fetch the dinner,' and with that he left the room.

At the age of sixty-five Alen was just beginning to admit to himself that he was homosexual and I was his first love. His mother, an astute woman, had sensed it all along. Alen had repressed his feelings until he met me and mum now reasoned it was better he brought his new love home instead of hiding him. Inspite of her age this old lady was still all with it ! Calling me to sit by her side she looked at me intently, saying, 'Alen loves you, you know that, don't you?' Unable to answer I just nodded and sat silent as she went on. 'Make me one solemn promise. Don't ever hurt my son.'

As she spoke the large oak doors to the dining room opened and Alen announced that dinner was served. We helped his old mother to the top of the long dining table. 'You are our special guest,' he said, seating me at the other end. Throughout the meal I felt ashamed. If he had wanted sex I could have coped with it, but no, Alen wanted far more. He wanted me to love him ! How could I ? I wasn't gay and besides, I was in love with a Maltese girl three thousand miles away. For the first time ever I was being unconditionally loved and now it was me dishing out the pain. Like him, yes, but love him? Impossible. The guilt began to outweigh the envelopes of cash. Of course that night I could have said, thanks old chap, sorry, I'm not gay. But I didn't. I needed to be loved and wanted. After dinner and a little small talk with his mother I got the usual cab ride home, holding yet another envelope of cash. The evenings at Alen's home continued but with one difference. Now the old lady retired to bed at ten, leaving us alone with each other. For sex? No ! Alen played the piano and sang love songs to me. His favourite tune was, 'People who need People are the Luckiest People in the World.' He needed me but he was hardly lucky to do so. Apart from dinners at his home we had the most fantastic days out together, strolling around town, visiting the new 'Biba' store and many other places. 1964 was an exciting time. Mods and Rockers were fighting on the beaches of Brighton, The Beatles and the Rolling Stones were kings of pop, it was all happening. From our front row seats at Wimbledon we watched Maria Bueno beat Margaret Smith in the women's final. If tennis and strawberries made me feel like a prince soon I was to be treated like a king. A few weeks later Alen took me to the Beatles movie premiere 'A Hard Days Night' at the London Pavilion.

It was after one of the grand evenings with Alen when I suddenly realised that Camilla was due back in exactly two weeks and expected to live in the luxury new home I'd lied about. This quickly brought me down to earth with a bang. Part of me knew that even with a luxury home the rows would continue but in the same way Alen loved me I loved Camilla. I wanted her back. Suddenly I remembered Terry Marvin, thinking this man about town with all his connections will surely help me find the right place. I hadn't seen him for a year and discovered he'd moved but eventually found him living in a penthouse opposite Hampstead Heath, one of the best parts of London. He told me he'd opened his own heating firm called 'Highheat' and proudly showed me his new Rolls Royce. I wondered how his firm had made so much money in a year. It didn't quite add up. 'Spending it all a bit quick,' I smiled. Terry, a lean man with dark hair combed back wasn't super handsome but he had a flair about him. He was one of the boys and knew practically every gangster in London, which impressed me no end. Again Terry suggested that I joined him in business. Now I was more than pleased to do so but explained that first I had a far more pressing problem. I had to find a luxury home within a week to get my wife back from Malta. 'So you hooked her after all !' he laughed on hearing about my troubles. 'Should have invited me to the wedding.' Thinking back to the empty church I thought at least we would have had someone there. 'Leave the flat to uncle Tel !' he said with his usual air of confidence That's exactly what I did. Tel's enthusiasm rubbed off on me and being back around him felt good. Two days later he handed me a set of keys smiling, 'New luxury home near your uncle Tel, Stevie Boy.' The fancy flat in a luxury block in Hampstead Way was set back off the road in wonderful landscaped gardens. It was a large and beautiful apartment with three bedrooms and two living rooms. Afterwards he invited me down to his new offices, urging me once again to become his partner. He kept repeating, 'We will make fortunes together.' Over the next few years we did just that. The following day we finalised an agreement and I paid him three thousand pounds to become a fifty percent shareholder in Highheat.

In typical Terry fashion the two of us went to celebrate our new partnership at a fashionable night club. That evening, loosened up by drink, I told him the entire story about me and Alen. Terry listened intently. We were already quite drunk when three men came over to our table. Two of them had very dark features and looked almost identical. The third was short with red hair. Ignorant as to who they were I carried on talking when suddenly I recognised the wild rabies look - it was the man from the basement club I'd encountered many years before with Gentleman George. But now there were two of them, he had a twin. 'Stephen, my boy,' Terry said, 'let me introduce some close friends of mine, Reggie and Ronnie Kray.' They both shook my hand. 'And this is Tommy Cowley,' Terry continued, pointing to the third man. This was my official introduction to London's top crime bosses. I was relieved when I realised that Ronnie didn't recognise me as the cocky little kid who'd insulted him all those years ago. They had one drink and after a private word in Tel's ear left.

I was glad the flat and everything was sorted out and I could relax for a few days before flying over to Malta to bring Camilla and the baby back. A day or so before I was due to leave I had dinner at Alen's home. Omitting the part about a wife and daughter I excitedly told him about the new flat. To cover for the Malta trip I pretended to be going for a week's holiday in Spain. Alen offered me an antique desk as a house-warming present but when he suggested to have it delivered while I was away I refused, saying it would be better if I collected it later. The secret lives of Alen and Camilla were already causing complications. The following morning Alen took me to his company offices, London's biggest stockbroking firm 'Copel Pure Lindon Dark and Co'. Alen was a senior partner and had a great deal of control at his firm. That day he handed me a company cheque for a considerable amount of money. 'Your

shares went up,' he said laughing, 'You're getting rich !'
He'd secretly bought and sold shares in my name. Being
Alen's first love his generosity was uncontrollable, he
just could not give me enough. He often wrote intimate
love notes to me, sometimes on his company note
paper, leaving himself wide open to blackmail.
Thanking him I said goodbye, promising to ring as soon
as I returned from what he thought was Spain

Chapter 7

A BOATLOAD OF DRUGS

Two days before departing for Malta I went out with two young men I'd recently met, Con and Keith. They were wild types, living it up day and night high as kites on amphetamine. No way did I want to wind up in the same state they were in, remembering the drug-induced horrors of Dr. Newam. My all-day drinking was inflicting enough damage but speed drugs? I didn't want that again !

It was a sunny bank holiday Monday when at Hampstead funfair Con offered me a pill. I refused, telling him I was once addicted to amphetamine, 'Thanks, I'll stick to my brandy.' But he stuffed two pills in my pocket anyway, saying, 'These are different, man, they're not addictive !' We all got onto the roundabout, laughing and calling out to each other. The music was blaring as they shouted again and again, 'Take the pills, take the pills !'

Why I did I will never know, but I swallowed them both. Those two pills were the first of over half a million tablets I was to take during the next twenty years. Like the roundabout my life began to spin round and round for ever more. At first I thought the strange feeling was the horse going up and down and got off the ride. Minutes later, as the mind altering drugs took control, I climbed back on the merry-go-round. Paying over and over for new rides I stayed on it for hours.

I was back on drugs, I was addicted.

Eventually I got off and searched for the boys to ask them for more pills. Out of our minds we all took several tablets and started to behave like lunatics. At the bow and arrow stall, stoned beyond belief, we fired arrows into the air above the passing crowds, causing havoc. Our frenzy continued as we threw ice-cream over bumper car drivers. It just went on and on until a crowd of angry stallholders chased us from the fair.

Too drugged to stop the action we carried on that evening with a wild party at my new flat. Girls were everywhere, all stoned, drunk and half naked. I must have passed out on a combination of drink and drugs and woke up feeling terrible with the sun coming in through the windows. Naked bodies were scattered all over the place. I was wearing only a vest with my dick hanging out and couldn't recall a thing. Attached to my vest with a giant safety pin was an envelope and inside it were seven yellow pills and a note saying, 'Pills for Malta ! Love Con.'

Oh my God ! Oh no ! I suddenly remembered ! I was supposed to be flying to Malta that morning. Hardly able to move I took all seven pills in one go. Ten minutes later, beginning to wake up properly, I rang for a taxi and was soon on route to the airport. In the back of my cab I felt the almighty buzz of the drugs come over me, getting stronger and stronger, like a kettle coming up for the boil. As we passed Gloucester Road I was already out of my mind and made the driver stop at Alen's. It was seven in the morning but that didn't deter me from banging on his door. Alen was shocked to see me looking rough and acting so strange. 'What's wrong, Stephen? I thought you were in Spain.' 'I'm on my way there now ! I'm in terrible trouble and need a thousand pounds quickly,' I screamed. The taxi was still ticking over in the street as his mother called out,

'Who's there, Alen?' 'Oh, nothing,' he called back, 'it's a registered letter.' He gave me a personal cheque and looking very worried said, 'What are you doing to yourself, Stephen? Please ring me when you get back.' Jumping into the taxi I waved to Alen who looked so lost on his own doorstep. I didn't need his money and the cheque was no use in Malta. This was the first of many lunatic things I was to do for no reason under the influence of drugs.

At the airport my plane was delayed for hours and when it eventually took off I was already feeling the drug come-down. The excitement and happiness was replaced by tiredness and doom. Since I had no more pills I drunk brandy throughout the flight to ease this awful sad feeling. In Malta I took a taxi to Camilla's mother's flat, arriving there in a terrible state. Everybody looked shocked to see me like this but feeling too ill to care I just drunk myself to sleep. The next day, instead of being happy to see Camilla and my little daughter again, I was only interested in drugs, nothing else mattered. Isabella and her girls couldn't understand what was wrong with me.

Here in Malta the true horror of my dependence showed for the first time. The chemical high of the last few days had re-lit the addiction and all I craved for now was the buzz from the drugs. My craving turned into desperation when I realised I couldn't get any pills in Malta. I tried getting drunk, but drink no longer gave me the feeling I now so desperately wanted. After about five hours in a bar I returned to the flat, mumbled something about urgent business and left for the airport to catch the next flight back to London and the drugs. My wife and her family looked puzzled but seemed to believe me. Camilla still agreed to come back to

England a week later. The photos of the new flat had done the trick.

Landing at Heathrow just the thought of my first dose of drugs turned me on. From the airport I phoned Keith for more pills and he put me in touch with his own drug dealer. Two hours later I met this man who offered to get me a hundred pills later that day. 'Don't be fucking stupid !' I screamed. 'I need to stock up !' I offered him money to introduce me to his supplier and seeing the handful of notes he agreed.

A meeting was set up between myself and a mystery man near Barnes Bridge. At first it was all 'Cloak and Dagger' with him making sure I wasn't from the police. 'How long have you been a dealer? How long have you known Patrick?' he wanted to know. 'Oh, sometime,' I replied. How was he to believe I wanted all the drugs for myself? Still looking at me with suspicion he asked, 'How much do you want to spend?' I showed him two thousand pounds and patting my pocket indicated much more. Now he took me seriously and asked me to follow him for about a mile down the river. As we walked he kept turning round, making sure we were not being followed. Eventually we reached a house-boat and locking ourselves inside we went down into the hull. There he showed me suitcases with hundreds of pill-bottles inside. 'What kind of pills are all these?' I asked. 'All uppers, amphetamine,' he said, handing me two tablets to sample. I took them and we sat down. In a very short time I was buzzing, my head was exploding. 'Well?' he grinned, seeing the pills were working on me. 'How much?' I asked. 'For how many?' 'For every pill on this boat !' I shouted. After much bargaining we settled on a price and I went to fetch my car alongside the barge. Together we loaded all the pills, completely filling the car boot. There were over

300,000 tablets and driving away I was one happy addict ! I had ten years supply of drugs. From now on all the gay doctors and dealers could go and fuck themselves ! I was never going to be short of pills or happiness again. If I'd been offered a million pounds for those drugs I would have refused. Those pills were my confidence, my self-belief and with them I could steal enough money to buy all the love I needed.

A few miles along the road I suddenly noticed a police car behind me. I've been set up ! I thought. Caught with so many drugs I would have gone to prison for a long time. How would any jury believe they were all for me? Trying to act cool I pulled off the road into the 'Ace' cafe only to see the police car pull in behind me. Should I run? My heart was pounding as I walked into the cafe and sat at a table waiting to be arrested. But when the two policemen entered they just bought sandwiches and left. I breathed a sigh of relief and when I'd calmed down enough drove home to quickly unload the drugs, locking myself inside the flat. There were so many ! Hundreds of bottles ! The sheer size of my purchase was mind-blowing. Standing back like an art collector admiring his paintings I stared at my pills, a room full of drugs. Ecstatic I kissed every bottle and started to count each pill one by one putting them into piles of five hundred. I soon gave up counting, it would have taken days. Instead I filled my pockets with tablets and went out for one wild night.

Stoned out of my mind I met up with Keith and began a seven day drug-binge, the worst yet in my life. One day blended into the next as I swallowed handfuls of pills at a time. High all the time I couldn't control my brain.

Towards the end of this lunatic week, in the middle of another party, I suddenly remembered Alen's special dinner. I should have been there ! Leaving a new crowd of naked bodies strewn about the floor I ran out and drove like a madman to his flat.

I arrived to find him with his mother cutting the cake. He looked upset and said, 'I thought you'd forgotten and weren't coming.' I apologised with some feeble excuse which Alen only half believed. Suddenly, realising I hadn't bought a present, I rushed back out to the local shops, returning with chocolates and champagne. They weren't even wrapped but Alen, so pleased to see me, forgave anything. His mother, however, gave me sterner looks. Throughout the dinner I tried to act normal as Alen made conversation between the three of us. 'What are you doing tomorrow, Sunday morning?' he asked. 'Sunday?' I shrieked. 'What's the date?' 'It's the first of the month today,' his mother answered. Oh God, no ! I thought, hearing the grandfather clock strike eight. Camilla was arriving at Heathrow airport in an hour's time.

'Alen, I will explain,' I shouted, 'I must go.' Jumping up in the middle of the meal I ran to the street door. In the hall I turned, dashed back and throwing my arms round Alen kissed him in front of his mother, shouting, 'I love you, I really do !' I rushed back out the front door, leaving Alen and his old mum frozen with shock.

Driving towards the airport I felt very confused. What was happening to me? My whole life was spinning round. I didn't know who I was supposed to be anymore ! Was I Camilla's husband meeting her with our new baby girl, Alen's lover cutting his special cake, or Keith's playboy buddy at another wild party? Confused I took even more pills.

At the airport police were everywhere, still looking for Charlie Wilson, the Train Robber who'd escaped from Winston Green Prison a few weeks earlier. I was stoned as I watched my wife and baby come through the customs. Camilla was very suntanned, looking more attractive than ever and the baby was like a little smiling doll. Meeting them seemed to shock me out of my other identities, as if Alen and Co. didn't exist.

To enable us to move straight in I'd arranged for the entire flat to be carpeted and partly furnished. On the journey back from the airport I said nothing to ensure there were no arguments but after a long period of silence Camilla dropped her latest bombshell. She wanted a separation and intended to live in the flat on her own with the baby. I went absolutely berserk, screaming that if I could not live with them there would be no flat and she could catch the next flight back to Malta. I had nothing to lose and meant it. Camilla realised my state of mind and agreed to stay with me or at least live in the same flat. The drugs and Camilla's ultimatums made my head spin with even more confusion.

Parking outside the flat we were about to get out of the car when a girl, half-undressed and looking very dishevelled, came out of the main entrance ! 'Look at that slut,' Camilla said. 'She's not even dressed properly !' Horrified I recognised the girl. She'd been at my party with Keith the previous day. Oh my God ! Who else is still up there? I thought.

'No no !' I shouted, pushing Camilla back into the car. 'I've forgotten. Terry's got the keys ! We must collect them from his office.' At the Highheat offices Camilla was kept waiting on the pretext that Tel had left the keys in a engineer's car who was bringing them back to the office soon. While we drank tea Tel performed yet another of his miracles, clearing every naked body from my flat, giving them strict instructions never to return.

With all the evidence gone Camilla, baby and myself finally moved into our new home to resume our stormy life. Soon I was out for the count and slept for two solid days. When I woke Camilla said that mystery people had kept calling at the door, asking for the party ! 'Must be another flat !' I replied coolly.

Chapter 8

HELTER SKELTER YEARS

My wife and daughter were back, I had a luxury flat and Alen was constantly showering me with money or gifts. Added to all this Terry, my Jewish gangster partner, now introduced me to the worst of criminals so times were hectic, to say the least. Taking so many drugs life became like a helter-skelter ride, moving at such a fast pace I no longer knew what I was doing. Camilla, however, seemed content in her new surroundings and as long as she had money to spend didn't ask any questions, even when I disappeared for days.

I now owned half of Highheat, although I didn't have a clue as to what was going on behind the scenes. My partner Terry was a devious character with little intention of playing it straight. He only saw me as a gullible kid with too much money, ready to be exploited. His neurotic obsession had always been to become the Godfather of London's criminal underworld and to this end he had taken Tommy Cowley onto our books. Tommy, the right hand man to the crime bosses the Kray twins, was just as evil as his masters. The Kray's who had by now become the undisputed kings of the underworld in London were feared by everyone. At thirty they were at the peak of their careers with an army of men enforcing their reign of terror. Reggie was a violent man but his brother Ronnie was worse, an insane psychopath. Terry with his gangster complex had been easily hooked by the Krays because he was really the exact opposite of the Al Capone figure he so much wanted to be. He was just a dreamer, petrified of the Kray twins who made him do exactly as they wanted. Nevertheless, having them in the background enabled Terry to run his own show, frightening criminal novices like me. Tommy Cowley, of course, did no work and was on the company books simply because the Krays wanted him there.

One day I accompanied Cowley to the coast to collect a bad debt from a hotel owner who refused to pay for Highheat's defective work. Cowley, a short James Cagney look-alike, insisted two young girls from the company offices came with us. At the hotel Cowley threatened the owner with the Kray name and immediately we were paid in full. 'Sorry I was late paying,' the man said as he handed Cowley the money. I was amazed at the fear the Kray name inspired. Cowley helped himself to a considerable amount of cash, saying it was money for the twins and gave the rest to me for Terry.

Mission completed we finished up drinking in the hotel bar with the girls when three men, twice Cowleys size, started to argue with him. I got frightened and as usual took more drugs. Once again Cowley mentioned the Kray name and the men backed away. I couldn't believe my eyes.

Earlier the hotel owner had given Cowley two adjoining bedrooms free of charge and now all a bit drunk, we took the girls upstairs. The girls were already half undressed and we'd just got going sexually when Cowley left the room and returned with one of the men from earlier. 'She's yours to fuck !' he said to him, leading me and the second girl into the adjoining room. Both girls seemed to be very frightened and just did as they were told. Some minutes later Cowley looked at me with a mad expression in his eyes. 'This is what happens to people who annoy us !' he said, bursting back into the room where the man was now on top of the girl. Using a brass lamp he hit him over the head, cutting him very badly. The naked girl screamed hysterically as Cowley pulled the man to the floor and struck him again and again. His nose was practically severed from his face and his mouth was full of blood as Cowley kicked him senseless. Ripping the sheet into strips Cowley turned to me and screamed, 'Tie the bastard up !' It wasn't necessary. The man, now laying in a pool of blood, wasn't moving. Scared stiff I obeyed and tied up the body, getting blood all over my hands. Cowley now unzipped his trousers and jumping on top of the terrified girl screamed, 'This is how you fuck a woman !' The girl, herself splattered with blood, cried but stopped as Cowley hit her round the face, shouting, 'I'm fucking you, enjoy it !' Halfway through the sex Cowley jumped off to kick the trussed up man again who just stared blankly, then jumped back and continued to fuck the girl. Reaching his climax he screamed, 'Cut the bastards prick off !' Petrified I ran back to the other room to hide in the wardrobe with the second girl.

Later, when everything had calmed down, Cowley took the girls and me to a local night-club. After what had happened we were just too scared to leave him. The two other men from earlier came in, saying how sorry they were for what had been said and pleaded with Cowley to take some money and not to mention anything to the twins. I now had witnessed first-hand the violence that enforced the Kray empire. That night back in London as he dropped us off Cowley glared, saying, 'You saw nothing !' 'Nothing,' replied a chorus of frightened voices. He then turned to me,

'Next week you will do the Krays a favour !' I sat there, dried blood still on my shirt, too afraid to speak and just nodded.

A week later I found myself in the witness stand, giving false evidence for ex British boxing champion Sonny McCothey who was on a theft charge. Standing in front of the jury I asked myself why I was doing this. I didn't even know McCothey, I'd never bloody well met him. Looking up to the public gallery the answer stared me in the face - Cowley and the Kray twins smiling.

Over the next few months I witnessed much more violence as Terry paid to put people in their place. It gave him pleasure. Once a man who had left Highheat to start his own company was held out of a fifth floor window by his feet and told he would be dropped unless he closed his firm down and re-joined Terry. Two days later he did. On another occasion a mini cab driver was viciously beaten simply because he wouldn't give Tel details of where he'd taken me the previous day. This man nearly lost his eye and was hospitalised for many weeks. Terry, who never hit anyone himself, employed second division thugs to do the dirty work for him. This way he continued his Godfather fantasy, but in terms of violence the Krays were in a different league. They were the real bloody thing.

The continuing high quantities of drugs now began to take my life into another dimension and without realising it I slipped back into the world of serious crime. It wasn't the money I was after, I didn't need any. It was the buzz, the escape from normal life.

Through Terry I had met a character whom I shall call Billy. He was part of a blag team famous for a series of large-scale wage snatches. It all came about because

Terry had witnessed me driving my Jaguar at ridiculous speeds down one-way streets, dodging other cars just for kicks. I could only do this because amphetamine quickened my reflexes and made me oblivious to the risks. Having heard about my exploits Billy asked me to take him on one of these wild spins and on his word I was catapulted into the role of getaway driver on a big wage snatch. There was a lot of money involved and while we were just talking about it I felt big. When I realised we were actually going to do it the horrors set in because, without amphetamine to give me the bravado, I was still like an insecure kid, scared of the dark.

During the days of the run-up to the robbery I kept imagining crashing the getaway car and killing someone. I wanted out but it was too late and Billy came on very heavy when I expressed my doubts. On the morning of the job, very scared, I took so many pills I nearly overdosed and was totally spaced out as we picked up the robbery cars. An older man who'd never wanted me to be part of the team realised the state I was in and said, 'Fuck up, son, and you're dead.' I was very frightened and wanted to run away but things now began to happen thick and fast.

In the rear-view mirror of the getaway car I watched as the gang rammed the wages truck with our second vehicle. I began crying when I heard shouting and the breaking of glass. The driver was forced to open the wage truck at gun point. It was all over in seconds and as the men piled into my car I felt a gun press into the back of my neck. 'Fuck up and you're dead, son.' The familiar words came from a hooded face behind me. My foot hit the accelerator so hard we shot off like a rocket but in a weird way the car didn't seem to move. Everything seemed to happen in slow-motion.

One of the robbers was being dragged along outside and as someone pulled him through the window into the moving car he screamed abuse at me. The older man hit him in the face, saying, 'Later, let the kid drive.' We had a pre-planned route but on turning the first corner a delivery lorry blocked the entire road. I mounted the pavement with my hand on the horn. Suddenly a woman with a pram came out between two parked cars but at the speed we were driving it was impossible to stop. She somehow pushed the pram out of the way and miraculously leapt to safety herself. As I hit and bounced off various parked cars I felt like being in a film where everything has already happened.

Constantly turning left and right we were soon in the clear and I realised that barring a stupid accident I'd made it. I started laughing and crying at the same time. On reaching our third car we all piled out and I vanished down the nearby underground station with the older man. Sitting on the train he said, 'Well done son, you drove well !' His words meant more to me than all the cash I was to receive later that day. It was this recognition I had always wanted, not just the money. Since I was a child I just wanted to be accepted and belong to someone. Sadly, for me it had to be a gang of robbers.

I locked my share, several carrier bags of cash, in the flat out of Camilla's sight. It took me several days to get over that robbery but I did and with the help of my drugs went on to commit many more crimes. Under the influence of amphetamine what I was doing didn't seem real anymore, it was all just a game.

A few days after the robbery we drove to London Airport to meet Camilla's mother Isabella and her daughters visiting for Christmas. Isabella was stunned to see how thin I looked. I had lost three stone in weight since I'd last seen her. My addiction, the crimes and the violence were taking its toll but inspite of everything I wanted to give Isabella and her girls a normal holiday. During our Christmas dinner I stared at my family. Because of the bloody drugs I'd forgotten that Camilla and Tessa even existed. That afternoon Louisa pushed Tessa on a swing and she fell off. Her crying jolted me back to reality and picking up my daughter I realised I hadn't looked at her face for so long. For the rest of the holiday I desperately tried to become part of the family and cut down the drugs.

We saw the lights in Oxford Street and the giant Christmas tree in Trafalgar Square. During those few days of sanity we also visited the Petticoat Lane street market and as we pushed through the crowds I thought, just look at all these ordinary people leading ordinary lives without drugs. Why can't I be like them? The girls always clung to Isabella, she was all they had. Watching them all chat with Camilla and their mother I found myself wanting so much to become part of that normality. Later that night I listened to the new Rolling Stones record I'd bought, 'It's all over now.' It made me feel sad, as if I knew my sanity wouldn't last.

Saying goodbye at the airport as they flew back to Malta I held hands with Isabella for what seemed an eternity. She looked pale and tired. There was something in her eyes, as if she was trying to say something

At home, with the Christmas cease-fire over, our domestic war re-exploded and one night after dinner with Alen I got home to find Camilla screaming her head off. She had failed her driving test. I'd bought her a brand new Triumph sports car which had sat outside for weeks waiting for her to pass and having failed she now ranted and raved as though it was me who'd hit the bloody kerb in the three-point-turn. Certain money was paid to ensure that even blindfolded she passed the second time round. I was prepared to do anything, pay anything, to keep the status quo.

Some months later, early one morning, Camilla began screaming again, demanding a house. 'We can't bring a child up in a flat. She needs a garden to play in !' 'Calm down,' I replied, 'I'll buy one before I come home tonight.' Taking a carrier bag of cash I went to see Terry as always in times of trouble. 'I must get a house today,' I cried, 'I daren't go home without one. I can't face another row.' Luckily Tel knew a solicitor, desperate to sell his house in Totteridge. 'If it's got a garden I'll buy it. The money's in the car,' I said. We rang the owner and immediately went over to see it. He wanted to show me round but I just said, 'My wife can look later. Name your price.' He looked bewildered but named a sum, more than it was worth, which I accepted without query - I just wanted peace. Apart from a small amount I paid them in cash from the carrier bag. Thank God no rows tonight, I thought, driving home with a photo of the house.

We spent a fortune renovating our new home. I had no interest in the decorations, to me it only represented dipping into another carrier bag of cash. The huge detached house had five bedrooms and a long sloping garden backing onto open farm-land. This unrestricted view was a rare thing in London but I was too stoned to appreciate it.

My father became involved and helped to organise the numerous builders. He was changing towards me, trying to get closer. Helping Camilla with the house was the first time he had ever shown any interest in anything I did. Was his friendship due to my new-found affluence or had he discovered me as a son for the first time? I didn't want to know the real answer. I enjoyed his attention too much. Dad's shop had gone broke and because he was now too ill to work properly I'd begun to send him twenty-five pounds a week. Recently I'd also bought him a new car, all part of my 'Money buys Love' formula. Like many others he wondered how his twenty-one year old son had suddenly acquired so much wealth.

To celebrate moving into the new house I took my parents and Camilla to dinner at the fashionable 'Talk of the Town.' Sitting in the best seats by the stage we looked like a happy bunch. Still clinging to the dream of creating a family who loved me I wanted to get my wife and parents closer to each other. Inspite of all the drugs and crimes a part of me wanted to slow down. We were just starting to enjoy our meal when I felt a hand on my shoulder.

I turned to find Tommy Cowley standing behind me. 'You're wanted at our table,' he said. To my horror I saw the Kray twins and various other sinister faces looking at me. 'I can't come now, we're in the middle of a celebration,' I replied. 'Now !' he sneered, 'If you want to ever celebrate again.' 'I'll be over in a moment,' I replied. Forcing a smile I excused myself from Camilla and my parents who sensed something was wrong. First I went to the toilet where I was violently sick. After composing myself I went back out to be greeted by Ronnie Kray's famous rabies grin. Looking up at me in a very disinterested manner he said, 'We've got someone for you to meet later this evening,' telling me to come to an address in Chelsea in an hour's time. 'Don't be late,' he smiled. 'But what do you want?' I asked. 'We have some business for your stockbroker friend,' Ronnie replied. I was stunned. Terry must have told them about my relationship with Alen. The bastard !

I returned to our table and sat down, too shocked to speak. In my mind's eye I could picture Alen playing the piano for me. Was I to sell the only person who ever loved me down the river? 'What's wrong? You look ill,' my mother said. 'Oh, it's nothing,' I replied, taking more drugs in front of everybody. I was too far gone to care. Explaining I had to go somewhere urgently I put Camilla and my disappointed parents in a cab home and drove over to Chelsea.

The meeting was being held in an exclusive block of flats. Getting out of the lift on the fifth floor I was greeted by a balding American of about fifty. He didn't look anything like the usual heavy mob, more like a banker. He showed me into a crowded room and after sitting me down proceeded to spell out the ruthless deal. Everyone remained silent throughout his speech. 'Copel Pure Lindon Dark & Co.' were needed to front a big share swindle. I didn't have to understand all the technicalities because my role was simple. I was to lure Alen into a hotel where incriminating sex photographs would be taken. The Krays would use these pictures to blackmail him into doing as they wanted. The American explained that several million pounds were involved and I would be paid very handsomely. 'I need time to think,' I pleaded, feeling sickened by it all. Ronnie Kray stood up and came over to me. 'Thinking is bad for your health,' he whispered, knocking my head with his knuckles.

How could I do this to Alen? But what choice did I have? I left that Chelsea flat with my mind in turmoil and spent the night driving around town. Why couldn't I be like other youngsters of my age, enjoying the swinging new London with its Carnaby Street shops, coffee bars and clubs? I passed the cinema showing the premiere of the Beatles film 'Help.' 'Oh fuck', I cried, 'Help me someone ! What's happening?'

Early the following morning I rang Alen, explaining I needed to see him urgently. He asked me over for lunch and an hour later I was at his door. 'You look terrible !' he said inviting me in. While he went to the local shops he asked me to have coffee with his mother. The old lady and I sat in the drawing room just looking at each other. After a while she spoke. 'Are you going to tell me what the trouble is, then?' It was uncanny, as if she already knew. Sitting in Alen's lounge with that refined old lady seemed so far away from the evil world of crime I was now trapped in. Suddenly she stood up and using her walking stick crossed the room to stand in front to me. Putting her hands on my shoulders she said sternly, 'If it affects my son, tell me.' Looking up I asked, 'What would you do if you were being forced to do something terrible to someone who loved you?' She sat down next to me and replied, 'I simply would not do it ! If you find genuine love just once in this life you are a lucky person. It's worth dying for. My son Alen loves you. What ever it is, don't do it !'

I sat in silence. She was right. Some things were worth dying for. I promised to stop it. 'You will feel so much better about yourself and won't need so many of those pills you secretly take,' she said quietly. As she spoke Alen came back into the room. 'You look better,' he said. 'What did you do with him, Mummy?' 'I just made him face life for once,' she smiled. As we ate lunch a feeling of freedom came over me. An old lady had taken away my fear of the Krays. I was more afraid of her now. She'd spoken with the voice of my conscience.

Through Alen's mother I'd found the resolve to fight. I booked into a hotel near Kings Cross owned by Maltese people I knew. A few hours later with the help of an expert, I wired up a sensitive recorder under the bed to record everything that would be said in that room. That evening I phoned Cowley, saying I wanted to discuss more about the deal before going ahead with the photo-session. An hour later he and the American arrived in my hotel room. Foolishly they talked at length about the entire plot, answering all my questions as I drew them out. They left when I told them I was now satisfied. We had agreed they would take the photos the following evening.

Immediately I made three copies of the tape, putting each into separate envelopes. I addressed one to Scotland Yard Police Headquarters and one to the News of World Newspaper. I took the third to a solicitor I knew, explaining what had happened. I gave him the two envelopes with the other tapes and told him to post them if the Krays or Cowley harmed me. The evidence was sufficient to put many people behind bars.

The following day, stoned out of my mind like a kamikaze pilot on his final mission, I waited in that hotel room for the showdown. I sat on the bed holding a gun, too mad now to care. As Cowley and another man burst in with their cameras I jumped up, screaming, 'It's all recorded ! Read these letters !' Putting the gun to my head I shouted, 'What the fuck can you do now. Kill me? I'll kill myself ! Then the police will get all this and you'll all go to prison !' Care of the drugs I had become a suicidal lunatic, afraid of nothing. Upon my death the solicitor would have posted the tapes and alerted the police. 'Calm down,' Cowley said, 'Let's talk to Terry.' Tommy Cowley might have been a thug but he was not a stupid one and wanted the whole deal forgotten now his freedom was at stake. Promising to never go near Alen again they left me alone in my room. This time drugs, like my parents wine with the bully boy all those years ago, had been on my side, making me insane enough to bluff the gangsters.

My fear of a frail, one-hundred-year-old woman had checkmated the Krays.

Relieved I drove home, totally drained and exhausted. I had not been to bed for days and just wanted to sleep.

Just as I lay down on my bed I heard the phone ring, followed by shouting and crying from downstairs. Then Camilla burst into the room and said in a choked voice, 'Mum's in hospital. She's dying.'

Chapter 9

DEATH IN MALTA

Having just lived through one nightmare the news from Malta was devastating. Roseanna, the eldest of Camilla's sisters, was staying with us at the time and at fifteen was old enough to look after Tessa for a couple of days. In a state of shock Camilla and I drove to London Airport to catch the next available flight to Malta. We had to take care of Isabella and her kids.

At Heathrow I left Camilla in the bar and went to organise our tickets. The terminal was packed and queuing at the ticket desk I suddenly heard Camilla calling me above the airport noise, her voice was frantic. 'Mummy's dead, Stephen, Stephen, help me !' I looked up but couldn't see her in the crowds. Again I heard the screams, 'Mummy's already dead !'

I'd been awake on drugs now for three days and felt numb all over. The ticket clerk turned to me, 'Next please,' but I just screamed, 'It's too fucking late now. Isabella's on a flight to heaven !' Turning round I pushed past the crowds with their suitcases, hearing Camilla's cries again. Running to the other side of the building I saw her leaning over the glass railings on the floor above, crying uncontrollably.

Oh God, it had really happened. Isabella was dead !

The drugs held back my own tears, I was too stoned to cry. I'd loved that women but now I had to help Camilla who was inconsolable. Stunned with grief

I suddenly realised I also had to rescue three little orphans alone somewhere in Malta.

Gathering what was left of my drugged-soaked senses I took control of the situation, telling Camilla that she should stay at home while I flew to Malta to bring her sisters back to live with us in England. My intentions were good but by now my addiction was so bad I needed help myself and certainly wasn't a fit person to become the children's guardian.

After booking myself a later flight I helped Camilla to our car. She was out of her mind with grief and cried so much as we drove home I feared for her safety. Trying to calm her down I began an hour-long God-inspired monologue. With the drugs fuelling the drama inside my head I explained that death was a wonderful journey, the ultimate trip to our home in the sky. 'Your mother's heart died with your father's death. Since then she only lived for the children', I told her. Pointing towards the sky I exclaimed, 'Look, there's your mum with her arms round your father. God's beckoning them inside, they are both so happy.' My description of heavenly bliss continued until we pulled up at our house. The words had helped and Camilla seemed calmer. Roseanna went quiet with shock when she heard the news. Fortunately a neighbour offered to stay with them both and soon I was leaving again for the airport.

With my emotions swimming in a sea of drugs I drove off shouting, 'God's with me, I'll save the girls !' An hour or so later, in an even worse state, I was on my 'Mission Saviour' flight to Malta. Landing at Lucca airport drugged beyond recognition I took a taxi across the island to Isabella's new home in Sliema. Nobody was there, the flat was locked. It was midday and the sun was beating down as I stood in the street, lost, not knowing where to turn next. I felt dizzy and sat down at the kerbside when a man came up and spoke to me in Maltese. He recognised me from my previous visits and led me to a crowded bar where he spoke with some men who all turned to look at me. I didn't understand what they were saying but heard the name 'Isabella' many times. A drink was handed to me but getting exasperated I screamed, 'This is not a fucking celebration. Where are the children?' I ran back out into the street where a woman on a balcony called out to me, 'Mr. England man, wait, I will show you.' She came down, explaining that the girls were being looked after a block away and took me to the top of a narrow street which went steeply downhill in long flat steps. 'The girls are down by the fountain,' she said pointing and turned, leaving me alone. Isabella had only died the night before and nobody had yet told the girls. Fate had dealt that job to me.

Washing hung overhead between the high buildings and there were several shops with fruit piled outside. I passed a woman cleaning her step and seemed to be walking forever when I suddenly stopped. The three girls were playing in a small square further down and hadn't seen me yet. I mustn't cry, I thought, rehearsing a second God-inspired monologue. 'Your mum's in heaven, eating breakfast with your father. Eggs, lots of them.' Fuck, this has got to sound real, I thought to myself as I got closer. I couldn't face it and with tears filling my eyes took refuge in a small bar to take a large brandy and more pills. I offered to pay but the man just waved, meaning he didn't want any money. He knew why I was there and giving me another drink hugged me as I left for the longest walk of my life. Villagers were at their doors now, watching the Englishman who'd come for Isabella's kids. Unsteady but with my head held high I walked slowly towards them.

The square suddenly emptied. People were leaving me and the children alone. The girls were sitting on the steps of a fountain, drawing on the ground with chalk. When they saw me they looked up and in a chorus asked, 'Where's Mummy?' Shaking my head I sat next to them. The sun was still beating down heavy on us as I began my story, 'Mum's in heaven now.' The children stared at me in disbelief but listened intently to all the details. Stoned out of my head I began drawing pictures with their chalk, like a kindergarten teacher. 'This is your mum and your dad in heaven', I said, pointing. 'And this is their breakfast with eggs.' 'So many eggs !' Louisa said. Josephina suddenly began screaming, 'Mummy's dead, Mummy's dead !' She and Laura grabbed me and started to sob uncontrollably. I looked up to find Louisa had walked away across the empty square. She was staring up to the sky, shouting, 'Why did you go to heaven today? Couldn't you have gone later?' She turned towards me still shouting, 'Why did she go today?' 'I don't know !' I replied angrily. 'God's got the bloody time-table !' Slowly Louisa walked back and sat next to me. She never cried.

For a long time we sat on the ground under the fountain, holding hands in a circle. The villagers kept away. Time stood still, the drugs, drink and hot sun were getting to me. Leaning back I closed my eyes and fell momentarily asleep. When I came to I saw the bar owner and other villagers standing all around us. Several women were crying. Someone gave me a glass of brandy and pulled me to my feet. A woman came up, kissed the girls and then gave me the key to Isabella's flat.

I thanked the crowd and with three sad little faces alongside me walked to the flat. This is where Isabella had laid for days. The entire flat smelt of death, the bed-sheets still felt wet. Why, oh why could I not have been here last week? I thought, wanting to scream. Why didn't someone tell us? The flat looked empty, so many things had gone. Later a neighbour came in and told me the girl's cousins had stolen it all that very morning. 'Those bastards will pay for this !' I shouted. My head was going round in circles. Where was Isabellas body? Who will bury her?

I sat there overwhelmed by the magnitude of this situation when I heard shouting from the street below. Looking from the balcony I recognised Isabella's father and went down to meet him. He was a strong old man of about eighty with a wrinkled, sun-tanned face. Holding me by the shoulders his eyes filled with tears and he said something in Maltese. Suddenly he let go, clenched his fists and dropped dead at my feet. 'Oh fuck, no !' I screamed. What was going on? Why was everybody dying? The villagers quickly rallied round to help and kept the children out of sight. Later, to calm down, I took the girls to the beach and we sat there till nightfall, throwing pebbles into the water. Nobody spoke very much.

I should now have concentrated on getting the kids off the island but in my deranged brain there first was a score to settle with uncle Tony, their late father's brother. Isabella had written, explaining how Tony had cheated her out of her share in the parents will. Following her husband's death she had been too grief-stricken to fight it out with him. High on drugs I wanted revenge and with a gun I would have shot the man dead in broad day light like in a John Wayne movie. Fortunately I had no gun but instead that night I took three confused girls across the island to their uncle's bar.

It was around midnight as the cab parked in the village square. Making the girls walk ahead with bare feet into the bar I followed them like a stoned desperado screaming, 'Are these your brother's kids? Look, they have no shoes on their feet ! You bastard ! You cheated them out of their inheritance !' I ranted on and on. 'I'll blow up your bar. The whole fucking village.' I meant well but I was a sick addict, totally out of touch with reality. My behaviour only confused the sad little girls who'd just lost their mum and got them no money. They should have been asleep in bed. Eventually, after exchanging more threats, I took the children back to the flat.

The next morning I arranged to have Isabella buried and wanting only the best had her body embalmed. I paid for a funeral with a black coach drawn by six black horses. By the day of the burial I was in a terrible state, not having slept for many days. I went on my own to see Isabella's body at the funeral parlour wanting to say goodbye to the woman who'd loved me. Her face looked white and very drawn but at peace with an expression as if she was saying, 'Look after my little girls.' A priest came in, quietly held my hand and we prayed together.

An hour later I stood outside with the kids and watched Isabella's coffin being loaded into the carriage. The sun got hotter and I heard voices shouting from the sky, 'Stephen, Stephen, take care of my children !' Everything started to spin round and I passed out in the street.

A day later I woke in a neighbour's house with the girls faces looking down on me. 'We want to go to

Camilla,' they all cried. Now I discovered another problem. They had no passport, having previously travelled on their mother's. Since I wasn't their legal guardian I would not be allowed to take them off the island. For the next three days I visited every official building many times in my futile quest for passports, even getting to see Mintoff, the Prime Minister of Malta. He explained he was powerless to help and the matter would have to go before the courts. In typical Mediterranean 'manana' style the next court sitting was in three weeks time. Stoned and very upset I grabbed hold of Mintoff and began to threaten him. Immediately two officials pulled me off and called the police who dragged me screaming from the scene. They locked me in a cell where I broke down and cried. I was beaten. All my bravado couldn't help me this time. All I had left was God. I knelt down, closed my eyes and prayed. An hour or so later when I woke God had already answered my prayers.

A woman was at the door of the cell with the three girls. She introduced herself as Miss Spittuna, a social worker. 'I will help you,' she said shaking my hand through the bars, 'I'll get you a passport. My cousin works in the emigration office.'

The police refused to release me but allowed the children into the cell instead. Having not slept properly the previous night they were tired and soon we fell asleep together on the cell floor. A few hours later we were woken by a smiling Miss Spittuna. The passport she waved at us had all three girl's faces on one photograph. 'It isn't strictly valid but it will get you off the island', she explained. I paid a fine which went straight into a policeman's pocket and the door was unlocked. With great relief we walked out into the sunshine.

Before we left for England I wanted the children's grandmother to see the girls one last time. Now sick and old it was unlikely she would live to see them again.

We went shopping in a big store in Valletta where I dressed the girls in new clothes from head to toe, yellow dresses, black patent shoes and white ankle socks. To top it up I bought them bright red coats and matching berets. Isabella's kids looked like princesses. Unfortunately they were led by a rather stoned prince as we walked through the small village to see the old lady.

Arriving at her house another elderly woman let us in. The grandmother was sitting up in bed in her darkened room to greet us. She hugged each child. Other village children looked in through the ground floor window. Finally the grandmother beckoned me over and kissing me said something in Maltese.

On the plane Laura, the youngest child, unable to comprehend that death was forever turned to me and asked if Mummy was already in England with Camilla. Too choked to answer I hugged her and taking more drugs forced back my tears.

Hold on, don't cry, I said to myself as we came down to land at Heathrow airport. At British passport control we met the problems I had envisaged. The officer took one look at the passport and went off somewhere to return with his superior. This man took us to an office where he asked me many questions but in view of the tragic circumstances he eventually turned a blind eye and let us through. At long last I collected my car and drove three tired children home to Camilla who brought them up from that day, acting as their mother.

This was an enormous responsibility for Camilla, herself only a young girl of twenty-one. To her lasting credit, she was to cope well.

Isabella's girls were safe at last. They grew up together, not separated in different orphanages. Throughout the difficult years ahead they kept close, got married and saw each others kids grow up. Isabella would have wanted that.

When all the children were safely asleep in bed I went into the garden alone, looked up to the sky and cried my heart out. It was my turn, I had waited long enough.

I had loved that woman and Isabella had loved me.

Chapter 10

THE SERMON ON THE PLATFORM

Following Isabella's death the children settled in remarkably well. They had each other for strength and Camilla looking after them was something they already knew, so they felt safe. Roseanna now worked as a live-in mother's help in Hampstead while Louisa, Laura and Josephina were living with us. They were quite happy in their new local Catholic schools. Our house in Totteridge was very large and five bedrooms provided plenty of space for everybody. With two cars in the drive and the local gardener calling twice a week it all seemed very respectable but nothing could have been further from the truth. Behind the front door lived a deranged lunatic with his carrier bags of stolen cash and hundreds of pill bottles. The ever spiralling drug intake made me increasingly withdrawn as the craving for the high took over my entire life.

Terry and his betrayal of me to the Krays had upset me more than I realised. At the time I hadn't really comprehended the severity of the Alen blackmail and it took me a while before I faced up to its full implications. This in turn led to the first of many bust ups I was to have with dear Terry and in the weeks that followed I sold back my interest in Highheat. We parted screaming abuse at each other but in many ways I was pleased to leave him because it freed me from all responsibilities and gave me more time just to take drugs.

During the first few weeks of my stay-at-home period I still mixed with Camilla and the girls to some degree, eating downstairs and occasionally poking my head into the living room but soon this all changed. As time passed I began to lock myself into my library to take drugs and never came out for days on end. My only contact with the outside world was my three year old daughter Tessa. Having passed out on the library floor I was regularly woken by her shouting outside the door, 'Daddy, daddy, let me in to play !' Often Tessa stayed in my room all day, drawing pictures and because she wouldn't leave Camilla had to send her meals upstairs on a tray. My daughter and I were to spend the next six months together in that library, creating a permanent bond between us. From Tessa I received the love I never got from my wife. Nevertheless, this room without me realising, became my first prison on drug island. It was a comfortable cell with thick black carpet and high shelves on every wall. On display were over ten-thousand books, not that I ever read many, I'd collected them just to make me feel good. Obsessed with hiding things I cut out a square in the middle pages of many of the big books, creating secret hiding places. On one shelf I kept the pill books and on another the money books. Often, drugged out of my skull, I forgot which books were which and pulled dozens to the floor searching for something. There was a white desk and two black leather chairs, dad's chair and baby Tessa's chair. The only other furniture were two locking filing cabinets, one for my pills the other for Tessa's drawings. I was creating my own world of make-believe inside one small room, oblivious to outside events such as Harold Wilson winning the March elections. As long as I took my tablets the world looked wonderful whichever government was in power. Although I was living in a house with five other people it was as if they didn't exist. Spaced out I floated around in a life of my own.

Permanently stoned out of my mind I developed a vision of the entire world taking happy pills. Politicians, judges, police, everybody, all singing along in perfect harmony. There would be no more wars or famines, the world would become a better place with us all high as kites. This wasn't some silly dream, I really believed it was my divine duty to get the human race on to their daily dose of Dexedrine. What better place to start than my own street? But how was I to get them all to take their drugs? I couldn't knock on each door saying, 'Drink a glass of this cola !' This wasn't Halliwick Hospital. There had to be another way.

One morning, watching the milkman doing his round, I found the answer. I could mix the amphetamine with his milk. Realising he could never be bribed I needed to put the drug cocktail in my own crates of milk then get him out of the way for long enough to switch my bottles with his. Ringing the dairy I had ten crates delivered to my garage where I carefully removed the tops of each bottle, mixing in the liquid amphetamine. Totally stoned I worked throughout the night to complete the task but by the early hours of the morning I was in a terrible state with milk spilt everywhere. My giant speed milkshake had gone horribly wrong and towards the end I took sleeping pills by mistake and passed out. The gardener found me asleep on the lawn but after a couple of bottles of my own special milk I soon recovered. Unfortunately by then all the neighbours had left for work with the same boring cornflakes and their introduction into a new way of life was officially cancelled.

After this episode I began going out on lunatic shopping sprees which under the influence of drugs I just couldn't control. On speed you can't stop talking and in shops I was guaranteed an attentive reception. No shopkeeper is going to tell you to buzz off and spend your money elsewhere. For me it became impossible to stop buying things. Not things I needed, anything would do. Shoes, pens, fruit, paint, cooked meat, it didn't matter as in a frenzy I ran in and out of every shop. Buying and talking non-stop I moved down the High Street carrying umbrellas, wood, blankets, vegetables, drills, books, clothes, accumulating more and more. Eventually, when there was simply too much to carry, I'd get a friendly shopkeeper to store my mixed bunch of goodies only to forget where I'd left them. One day, buying a packet of cigarettes, I was presented with five bags full of shopping. I had no recollection of ever buying them. Another day, entering an undertaker's shop I said, 'Hi, nobody's died yet but I need to arrange my own funeral,' paying for the most expensive coffin they had in stock. In retrospect it was sad. I was so fucking lonely I needed to talk with anyone about anything, even my own death. One afternoon in a barber's shop I began to get weird looks and when it was my turn the barber told me he had already cut my hair earlier that morning. 'I just want two more snips off the top ! I'll pay you again,' I replied, feeling very stupid. Two snips later I paid a very happy barber who called after me, 'Come back any time. We are open till six today!' On the day England played Germany in the World Cup final I went to watch the football match at Wembley but mixing acid with speed was so gone I thought England had lost 4-2. Lots of English fans gave me peculiar looks as we left the stadium with me commiserating them saying, 'Don't be sad. It was a good game.' It was only later in a pub seeing their smiling faces that I discovered Jeff Hurst was on our side.

And that's how life continued for the next year or so - in one purple haze. It was midsummer 1967. The Beatles were meditating and their manager Brian Epstein had just died, when on a wave of flower power my own goodwill era began.

One night when everybody else was fast asleep I received the ultimate call from the governor himself, not on the telephone but on a direct line into my spaced out mind. At first the line was crackling so I took more pills to get a clearer reception. As the drugs took effect I was reconnected. God was on the line. 'Blimey, Hello God,' I said. 'How are you? This is indeed an honour.' 'Be quiet,' God said in a very authoritative manner. 'Listen carefully,' he continued. 'Give it away to the poor like Robin Hood did. You never gave a cent away in your handbag-snatching days, that's why you got caught. Give it away and I will steer you clear of trouble. You will only have luck, my son !' Did he say my son? I was flabbergasted. Yes, he did. He was telling me I was Jesus ! Now Camilla and the neighbours might see some good in me, at least her priest would look up to me. Kneeling on the floor I now received orders to commit the ultimate sacrifice to prove my allegiance to the biblical mob. With no son like Abraham it had to be my daughter. I went to Tessa's bedroom. She was sleeping. I kissed her on the head and then, closing my eyes, I stood over her and put my cars keys by her side declaring, 'I'll walk to the poor !' 'He's one of us,' I heard God say in an East London accent as I left the house with a bag full of cash. Two streets away as I walked past a phone box God spoke again. 'Stop walking. You have proved yourself. Take a cab !' I was relieved because even for a twenty-two-year-old Euston was a long walk away.

Twenty minutes later the cab pulled up at Euston Railway station and I was ready for my 'Sermon on the Platform'. In saintly drug overdrive I began to look for the poor. The area around Euston is always full of tramps with a body on every street bench. Wonderful ! I thought surveying my flock. My first beneficiaries were a very old Polish man and his sixty year old daughter. He was a frail old boy, bent over, with long white hair. The woman was small, wearing a man's overcoat so long it dragged behind her. This poor, decrepit couple had lived on the streets for years, sleeping in shop doorways and eating dustbin left-overs discarded by our caring society. These Polish immigrants were not winos, just two lonely weak old people. Charged up with heavenly pills my mission began. 'The Good Lord has sent me to feed you, follow me,' I said, leading them towards an early morning cafe. They followed very slowly with the small lady constantly stumbling over her long coat. Unable to operate at this snails pace I picked the woman up, carrying her over my shoulder into the cafe. This frightened them both but with free food on offer they bravely stuck with their spaced-out benefactor. Lining up to be served we looked an odd trio amongst the early workers, unaware of the miracle being performed in their midst as they ate their huge two egg, two sausage breakfasts. With the Beatles singing 'All you need is love' on the cafe radio it was our turn to be served. 'Have whatever you want,' I said, putting three teas on our tray. Instead of filling themselves on a hearty English breakfast my Polish friends, frightened to abuse their heavenly host in asking for too much, opted for one rock cake each. As we waited to pay the old man guiltily put out his grubby little hand, taking a third concrete chunk. 'One and a half cakes each, is that alright?' he muttered nervously. Oh fuck! My drugged emotions couldn't take it anymore and stuffing money into their pockets I ran out into the street. 'Buy a proper meal !' I screamed from the door. Outside confused and angry, I began shouting, 'Why are these people so poor? Why haven't they got fucking homes?' Continuing God's work I ran up to every tramp in sight, giving away money, making sure I moved quickly on each time before I could get involved in another sob-story. Many down and outs who didn't wake up had the cash stuffed into their pockets as they slept off the previous night's wine.

Hours later when I ran out of money I telephoned one of London's heaviest mobsters. This man was a killer but oblivious to the type of person I was talking to I screamed down the phone, 'Mick, get down here quick with some cash for the poor !' 'Fuck off, you little cunt ! Ring again and I'll cut your fingers off !' he replied angrily, slamming down the phone. Thank God I never had his address or I might have called round and actually had something cut off.

With Mick the Baptist not joining me I had no choice but to wait for the banks to open. Any bank would do, I had money in them all. By now I felt cold and wanted to drink a cup of tea in the warmth of a cafe myself. For a few pounds to tide me over I left my gold watch with a hotel porter as security. Later I cashed a cheque, miraculously remembering to retrieve the watch before continuing God's work. Leaving the hotel I spotted a woman, who I thought I'd earlier given money to, rushing towards the station cafe. I chased after her and stuffing more money into her hand shouted, 'You must be fucking starving love, have some more !' I was mistaken. She wasn't my tramp, just an everyday traveller who replied in a shocked northern voice, 'No, I'm just late for my train !' Frightened by my behaviour she now ran on even faster.

Unable to tell the difference between tramps and everyday people anymore I just gave away money ad-lib to anyone and everyone, soon arousing the attention of the railway police. When a station inspector challenged me I quickly vanished down the underground to catch the train back home to Totteridge. On the tube I took a large dose of sleeping pills, only just managing to reach the house before collapsing, which was lucky. Many times I didn't make it and was found asleep in the front garden by Louisa or Laura as they left for school. Entering the house I was confronted by Camilla screaming, 'I need more house-keeping money !' Annoyed I rushed upstairs to the library, shouting, 'Do you think we're made of fucking money?' From outside the locked room she argued with me but it was too late, I had peace. The sleeping pills were working. You can't argue with someone who's unconscious.

With my philanthropic mission behind me and the airways closed I slept for two solid days on the library floor.

Chapter 11

LEAVING CAMILLA

Following this spiritual period I was again craving for excitement, looking for the ultimate buzz. My latest drug induced fantasy was to become the fastest driver in the world. Amphetamine made the whole thing obsessive, locking my brain into fast cars at the exclusion of everything else. As usual, until I got it out of my system, nothing else existed.

I'd become friendly with Steve Ladd, a driver who worked for Highheat. He was two years younger than me but a game kid and an expert with cars. Every weekend he tuned the engine of my red mini cooper. Steve had an older car and we often raced each other on quiet country roads. He was a very fast driver which upset me and having to be the best at everything I challenged him to the ultimate car race. To ensure there was no advantage for either driver I bought a second identical mini cooper, a blue one, telling Steve that he could keep the car of his choice if he won.

Together we planned a five mile race along country lanes at dawn when the roads were guaranteed to be empty. The finish line would be the far end of a narrow bridge which was just wide enough for one driver to cross so the first car on the bridge would automatically win. For two days prior to the race I kept myself asleep and was woken by Louisa a couple of hours before the start in order to swallow the largest dose of amphetamine any human ever took and still lived. It was still dark as I left the house and Louisa wished me luck, giving me a bunch of wild flowers she'd picked from the bottom of our garden. At the start I was so high you could hear my heart beating while Steve, wearing an Indian waistcoat, was completely relaxed, smiling as he sung, 'Those were the days my friend.'

The race started and soon we were both driving like madmen with our cars touching each other at speeds of up to 80 mph. As we approached the bridge our cars were still level which meant one of us would have to break or we both would crash head-on into the stone wall. It was a game of chicken, coward to lose.

Steve looked at me and smiled. I smiled back. He waved. I waved back. He accelerated. I braked, swerving off the road into a field. Steve had won, leaving me with a slightly dented car but a very shattered ego. Glancing at Louisa's flowers on the seat next to me I cried, taking more pills to console myself as I watched Steve walk back over the bridge. Drugged I always became very emotional and throwing the pills to the ground screamed, 'You went for broke. Even with these fucking drugs I still chickened out !' Steve picked up the bottle, put his arm round me and said, 'Let me teach you not to be scared. Let's drive over the cliffs at Brighton together ! Throw away these stupid pills and you'll never be afraid again. Nobody needs that shit inside them !' Arranging to meet the following weekend we parted and he drove off smiling in his new blue car.

The drugs now began to change my entire personality. I was behaving so mad that other people found it increasingly hard to be anywhere near me. This included Alen who was very annoyed when he found me taking pills in his lounge. Dinner that Saturday evening had been a very sombre affair with Alen discussing the recent assassination of Martin Luther

King in Memphis. 'It's a tragedy for mankind,' he'd said. 'Look, life is so short. Why are you doing this to yourself? Why do you need that rubbish inside you?' 'I'll do whatever I fucking want,' I shouted defiantly, taking even more pills in front of him. Whereas before I'd always been nice to Alen I now screamed abuse, telling him not to interfere. His mother woke up hearing the noise and came into the lounge to see what was wrong. 'Tell your son to mind his own business,' I screamed rushing out past them both. 'I've got to go. I'm driving over a cliff tomorrow !' It was now all so different from the piano playing evenings of old. The drugs were seeing to that.

Swearing never to see Alen again I drove down to the coast. Steve had driven there in an old car we'd bought specially for our mountain drop. He'd cut off the doors to enable us to jump out unrestricted. The idea was to drive over the cliff and leap out at the last possible moment when the car was actually in mid-air. Most important - I had promised to do it all without drugs.

It was quite late when I met Steve high up on the cliffs outside Brighton near Seven Sisters. 'You only live twice,' he joked, referring to the recent James Bond movie. When we were both ready, wearing crash helmets, I drove the car over the grassy slope towards the cliff, trying not to let Steve see my fear. As it shot over the edge Steve held my arm and shouted, 'Wait, we're still safe !' Seconds later he pushed me out. Dazed I looked around but Steve was still in the car, laughing. An inch before the sheer drop he leapt to safety himself. The car exploded on the rocks below. I lay there paralysed with shock, watching Steve climb back up towards me, his head bleeding slightly. 'You did it without pills !' he shouted, putting his arms round me as we both lay on the grass. He was exhilarated, laughing and joking as we drove back to the hotel where he'd left two girls waiting to celebrate with us.

We all had dinner and after lots of drinks parted to go to our rooms. 'It's easy ! You don't need pills to do anything !' he laughed, getting out of the lift. Quite drunk and unable to get interested in sex I left my half naked girl on the bed in my room to go to the bathroom. Looking into the mirror I sobbed, taking a bottle of pills from my pocket. I had lied. I'd been on drugs like every other day of my life. I was an addict. With the pill bottle I smashed the mirror into tiny pieces.

Steve and I were both lunatics, the only difference was that he did it all without drugs. He went on to become a famous stuntman, getting into the Guinness Book of Records. His record breaker was a drive through the longest tunnel of fire ever. He got through and beat the record but wanting to double his glory drove back. Halfway through the tunnel his car blew up, exploding into a ball of fire. He died as he had lived, free of fear and free of drugs.

Meanwhile Terry, inspite of being such a devious bastard, continued to be my hero figure. I admired or despised him, depending entirely on how my drugs were working that day. I was living in such a hazy world I soon forgot all about the Alen blackmail, nothing seemed real to me anymore.

One morning Tel telephoned, inviting me over to his house for tea with the mobster Reggie Kray. Up to that time I'd only dealt with his twin Ronnie but oblivious to danger, I agreed to go. The only precaution I took was to write a note which I put in a sealed envelope. It said I was at Aylmer Drive, Stanmore, having tea with Reggie Kray and Terry Marvin. I gave this to the minicab driver who took me there with strict instructions to wait outside and if I didn't come out within an hour to take the letter to the local police. There was no reason for me to go or for Terry to invite me, it was all part of his gangster-complex. The only sane one of the trio was Mr. Kray, receiving a fat wad of cash in return for playing a part in Terry's Al Capone fantasy life. Terry gave the Kray twins fortunes just to be part of their world and one afternoon I saw him give Ronnie ten thousand pounds, two hundred thousand pounds today. On the way over I took a double-strong dose of amphetamine for courage, arriving at Terry's house out of my head.

Reggie, sipping his tea, told his favourite story in which a crab cheats a scorpion only to suffer death when the scorpion takes revenge. The purpose of the story was to warn me that if I ever was to double cross them or Terry I, like the crab, would get stung. Throughout the tale Terry sat there with his usual soppy grin. Reggies cryptic warning was supposed to put the fear of God into me but high on drugs it was all just good fun. Totally spaced out I interpreted the story as a five-year-old would, unaware of the danger like a baby is to fire. London's most ruthless gangster was making serious threats but I just replied, 'That's a good tale ! Do you know any other animal stories?' Instead of 'Listen with Mother' it was 'Listen with Reggie.' With the animal stories failing to frighten me, Terry got exasperated and held a shotgun to my forehead, angrily asking, 'How does that make you feel?' I thought this was an extension to Reggie's animal stories and that we were now into quiz-time. With the gun now pressing against my nose I paused and rolled my eyes searching for the right answer. 'Well?' Terry shouted, 'How do you feel?' 'Hold on, don't tell me, give me a minute, let me guess. Two cold rings on my forehead.' I released the safety catch and said, 'Perhaps I'll feel different with it off, more danger.' Shaking Terry dropped the gun which exploded on the floor. 'That was lucky,' I laughed. Reggie had by now a belly-full of this retarded grown-up fantasy party. He just wanted to collect his entertainment fee and go home to Ronnie. 'Could you excuse us. I've got some private business with this gent,' he said, nodding towards Tel. I left very drugged but quite happy, still trying to work out the gun-quiz answer.

A week or so later I met Reggie Kray again in Terry's offices. He saw me taking tablets and took me privately to one side for the strangest lecture of my life. 'Those drugs will kill you. They are evil,' Reggie said. 'Listen son, we only ever hurt our own, not innocent young kids. That's why me and Ronnie would never get involved with drugs. It's too evil for either of us. Get help.' I was amazed. I was now being guided by London's most dangerous mobster. The morals of Reggie Kray were higher than those of many others I knew. This man actually cared for society. In May when I read the Kray twins had been arrested I was somewhat confused, thinking, were they so bad after all? Terry, however, was financially better off after their arrest as his astronomical payments to Ronnie stopped. But this was only a temporary saving. Soon he paid other gangsters instead to remain one of the boys.

Meanwhile back at home it was time to face reality and I felt sad. All Camilla ever thought about was a clean house or going to church. She talked to me like I was a stranger and when she looked at me her eyes seemed to say, 'Oh God. Why have I wound up with this jerk? I pray he won't want sex tonight !' Heartbroken I often screamed, 'What am I, just the fucking money machine? If I had no money you and your bloody sisters would soon leave !'

Often I watched Tessa from the window as she played in the street with Caroline, a girl of her age who lived a few doors down. Occasionally I saw Camilla smiling with the neighbours. Why can't she be nice to me, I wondered, peeping from behind the curtains. The only peace I ever had was when I was asleep. Often I slept for up to two complete days after several nights awake on speed. If anybody rang during my sleeping periods Camilla would simply say, 'Ring back in a couple of days when he wakes up.' With me locked in my room Louisa, Laura, Josephina and Tessa carried on playing as normal - on such heavy doses of sedatives nothing disturbed me. I wasn't just asleep, it was like I was dead. There was a permanent sad cloud over me and I could only see the sorrow in the world. That June when Bobby Kennedy was shot I thought back to my own misery when his brother Jack was assassinated. Nothing had changed and it seemed only drugs gave me the will to carry on.

Already quite mad and impossible to live with when I was awake I had constant rows with Camilla. One of our worst ever was over my building of a giant wendy house in our lounge. I'd already worked around the clock for several days, cutting wood and hammering in the garden. On the third day at around midnight a neighbour arrived in his pyjamas, screaming that the bloody noise was keeping him awake. I'd promised Tessa it would be ready by the weekend and determined to finish carried on sawing in our lounge. Camilla now woke up and came downstairs. Seeing sawdust all over the expensive carpet she went mad, forcing me to stop. The following morning the row began all over again as she vacuumed up. The shouting got so bad the kids were frightened and ran to a neighbour where they stayed all day as we continued fighting.

I never once hit Camilla but to stop her screaming I always broke one of the windows at the front of the house. The shock of the shattering glass which all the neighbours could hear never failed to shut her up. It was a guaranteed remedy for peace and became such a regular occurrence that the local glaziers developed a time saving system. They measured and numbered each window so I could just ring and say, 'It's number six today.' During the worst period they came out as much as four times a week. 'Oh, number two again. That's going well this week,' the glazier would joke over the phone.

There were the odd breaks in the storm with quiet nights when we had sex. Nine months after one of these our second daughter Antonia was born. When Camilla became noticeably pregnant things got a bit more human, even the neighbours occasionally asked me how my wife was. On the day Antonia was born Tessa, now aged five, was very excited when I took her to the maternity hospital to see her new baby sister. Mother and daughter looked beautiful but Camilla's expression made me feel she didn't even want me to pick up the baby. That afternoon two women neighbours rushed up to me in our drive and asked, 'Well?' 'A little girl', I replied. Turning to each other they said, 'We must visit Camilla tomorrow', and walked away without offering their congratulations. I felt like the porter from the hospital delivering the news, as if I had nothing to do with the baby and didn't belong anywhere.

Sadly this was true. Seeing the world through a cloud of drugs I didn't.

By the time Antonia was born I had become a walking bottle of pills as my addiction worsened. I never spent time with her or played with Tessa anymore. Unlike her older sister, who at least had seen a drugged dad for a few short years, poor Antonia had no father at all.

No child deserves a dad so bad, so addicted.

For a few weeks following Antonia's birth things were a bit quieter but soon the rows resumed as usual. Nothing lasts, I thought to myself, reading that John Lennon and Cynthia were getting divorced. Even the Beatles were rumoured to be breaking up. The only positive thing in the papers was Jackie Kennedy marrying Onassis is but even that seemed a bit quick.

My parents began visiting every Sunday afternoon but I was asleep upstairs throughout most of their visits. One day I woke hearing shouting below. My mother was suggesting that Camilla changed her religion to Jewish. My father had voiced his disapproval of the cross of Jesus hanging in our hall. There was lots of noise but by the time my wake-up pills took effect and I managed to stagger downstairs my parents had left. Camilla, in one of her mega hysterical fits, had banned them from ever visiting or seeing our children again and from that day on they never did. It was a shame because my father really loved seeing the children, perhaps he now realised he'd never seen his own. I felt very upset for his sake but unlike a normal husband who would have challenged his wife's decision I merely took more drugs, broke a window and went out. By now our marriage was a farce and our home was just a place to sleep and store my pills.

Dad had lost all his money gambling. He had his house left but that was all. My parents only income was the small rent from his old shop plus the twenty five pounds I gave them each week. All along I kidded them the money came from Terry paying my father not to set up a competitive business. It was a ridiculous story which nobody believed but it saved him from having to say thank you to me. Using my age-old formula I was buying love from my mother and father. Even addicts want their parents to care. One day my dad and I had a row and in a fit of temper, drugged to my eyeballs, I screamed, 'The fucking money comes from me. The handbag-snatcher is feeding you two peasants now.' As the words came out my mouth I was already regretting them. I loved and hated him at the same time.

A week after my outburst I took my father to hospital and was devastated to be told by the doctor that his body was riddled with cancer. When Camilla heard about his illness she was unmoved and defiantly still refused to allow him to see the children. 'My dad is dying, you slag. How can you do this to him?' I screamed, but it all made no difference. She stubbornly refused to make peace. That morning, sitting on the stairs, I cried my eyes out over this impossible situation. 'Get out you bitch,' I shouted. 'And take your fucking sisters with you !' I couldn't bear to look at the woman I loved reacting with such cold indifference to my father's cancer. I was so upset I went berserk, forcing Camilla and the children to move there and then into a nearby hotel. As I drove them there I became hysterical, screaming, 'Fucking money ! That's all you bastards ever wanted off me !' and in a fit of rage threw several thousand pounds out of the car window. On my way back I realised what I'd done and looked for the money but it had gone. For someone walking near Totteridge Lane that afternoon it was their lucky day.

I started to despise money, finally realising the falseness it had bought me.

On the second night alone in the house I was watching Nixon celebrating his election victory in America on TV when the door bell rang. I was confronted by two policemen with a search warrant for drugs. It didn't take Einstein to work out who had tipped them off. I panicked, thinking there were still hundreds of pill bottles upstairs and the courts were never going to believe they were all for me ! I would be charged as a drug dealer. Miraculously the police accepted just one big bottle, believing it was all I had. They took me to the local station where I was charged with being in possession and released on bail to appear in court the following week.

Back at the house I rushed upstairs to move all the other drug bottles, afraid of a second police raid. Unlocking the pill cabinet I found to my horror there was only one left. Frantically I searched all my other hiding places, including the loft but soon realised it wasn't necessary to be nervous about the police finding more drugs. There weren't any !

I'd swallowed the whole bloody lot ! Ten years supply of drugs, an entire boat load, had gone in under five.

Now it was real panic stations. I had mega problems - not being charged by the police, not my wife and children in a hotel, not my father dying of cancer. I had far bigger problems ! I was running out of drugs ! I had to find fresh supplies, but where from? At first I set up about six private doctors who prescribed amphetamine for me but it was nowhere near enough to satisfy my horrendous craving. Driven by despair, always short of pills, I broke into a local chemist which, at least for the time being, boosted my supply. I had to find another long-term solution and began to work on the ultimate plan - an armed robbery, but not for money. My idea was to hold up a drug manufacturing company. This was to be the 'Great Pill Robbery' with sacks of tablets going into army trucks this time. To an addict like me this was the ultimate dream - a life-time supply of tablets. Lots of stock gave me the same security other people get from looking at their deposit savings book. Thank goodness the 'Great Pill Robbery' never left the planning board.

The following week my father surprised me and was outside Barnet Court which was kind of him after my cruel taunts over the money. It was my first offence and I was given a fine.

Living on my own in that big house I became increasingly depressed. One day I got a phone call from the glazier, wanting to know if everything was alright because he hadn't heard from me for a while. 'We're all okay,' I said. 'My wife's away on holiday.' 'Ah, that explains it,' he replied. That afternoon, completely out of my head I started drinking on top of the pills. Alcohol and pills were always double poison and proved so that day when laughing hysterically I broke every window in the front of the house. I got on the phone, screaming at the glazier, 'Bingo, full house ! Numbers one to sixteen inclusive !' Minutes later the police arrived. 'Intruders, bloody rowdies ! They ran away,' I said to them, smiling. There was nothing they could do so they left. An hour later, with me in tears, the governor of the glazing firm himself helped with the work and tried to commiserate me. He was a craftsman and therapist mixed into one.

Some weeks later I allowed Camilla and the girls back home but now there was a difference. I'd at last accepted that she didn't give a fuck about me but inspite of everything I wanted to make a go of it for the kids sake. For the first time ever I started to behave normally and cut down the drugs. I didn't go out at night anymore, behaving as best I could. Even my library was closed down and we made it into a bedroom for Josephina. I believed this would improve the marriage but after a couple of months the exact opposite had happened. The rows had become ten times worse with the bloody glazier practically taking up residence. Camilla's sisters always sided with her and now hardly spoke to me. To keep the peace I began sleeping downstairs on the couch but most nights slept in the Jaguar at the local car park when the screaming reached thunder-pitch .

Life at home continued for a few weeks until, in between the smashing of glass, Terry was on the phone again. He enjoyed my company because my youth made him feel young himself. This time he asked me to accompany him to Manchester for a couple of weeks. 'I'll give you three hundred pounds to come with me,' he said. Thinking it would be a break from the domestic war I agreed. Exactly why we were going there apart from having a good chat I didn't know, except that Terry wanted to see more of the actress Billie Whitelaw, who was filming in Manchester. He had developed a crush on her and ironically, years later she played the mother of the Kray Twins in a film about their lives. To me his romantic obsession seemed ridiculous. He was far too old. People of forty-five don't have crushes, I thought.

139

The following morning he picked me up in his blue Rolls Royce, introducing me to John Black who was coming with us. John was a two-bit player with one of the big boxing promoters. Full of drugs I sat in the back listening with fascination as they discussed the big names, Jarvis Astaire, Jack Solomons, Micky Duff etc. 'It's the big time for us now,' boasted Terry. 'Who with ? Muhammed Ali ?' I laughed. 'No, with Jack Contel,' he replied proudly. At that time Jack Contel was unheard of, still fighting out of Liverpool, but within a few short years was to become Light Heavyweight Champion of the World. 'If we could control one World Champion and then get him to throw a fight we would hit every bookmaker from here to Vegas !' exclaimed Terry, going into his usual daily fantasy. Jack Contel, who never knew anything about this conversation, initially came to London under Terry's financial control. True to form, however, just prior to Jack actually becoming World Champion, Terry relinquished all financial interests under pressure from certain heavy characters. Unlike the real Al Capone dear Terry always buckled under such pressure.

In Manchester we stayed at the best hotel in Piccadilly and did absolutely nothing except sit about all day listening to longer versions of Terry's fantasies. It was good fun though, constantly ringing room-service for more goodies. There were no women, just wine and Terry - when he wasn't out chasing Billy Whitelaw.

It was during the two weeks of tranquillity in Manchester I accepted what I'd known for so many years. There was no point in continuing my marriage and with a mixture of sadness and relief I decided to finish it. Back in London when Terry dropped me off outside our house I felt sad, knowing this was the end.

In my own drugged way I idolised the children and still loved Camilla but had to take a bow from the battle-zone. I had nowhere to go but was determined to leave the next day. In a sombre mood I took extra sleeping pills to ensure peace on my last night.

Chapter 12

GOODBYE DAD

The following morning I called at Terry's office to collect my Manchester money and there I met Thelma, a girl I'd known for some time. There was nothing between us but she liked a good time and occasionally we met in the clubs at night. Thelma suggested a drink and later that evening she was accompanied by her flat-mate Jean, a stunning model with long black hair. Thelma introduced us, laughing, 'Watch this one, Jean, he's a lunatic'. Jean's warm, friendly smile instantly attracted me and when they left the club I followed them to their Baker Street flat. Going straight into Jean's bedroom I sat down for a chat. 'You must go home now,' she said after a while, 'I've got work in the morning and need my beauty-sleep.' 'I am home,' I laughed. 'I'm going to live with you now. I like you !' I did stay that night and we were to be together for the next two years, first at Baker Street and then in a small flat at the back of Harrods in Pont Street. I never went back to the house in Totteridge again, leaving all my clothes behind and since there were no more drugs in stock what was the point in driving down that unhappy street? Camilla herself never came looking for me and was quite satisfied to receive a cheque each week which enabled her to continue living in the house.

I didn't love Jean but had found peace woman-wise.

Probably even with Camilla it wasn't love, more like an addiction to the image of what I'd imagined her to be all those years ago.

Jean helped me through my Camilla withdrawal and all the hurt that went with it. She was an undemanding girl who just let me do as I wanted with no questions asked and ironically, I started to calm down, taking less and less drugs.

We began visiting my parents regularly and they liked this. By now Dad's health was deteriorating fast and he looked worse on each visit. Most weekends we also visited Jean's parents in South London. Her father who'd worked hard all his life hated me, a flash twenty-five-year-old with a new white Jaguar outside the door. 'Are you one of the Great Train Robbers?' he asked. 'No, I was too young. They wouldn't have me.' I joked. 'Well, where did that bloody car come from then?' he insisted. 'From a garage,' I would reply. Getting furious he asked, 'How did you pay for it?' 'With pound notes, Grandpa.' And so our not so friendly conversations continued on every visit. 'At least they've got honest jobs,' Jean's father joked one day as we watched television showing the first men walking on the moon.' This is a small step for man but a giant step for mankind,' Neil Armstrong said proudly as he stepped down from the Lunar module. 'I'm going up next week, the space ship was full,' I replied, continuing to tease Jeans perplexed father.

A short while later Jean and I moved into our small flat behind Harrods. I just roamed around Knightsbridge all day and although still taking drugs I was amazingly settled. I started to see Alen again who, inspite of everything, was still in love with me and had forgiven me once more. We resumed our Saturday night evenings at his home and even his mother, now well over a hundred years old, commented on how much better I looked. I never asked for money now but occasionally Alen still gave me expensive gifts. When I wasn't in contact with Terry it was Alen I looked to as a father figure.

Life continued like this for several months until one day I got a call from an old crony in Hong Kong. He had a deal for me and told me to ring a number in Frankfurt. When I did an American asked me to fly over to Germany for a chat. I caught a flight the very next morning and met a crowd of smooth operators in their smart offices in Central Frankfurt, who asked me to join them. I didn't know exactly what for - but it all sounded exciting and on the offer of good money I agreed to start a few weeks later.

First, however, I had to go back to London to take my father into hospital to die. The end was near and he wanted me to take him in. Love him or hate him, he was my dad and here was a problem I couldn't solve. All the money in the world wouldn't help. I had to accept that he would soon be dead and whereas in the past drugs had shielded me from sadness now my grief over his cancer got through. Man could walk on the moon but had no cure for cancer .

On returning from Frankfurt I could clearly see he had at best weeks to live. Addicted to gambling to the bitter end Dad still placed small bets at the local bookmakers every day. The glory times when he once played with Terry Savallas at 'Crockfords' were long gone, but in his own eyes he remained a big shot locally. Risking his last few pounds his compulsion, like my own addiction, was as bad as ever. Having chain-smoked eighty cigarettes a day throughout his life he was now losing his final bet against lung cancer. The top of his once fat body had wasted away, leaving his legs swollen like tree trunks as the cancer dug in for the kill. To overcome my sorrow in seeing him like this I increased the amphetamine intake, arriving so high and happy you would have thought we'd won the lottery. After each visit alone in my car I always burst into tears. One day I started to think, if he's going to die why can't he take my drugs and go out happy? Thank God this never got beyond the thought stage. Seeing him take so many tablets for his cancer gave me a strange feeling of unity as we took our pills together, both easing our individual pains. One morning I was exceptionally upset and took several of his pain tablets which felt good, giving me a new kind of buzz. After this I always stole one or two on my daily visits.

As a Freemason Dad was still in charge of organising the annual Ladies Night. His efforts had always been appreciated by the lodge members who showed him the recognition he'd craved for since childhood. His inner void had condemned him to a life of gambling addiction. Following that year's annual dinner, his last, he simply gave up his painful struggle to stay alive. The roulette wheel of dad's life stopped spinning as God called, 'Rien-ne-va-plus.'

The next day me and my father drove to the hospital. Arriving there we parked the car and went in through the giant swing doors. His ward was on the second floor and we had a long walk down the busy corridor to the lift. My dad's legs now were so swollen he could hardly stand and with every step I expected them to burst like balloons. I offered to find a wheelchair but he turned towards me and smiled, saying, 'We're walking this one together, son, just the two of us.' He held my hand tight as we inched along. The fifty yard walk took twenty minutes but with the drugs swimming round in my brain I felt like a little boy with dad holding my hand, as if he was taking me over to the park. Something he'd never done. It had taken twenty years and terminal cancer to get us so close.

With other patients, nurses and doctors rushing past I squeezed his hand even tighter, shouting, 'Dad, what a super walk ! What a fucking lovely day !' Concentrating on walking in so much pain he never heard me. A porter came up offering him a wheelchair. 'Fuck off ! It's my dad taking me for a walk. Can't you see that !' I screamed. After what seemed like hours we reached the lift and pressing the button he said, 'We made it, son.' He was crying. It was the first time I ever saw my dad cry. On the second floor as the lift door opened there was a nurse waiting with another wheelchair. I pushed her away, shouting, 'My dad don't need that. This walk's not over yet.' We tried to go on but he stumbled and two nurses put him in the chair to wheel him into the ward.

I rushed to the toilet in tears, swallowing more drugs with half a bottle of brandy to compose myself for our last goodbye. I had so much to share with my dad. Sadly as I approached him dying on that bed my words disintegrated. Everything I'd wanted to say for so many years just wouldn't come out and looking at him as he lay there I could see my reflection in his eyes.

It was strange. I felt a child again - a fucking lonely child !

My mouth opened to speak but all I could say was, 'I'm off to Frankfurt tonight, dad. See you soon !' Laying on his back he looked up and slowly shook his head, whispering, 'No son. You won't see me again. Keep your nose clean !' He meant for me to keep out of trouble. Shrugging my shoulders I replied, 'I'll try, dad,' and with that I turned and walked away.

Pressing the lift button I could still see him on his bed and so much wanted to go back and say, 'Dad, I love you !' Perhaps I would also hear him say the words I so desperately wanted to hear all my life, 'Son, I love you.' The lift arrived and as I stood staring at my Dad the door closed and it went down again. I pressed the button and waited, still looking at my father on his bed. The lift came again. It's too late now, I thought bitterly. All this should have been said twenty fucking years ago, not now ! This time the lift went down with me in it.

Two hours later I was on a plane to Frankfurt where I drunk and cried myself to sleep. How I wish I'd let the lift go down without me. Sorry Dad !

The following morning I woke up with a headache but after taking my morning amphetamine went to see the American boss-man. To him, like to so many others, unaware of my addiction, I appeared only hyper and excited. He greeted me with a 'Hi, Steve !' and I started the job. Strange outfit, I thought, I don't even know what they're doing ! My interview several weeks earlier had gone something like this, 'So you're a friend of Gerry. You can start in three weeks !' I suddenly realised they didn't even know my second name. The boss-man turned to his colleague and asked, 'Where can we send this kid?' Soon I was on a plane to Berlin, not knowing what was going on except that I was on two hundred pounds a week.

At Berlin airport I was met by another smooth talking American who booked me into a top hotel. 'Anything you want, including a woman. Put it on the cheque to us,' he said smiling. Three days later, having done nothing except eat, drink and enjoy German girls my American friend phoned, saying, 'You're going to

Cologne.' Here the same scene repeated itself, except, that with my new host we watched lesbians perform. From Cologne it was on to Hamburg. Every evening I was taken to fancy dinner parties where everybody had an attractive woman on his arm. I asked one of the bosses if I could bring my girlfriend over from England. 'Do what you like, son, just enjoy !' was his reply. The following day Jean arrived, having given up her modelling job overnight. This all-expenses-paid life-style continued until one day we were called back to head office in Frankfurt. The original boss-man was looking at a world map for English-speaking countries where he could send me because I spoke no languages. I thought of asking what we were doing but resisted, not wanting to endanger the job. 'Malta, I know Malta,' I suggested. 'Good idea,' he replied. 'Go with George.' He introduced me to a Londoner of about thirty-eight and it was agreed that George would drive me and Jean down to Malta.

As we talked a call from my mother came through to the office and I was handed the phone. Her words were, 'Bad news, Stephen. Dad died this morning.' The boss man offered me his condolences, 'Take as long off as you like. Fly out and join George later. You're a brave kid.' Brave? I thought. What a farce. I'd left my brother Paul to help my father die. I punished dad and left him to die without me because of the bedtime stories I'd missed as a child.

We arranged to meet George at the Phoenicia Hotel in Valetta and Jean and I flew back to England. Jean returned to her parents while I went to pick up my car which I'd parked in the garage of my house in Totteridge while I was abroad. At the front door I was greeted by my six-year-old daughter Tessa, saying, 'Granddad's ill !' 'In Heaven darling,' was my sombre reply. Tessa told me her mum was out in my car but I soon found Camilla in a local bar laughing with some friends. The whole pub went silent as I screamed, 'Give me the car keys. My dad's just died !' 'So what?' was her cold reply. Very hurt I felt like killing her.

At my parents home I found dad's coffin on the dining room table. I was devastated and took so many drugs it all became like an exaggerated film part with me playing the head mourner. Out of my head I actually lay on top of the coffin. On so much amphetamine it was impossible to comprehend my father was dead. I was too high to cry. An hour or so later my sister Annette arrived from Switzerland and along with my two brothers, my mother plus dad's dead body we were united as a family for the last time. Annette insisted on opening the coffin so we could see and remember our father. I was horrified at the thought of seeing his dead body and ran to the bathroom in order to take more pills. My mother followed me, pleading, 'You don't need pills to see Dad for the last time.' She hugged me. 'Throw them away ! Dad would have wanted that.' For one brief moment with my mother holding me I felt safe and threw all my pills down the toilet before going downstairs to see my dead father. A short while later the local Rabbi came to open the coffin. I was surprised to see my father looking so peaceful. All his pain had gone. He had no more bets to win or lose.

With no pills I soon locked myself in a bedroom where I passed out with a bottle of brandy. The next day we buried my dad at Waltham Abbey Jewish Cemetery with thirty members of the Earlam Masonic Lodge all paying their last respects. Somehow Dad's Masonic Lodge had given him what his wife and children couldn't. As the coffin was lowered I threw in a note which read, 'Dad, I really loved you, you were the only Dad I did not have.' When the other mourners left I stayed for a few moments alone by my father's freshly filled grave and cried, feeling his spirit blow away with the strong wind. Later, after kissing my mother goodbye at the cemetery I took a taxi directly to the airport where I met Jean. I was determined to stay off pills now and left for Malta without any. I had been off drugs for nearly two days and this for me was a world record.

Throughout the flight I slept and continued to do so in the taxi on route to our hotel in Sliema. For the next two weeks I stayed in bed most of the day half asleep, half drunk as the physical effect of the amphetamine withdrawal hit me. Stopping speed drugs so suddenly changed me, all I wanted to do was eat and sleep. This lethargic feeling lasted for weeks but gradually decreased as time went on.

With me sleeping so much Jean settled in on the sunny beach opposite, getting more tanned each day. Wearing lots of make up and long false eyelashes she always looked like something straight out of a fashion magazine. A month passed and George had still not arrived but at least I was a little more awake and began venturing out. One day I went to Gillard Street where Isabella had died three years earlier. I felt sad but this was a normal sadness. Off amphetamine it all looked so different. Although I was still drinking heavily I now saw Malta for the first time in years without drugs to distort the impressions. In fact in my sober moments I was nearly back with the human race as I began to notice ordinary things like the sea and the little fishing boats. There were no more vendettas with my wife's uncles or cousins. Off drugs you don't want these wars. As time passed I even drunk less, going to bed some nights boasting to Jean, 'I've only drunk one bottle of brandy today'. This was still alcoholic but compared with the previous years my behaviour was like that of a monk in a closed convent. For the first time in many years I started to read newspapers and was surprised to read that in England Edward Heath, having won the election, was now Prime Minister.

A week or so later George arrived, explaining he'd got involved with a woman in Italy. I quizzed him about our work but he just replied that as long as my money was arriving it all could wait for a few more days. He needed to unwind and since I knew Malta he asked me to show him the island. Leaving Jean to intensify her suntan George and I began an eight week party of carefree fun. This was something I'd never experienced before, having been robbed of my normal teenage years by gay doctors, jewel thieves and other dramatic events. My life had been like an express train racing from puberty to adulthood, passing life's stations so fast I never even saw them. Now, for the first time, I was having innocent fun with no villains, no threats, no screaming wife, just George, Jean, sunshine and brandy.

I met George every morning at eleven for the same routine. First we played chess by his hotel pool until three, then we walked down Valletta's main street to a bar where we played three hours of billiards. At around 6 pm the drinking started. I knew I would finish up drunk, I did every night, but taking my time over the first few somehow made me feel safer. After billiards we went all over Malta, in and out of every sleazy bar along with every pair of knickers in them. Jean, meanwhile, was always patiently waiting for me in our hotel room, applying more cream for sunburn.

One night we found ourselves in a bar in the middle of nowhere. It resembled a Spanish bull ring and seated about a hundred people. We looked down onto a small dance floor rather like a circus arena. Already quite drunk we both sat down on opposite sides, laughing and calling out to each other. It was all very weird, we were the only ones there amongst all those rows of empty seats. Eventually a waiter appeared but after serving us both with a bottle of brandy he vanished. The place remained silent for about another twenty minutes when suddenly music started and lights came on. Then a girl appeared, wearing a skirt so short you could see her bright red knickers as she walked round the entire arena before sitting down. Soon a second girl entered and sat down on the opposite side. A third girl appeared, a fourth, a fifth and in no time the arena was full of girls, no men, just young women smiling at us. At last the ring master came in and explained we could have as many women as we wanted, it was all included in the cover charge. Just coherent enough to enquire how much the charge actually was we were told not to worry and enjoy ourselves. We didn't need telling twice and were soon on the floor, having sex with about ten girls. In the middle of our orgy I noticed the other women who were not sexually involved with us were sitting at their tables, chatting or reading like it was a fucking launderette. Standing up I drunkenly screamed, 'Do you mind shutting up while I have my orgasm, at least pretend to be interested !' Much later we both passed out on the floor.

We woke as the sun rose the next morning and looking round I realised all the girls had gone. Both of us had hardly come to when the proprietor appeared with several large friends, presenting our bill. There was an enormous row and we paid an extortionate sum but at least left in one piece. Obviously we'd been their only customers that night and the girls had been bussed in specially from local villages after our arrival.

Life continued in carefree style under the sun until one day an American flew in. 'Sorry guys, we're closing Malta. Return to Frankfurt,' he said. Shame, I thought, feeling sorry to say goodbye to our three months of fun. I had already decided to leave Jean and put her on a plane to London. She was far too peaceful and I was getting bored with her, besides, I missed the action of London. George and I set off by car to drive back via Sicily and Italy. After a day or so in the car I got impatient and left George in Milan to fly on to Frankfurt making him promise if Jean ever rang he would say I was working for the firm in Australia. I was paid several weeks money owing to me, the boss man wished me luck and said, 'Sorry to lose you.' I often wondered what they were up to. The likes of George and myself were obviously of use to them in something too big for us to comprehend but one thing was sure - plenty of money came from somewhere to pay for it all.

With the dolce vita now over I caught the next plane back to London.

Chapter 13

HOME ALONE

I'd looked forward to London but arriving at Heathrow airport the emptiness hit me like a ton of bricks. Although I had plenty of money I was alone with nowhere to live. My father had somehow been a form of distant stability but now he was even further away, living in the sky. Stoned out of my head on amphetamine it would have seemed easy. Off drugs a future with no wife, no home and no dad seemed terribly daunting. I took a taxi to my parents' home, arriving just as my mother returned from work. She had taken a job to make ends meet. My sister lived abroad and with my brothers at college we were alone.

It was strange looking round where I'd grown up, nothing seemed to have changed since I was a child. Even my father's clothes and ties still hung where he'd left them. Sitting in the old kitchen drinking tea with mum I kept looking at the clock on the wall, expecting dad to come home from work.

That night I got very drunk to forget my troubles but the following morning when I woke confusion hit me. My mother was at work and alone in that house with all its memories I began to tremble, panicking as I thought about my future. Should I go to see Tessa and Antonia? Alen or Terry? What the fuck should I do? I was sweating and as usual when confused I reached for the brandy.

By 9 o'clock that morning I was drunk and apart from when I was actually asleep stayed drunk for the next month. Unable to face up to reality I found it easier to stay intoxicated, escaping back into my childhood. Home alone my drunken fantasies became very real as I pretended I was a child of eight again with no decisions to make. Running from room to room I held imaginary conversations with my childhood friends and as the brandy went down the more true to life my fantasy became. I got madder each day and one morning called for Eric, the little boy who used to live opposite, asking for him to come out to play. His old mother looked bewildered as she told me Eric was married now with his own wife and children. Confused I left that puzzled-looking woman standing on her doorstep and ran to the alley behind her house. I was cracking up, fantasy had become reality as I searched for my gang of kids whose leader I had been as a child. The nursery compound I'd burnt down had gone, making way for new houses, but our old hollow oak tree was still there. It was an enormous tree and as kids we used to climb up inside the hollow trunk to the branches above. Twenty years on and somewhat bigger I got stuck inside but eventually freed myself to climb through. As I sat in the tree a little boy came out from one of the houses and looked up at me. 'Are you Eric?' I drunkenly enquired. 'No, my name's Bobby,' he replied. 'What are you doing up there?' Before I could answer his mother appeared and pulled him back into their garden, scalding him, saying, 'I told you not to talk to strangers !' 'Eric where are you?' I shouted staggering back to our house.

I spent the afternoon pretending my parents were both at home and crawling into their bedroom I asked, 'Can I sleep in your bed tonight?' 'Providing you've kept out of the naughty room,' was their imaginary reply. This room was our small back bedroom where as a child I had once caught my mother kissing a builder working in our house.

At around four each day my mother returned from work and was puzzled as I greeted her, 'I've kept out of the naughty room !' 'Good boy,' she always replied to pacify me, not having a clue as to what I was talking about. She was intimidated by me and had to join in my games. Every evening followed the same routine. I went to bed at eight with the usual hot drink, half milk, half brandy. Mum, under duress, sat at the end of my bed and read from an assortment of newly acquired 'Robin Hood' books. She had no choice. If she refused I went berserk and threatened to burn the house down. At last I had her in her rightful place, reading bedtime stories to her little boy safely tucked up in bed. With no bully sister or little pest brothers this deranged twenty-six-year-old child finally had his mother's undivided attention. 'I'm so glad I stabbed our nanny Violet,' I would say, drifting off to sleep. 'I hated her. Be a good mummy and I won't kill you.'

With my childhood fantasy becoming real I was more than happy until one night in the middle of story-time the doorbell rang. My mother gave me the book to look at while she went down to open the door. Drunk and half asleep I looked at pictures of Robin with his arms round Maid Marion. I was drifting off when suddenly, to my horror, there at the end of the bed was Jean, fluttering her eyelashes. 'You read to him now,' said my mother, looking very pleased as she left the room. 'I'm a little boy. I don't like girls,' I screamed, hiding under the sheets. Moments later I felt Jean's naked body next to me. 'I know what little boys like,' she said as she started to suck my cock. My Robin Hood Books along with the childhood interlude were officially closed.

The following morning I woke furious, feeling betrayed by my mother and Jean who'd both left for work. Everything looked different. I was in a grown-up house in an adult street and my dad was dead. He wasn't coming home anymore. I brooded all day, drinking absolutely nothing, just waiting for those two bloody grown-up women to come home.

That evening, following their meal, they both sat on the red sofa watching television like my mother did every night. Two ordinary people leading ordinary lives. It was all so fucking normal. I hated it ! I wanted to scream ! I'll show them, I thought, sitting between them on that bloody red sofa. Jean started to write a letter and my mother began knitting while I sat there grinning to myself.

After about five minutes I thought, well I'm ready for take-off and with the clock in the hall chiming the same boring tune it had done since my world began I smiled, stood up and quietly left the room..

Apprehensively I walked up the stairs to the naughty room. It was my turn to be naughty. Climbing onto the window-ledge I reached inside the false ceiling where years before I had stored a large quantity of amphetamine pills. I stretched my fingertips and my addicted heart started pounding when I felt a bottle still hidden there. With some difficulty I pulled it out and was now staring at one hundred dexedrine tablets. Petrified of the drug horror-journey about to begin I wanted to cry for help, but it was too late and unable to control my lifelong addiction I swallowed the first handful of pills.

Back downstairs, without saying a word, I sat down between Jean and my mother, with a pencil and paper to record the changes inside my crazy head. I waited for an eternity but nothing happened. Jean still wrote, my mother still knitted and the hall clock ticked loudly. Then, suddenly Jean's writing became interesting and my mother's knitting began to fascinate me as the cocaine earthquake of speed erupted inside my brain. The whole room was coming alive. My mother's knitting needles now sounded like drumsticks.

I began to write down how I felt when I suddenly began to shake with fear. I was rocketing back to drug-island. Jumping up I ran into the street, throwing the remaining tablets down the sewer and returned to the lounge to sit back between the ever silent women. Desperately trying to cling on to normality I sat there but it was already too late.

Everything felt like it had done in gay Dr. Newam's bathroom all those years ago. I tried to force myself to remain calm and stay on the couch but couldn't. Suddenly I had a million things to do, places to go, people to talk to. 'What's wrong?' Jean asked as I leapt up and rushed back out into the street to retrieve the pills I'd just thrown away. I tried to lever open the drain cover with a shovel but it wouldn't budge. Looking down I could see dozens of yellow tablets floating on the murky black water. Now I remembered there were drugs in the loft and ran frantically back into the house. Pushing past a worried Jean I charged upstairs, climbing into the attic where I'd hidden so much cash and drugs over the years. I searched and searched, moving all the old jumble for about half an hour, getting more desperate by the moment, when at last I struck gold. In the far corner, hidden by the eaves, were two silver cash boxes but there were no keys. I rushed down to the garage to smash them open, behaving like I was possessed by the devil. Jean and my mother were too frightened to stop me and stood there in disbelief as I attacked the boxes like a deranged vampire. There was lots of noise and eventually one snapped open. Inside were only bank notes, about a thousand pounds, but no drugs. Jean pleaded with me to stop but furious I screamed at her to fuck off, throwing the money all over the floor in disgust. The second box was stronger and I only just managed to make a small opening through which I squeezed my hand to find more money but no drugs. Cutting my hand on the jagged edges I shouted, 'More fucking useless money !' At this moment two policemen appeared at the garage door. A neighbour had reported the noise. They asked me what was going on. With blood dripping from my hand and money all over the floor it was a strange sight, as I smugly replied, 'Just lost the keys, no crimes committed !' They took down my name and left, warning me, 'No more noise or we'll take you in for disturbing the peace.'

Drugs had kidnapped me again after the Malta sunshine break. My addiction was back with a vengeance. Grabbing a handful of cash off I drove to the red light district to buy more pills. Jean tried to stop me as I started my car but it was too late, I was too addicted, I was gone.

For the next few days and nights I roamed from club to club stoned out of my head with all the other drug freaks. I finished up with a crowd of hippies joining the other one hundred and fifty thousand flower people at the Isle of Wight pop festival. Here out of my skull I saw the purple haze man himself, Jimi Hendrix.

About a week later I eventually returned to Winchmore Hill in a terrible state. My mother and Jean, who was wearing a new pair of hot pants, were sitting in exactly the same position on the red sofa where I'd last seen them.

The alcoholic interlude of my life had closed just in time for the main drug feature to begin.

Chapter 14

MASTER PLANS TO FORTUNES AND INSANITY

Back on my mind altering amphetamine I began to dream of creating a global empire. Speed can initially trigger enormous creativity and inspired like this I began to work on a plan to build up a company with the view to have its shares floated on the stock exchange. I reasoned that with all my stolen cash I could always give the business the extra push to ensure success. As usual this new idea took over my mind to the exclusion of everything else. I booked myself into the Cumberland Hotel at Marble Arch to avoid any disturbances and began to type a detailed 730 page master plan, telling me what to do each day for the following two years. Day 1 - find offices, employ secretary, day 14 - advertise for agents, day 100 - open food warehouse and so it continued in intricate detail. It even listed how many drugs I should take but sadly I didn't stick to those particular estimates. The scheme itself was based on American Discount Shopping, new to Britain at the time.

Twelve months later my plan had materialised with over 5000 shops in the London area offering discounts on production of our card and a company turnover of a half a million pounds a year.

Only leaving my hotel room to buy clean underwear or more drugs my master plan took nearly six weeks to complete. Nothing else mattered or existed as I worked away with little or no sleep. Occasionally I rang Jean just to say I was still alive but refused to tell her where I was. Eventually I emerged a little bleary from room 33 of the Cumberland with a new red briefcase embossed with gold letters reading, 'Master Plan.' Like Ali who'd just got his boxing licence back in New York I felt like a million dollars, ready to conquer the world.

During the weeks I'd worked on my plan Jean had found a flat. By coincidence it was one block behind the Cumberland and a week later we moved into 21 Seymour Street, Marble Arch, from where page one of the plan was immediately put into action. It was uncanny, everything I'd typed out somehow now became reality. Page by page, day by day, it all came true. Jean continued her modelling leaving me to operate my drug-induced dream without interruption. Occasionally we had sex but I made it quick and always returned to my desk immediately after to continue my mission. Jean was a good person, she loved me and regardless of my lunatic behaviour she stayed on for more.

Within a few weeks I'd teamed up with a clever man, Jack Blamford-Ericson, who'd run a similar venture in seventeen different countries in conjunction with Brampson's, the big tour operators. Compared to the usual humdrum of business life I, with my wild ways, was a breath of fresh air to Jack. After he joined me the whole thing flourished at an even more remarkable speed and huge sums of money began to roll in. Every morning I smiled as I opened the red briefcase to tick of yesterday's successes. On page 75, or day seventy five, which ever way you look at it I went to visit Dr. Salomi at his surgery in Wimpole Street. He was just one of about twenty private doctors prescribing drugs for me and between them all they just about satisfied my addiction. Opening the red case I took out the remaining pages of the unlived master plan and said. 'I need help, Doctor. I must find a person who has administration experience in running a big business. It's all getting too much for me.' 'I know just the person,' Dr. Salomi smiled.

I begged him to ring this man there and then but he explained that his friend was only on the phone at weekends. Strange, I thought, not on the phone weekdays. Where does he live, on an oil rig?

That Saturday morning at the doctor's surgery I met a tall, well-spoken man about twenty years older than me, impeccably dressed in a blue overcoat complete with velvet collar. He introduced himself as Steven Delanncey-Tinker and told me he was currently completing a five-year-sentence for his part in the big car insurance fraud with Eric Kavoondra. I remembered the case. It had been very big news with millions of pounds involved. Steven, smoking with a gold cigarette holder, explained he was currently on day release from Wandsworth Prison and had to be back each afternoon by five-thirty. 'I have a wealth of experience but perhaps with my somewhat tarnished background am not suitable for you,' he finished. 'Start Monday,' I said, grinning from ear to ear. He did.

In his first week Steven told me we needed a company accountant, someone clever with the books. 'Especially now we've got decimal currency,' he joked. Of course he knew just the chap - Jimmy, his prison cell mate, who joined our fast growing company soon after. 'Don't worry, we won't go bust like Rolls Royce,' Jimmy said smiling at the end of his first day.

The next few months saw the business mushroom beyond my wildest dreams. Like the Master Plan had predicted it just got bigger and bigger and including our agents we were now employing over two hundred people. With the London side of the business running smoothly it was time to conquer the Home Counties, England and then, naturally, the world. Typical of any amphetamine freak enjoying new found success there was no stopping me now, or so I believed. After negotiating contracts with major food companies we opened the first of many showrooms as per page 163, taking a four storey office building in Church Street, Paddington. From there the number of agents selling our memberships quickly grew to over one thousand.

Church Street is situated in an old part of London with numerous antique or junk shops and with our well lit bright red facia we stuck out like sore thumbs amongst the local traders. With the old and the new side by side next door to us lived a couple called Ma and Pa who traded in junk. Their family had been odd job dealers for generations and Pa, aged eighty, still went out every day, pushing his cart to collect rags like his father had done with a horse. For them we were a strange but interesting sight as we arrived in our expensive cars Further down the street was a very up-market antique business, the best by far in that street. It was run by a gay man of about thirty called Martin. He was tall, quite attractive and rather camp, always smiling. Often he came out of his shop and said hello to me as I passed. Stoned out of my skull I started buying something expensive in his shop every day, not because I wanted it, just to show off. I was very flash and enjoyed buying expensive works of art as if it was fish and chips. If Martin with his posh enterprise had been prince of that street then I arrived as king. On Saturdays the street became a market and I was puzzled watching the traders put out their stalls with worthless brick-a-brack. Why did they bother? Their whole stock was only worth a hundred pounds or so. One Saturday,

164

drugged to the hilt, I bought the entire stock of three stall holders. What was small change to me was a financial miracle to them. I put all my purchases on a table outside our building with a big notice reading, 'Help yourself. It's free.' Within minutes crowds of people arrived, clearing the lot while I watched from inside the showroom in hysterics.

Around this time I started to smoke opium every day on top of my pills. I watched the fight in which Ali lost to Frazier at Madison Square Garden on close circuit and was so gone that as usual, I didn't know who won. I was the only acid-tripping boxing fan and after the fight got knocked out myself following an argument.

Steven and Jack took responsibility for the layout of our showrooms. They did it in style with dark green carpet on all four floors, brand new office furniture in each of the ten rooms and a switchboard in the reception. It looked the height of respectability and at that stage still was. The board-room was on the first floor and Steven brought in his own expensive conference table and twelve chairs, one of which was genuine Queen Anne. On the same floor in our accounts office girls processed the hundreds of standing orders now coming in every day. Up at the top was my private office with its expensive white leather furniture. Above the side board was a Victorian oil portrait of a gentleman who I claimed was my great grandfather, the founder of the firm. On the wall opposite was a world map showing the thirty different countries in which associate cards were valid, making the whole thing look very grand.

It was an amusing set-up, headed by a young man out of his crust, chain-smoking opium as he screamed orders down the intercom. The company's chief executives, who had to be home in Wandsworth prison by five-thirty, often borrowed the managing director's white Jaguar which they parked overnight in the prison yard. Everything continued to go uncannily to plan with only one fly in the ointment - me and my drugs. The amount I was now consuming daily had reached ludicrous heights, causing my behaviour to become increasingly erratic.

As my madness grew I had the old armchair my father died in delivered to our offices. From that day onwards everybody visiting our reception was forced to sit in that chair while I proudly announced, 'My dad died in that chair.' Unable to calm down at night I left Jean in bed to roam the all-night drug clubs, going for days without sleep. Very soon I had progressed from being a pest to an actual liability for my own company. As I staggered in from yet another all-night session Jack and Steven would always say, 'Stay at home to dream up new brilliant schemes and leave the running of the business to us.' One morning they suggested, 'Go over to St. Tropez and watch Mick Jagger get married. That'll keep you out of trouble.' Completely unpredictable I went on the missing list for days, bringing the entire firm to a stand-still because only I was authorised to sign cheques. Smoking opium in my office when I wasn't interfering with the running of the business I spent hours looking up the bum of one of the secretaries who wore the shortest of skirts. All day long I made her file documents in the lowest drawer of the filing cabinets so she would bend over further and I could see more of her crutch. Speed does weird things to you sexually. You get the erection but you don't want the orgasm. This girl realised she was a turn-on for the boss and soon started to wear no knickers at all but even though she was keen I never touched her. I just sat there, stoned, with my erection under the desk all day. At least for the time being her bum kept me from doing worse damage elsewhere.

Over the months that followed the company income increased but so did my drug intake and violent temper outbursts. Early most evenings I was horrified when I reached in my pocket to find that I had already swallowed my daily allowance of one hundred tablets. One morning Jean began to seriously challenge me over the number of tablets I was now taking. 'Do you want to be found dead like Jimi Hendrix or Janis Joplin were last year ? You will be next !' she shouted. She'd hidden some of my drugs and for me this was high treason. Nobody tampers with an addict's drugs and with my head exploding I threw Jean and all her possessions into the street. Jack, my partner, found her crying on the doorstep of his mews house and took her in for a few days after which she left. I never saw Jean in my life again and with her went my last chance of remaining sane.

From now on it was downhill all the way. The drugged mood swings caused me to have rows with everybody and I started firing people on impulse. My favourite daily expression became, 'And you can fuck off, too'. Steven and Jimmy left of their own accord and a few months later Jack was gone. People were no longer able to cope with the drugged, deranged psychopath I had become.

Living alone in the flat added to my turmoil with my drug, alcohol and opium consumption now totally out of control. Gradually I lost all interest in both the business and looking up my secretary's bum. I just wanted the drug buzz and sat at home getting extra stoned. Bill Stone, a young boy who till then had worked in the printing department of the company was promoted to chief joint-maker as I began to buy marihuana and opium by the shoe-box. I gave him instructions to mark the joints with a felt-tip pen using a coding system - one ring meant average strength, two double strong and three rings brain-buster. After a short while Bill, a skinny boy with dark, curly hair, threw the pen away with me declaring brain-busters only from now on. At this stage a major part of the company's income was still self-repeating so at first, regardless of my lunacy, the money like the joints kept rolling in.

Chapter 15

DRUGGED ANTS AND WOMEN'S ORGASMS

It was drug-time ! Thinking of nothing else anymore I became obsessed with the search for the ultimate high. To conduct my experiments undisturbed I told everybody I was going abroad on business and painted the windows of my flat black, like it was wartime. I had about ten different types of amphetamine and crushing them up spent hours mixing the powders in different proportions like a deranged Frankenstein. I was trying to create electricity inside my own head, convinced the correct mixture would give me a never-ending high.

I took so many drug concoctions that during one of my experiments my heart started to race uncontrollably and fearing a major heart-attack I rang for an ambulance. This incident gave me a fright and returning from hospital I decided to conduct all further experiments on animals.

My research began with goldfish in three different tanks to whom I fed food mixed with amphetamine powder. Soon it seemed the fish actually swam round faster but sadly some of them enjoyed the high too much, overdosed and floated to the top.

Drug studies are a lonely business and to help me with my work I promoted Bill Stone from office joint-maker to first assistant at the lab. He arrived for work with a carrier bag full of dope. 'Hash is better,' he declared, 'You'll see !' Unable to get the goldfish to actually smoke their own joints we used straws to blow the hash-smoke into the tanks, making bubbles. Getting frustrated I disposed of my straw to find a faster way. Putting my face into the water to blow the smoke direct I accidentally swallowed a fish and became violently sick. After this the experiment abruptly ended. Falling all over the floor with stoned laughter Bill mumbled, 'I'll have to resign. You'll have to get a new assistant. I just can't smoke any more.'

Some time later when we recovered enough to get off the floor Bill suggested, 'Parrots. Birds breathe air !' Soon we were returning from Harrods with three birds in separate cages, putting one in each room. Gathering our last ounce of strength we went from room to room, smoking hash, creating the fog designed to get our feathered friends going. It soon became apparent we couldn't stand up long enough to complete the experiment and it was decided we needed help - more smokers. Bill had just the answer. He knew eight hippies living in a squat off the Portobello Road and was sure the offer of free dope would enlist their help. An hour later he returned with our new workers crammed into two taxis. Soon they were all chain-smoking dope which for them was pure paradise. Bill, as foreman, had to work at a very fast pace, rolling fresh supplies from a carrier bag full of Lebanese Red, to keep up with our smoke-force. Now, even beginning to look like Frankenstein, I locked every window and door of the flat to ensure the marihuana mist stayed inside. Shortly after, however, I was forced to re-open everything when many of the hippies became paranoid, thinking it was a new type of drug-bust in reverse. With the entire laboratory staff looking ill and the parrots staring on in silence I declared another experiment over. The winning bird was presented to the best smoking hippie at the end of their five-hour hash treat. 'Cool man, far out, any time !' they said, crawling out of the flat. Later we discovered the remaining goldfish had gone. The chief suspect was the hippie's pet cat who'd looked very smug as he left with his pot-smoking master. 'I must have time off work,' Bill declared. 'What for?' I asked with dismay. 'To go to sleep,' he replied, leaving me alone, totally spaced out in the laboratory.

Several pills later I had yet another brainwave. Ants ! Much easier to watch, I reasoned. In the middle of that night I went down to the dustbins behind the Cumberland Hotel armed with a bag of crushed pills and a torch. Spreading the drug powder all over the floor I watched gleefully as the ants climbed over the white mountains of speed. The experiment was going quite peacefully until it was suddenly interrupted by two uniformed police-officers, enquiring what I was doing at two am with a torch. 'Studying ant behaviour,' I explained. 'You'll get nicked. Why don't you go to bed and study them in the morning,' one of them suggested. They turned to walk away and horrified I watched as one size twelve policeman's foot crushed the happiest crowd of ants the world had ever seen.

Wild birds ! Was the next feather-brained inspiration flying into my head. As dawn broke I was in Hyde Park, feeding the sparrows with lumps of wet bread soaked in liquid amphetamine. Many ate the bread but it was impossible to observe them in flight or judge their happiness.

Later that morning I found one of my hippie friends laying on the grass near the Serpentine Lake and re-employed him to turn on the ducks. They move slower and therefore would be easier to watch I thought to myself as I took my lunch time acid trip. I lent my bearded friend a gold Rolex watch to time the ducks and keep the usual charts for posterity but the junior professor of drug-studies soon vanished with both chart and watch. I was tired now and lay down on the grass staring upwards, waiting to meet Lucy in the Sky with Diamonds. As I drifted off one of the birds flew overhead. 'He's happy at least', I smiled.

'Wake up ! You can't stay here,' said the park warden. I'd been asleep by the lakeside all day. Now it was dark and walking home I thought to myself, no more animals, they're too bloody unpredictable. It's people I need, humans to experiment on. Staggering into a coffee-shop I sat down to find myself looking up a pair of beautiful long legs barely covered by the shortest of mini skirts. Staring at that crutch I had a wet dream-type inspiration. I would time and record the quickest ever female orgasm ! Throughout that night I recruited some old and new hippies along with a couple of rent boys plus two prostitutes. By the next evening the laboratory was well and truly back in business as different couples were given various drug-cocktails while I got ready to time their orgasms. Unfortunately my human guinea-pigs were too far gone to record split-second results but for the record, oral sex between three people always produced the quickest climax. We all took more drugs as the wild scenes went from mad to madder with sperm flowing freely.

In the kitchen during one heated debate in the middle of a drug-tea-break a long-haired blonde claimed she would climax quicker with cream being licked off her breasts. That's it ! I thought, cream is the answer !

Two stoned helpers were despatched and returned with a suitcase full of cream, porno books and vibrators. History was in the making ! We were about to witness a new world speed orgasm. Dividing the party into three groups I painted large team numbers in red on the bums of all the men with a thick felt-tip pen. For the contest all men were totally naked while women wore regulation knickers only. Before the race contestants were allowed to read porno books to enhance their mood but touching was strictly forbidden with security tighter than at the Olympic Games. On my orders the men spread cream all over the women and then it was ready, steady, go ! Using dicks, vibrators or fingers the race was on. I'm sure the blond girl cheated because seconds later, with her knickers still round her knees, she had an enormous orgasm. Objections from other teams were all overruled with me, the racing steward too stoned to face an official enquiry. Sensing a riot and to keep the peace I screamed, 'Whole team must orgasm !' A great deal of confusion followed but in the end, with all the contestants looking well and truly satisfied, the prizes, various Anne Summers sex toys, were equally shared.

The wild scenes continued each day but somehow I got sadder and more lonely all the time. Once I woke up in bed with two half-dressed transvestites. Fuck this for a game of soldiers ! I'd wanted to be with the wrens, I thought, taking my breakfast amphetamine tablets.

Totally obsessed with sex I now paid a call girl to sit on the subway train wearing a practically non-existent skirt with no knickers. I wanted to judge men's reactions when she opened her legs. Some men would stare, others would hide behind their papers. It all got a bit out of hand when one woman started to beat her husband over the head with her umbrella and dragged him out of the train, screaming, 'You dirty bastard. You only go to sleep when I get undressed.' At least one builder had the balls to say, 'If you've got somewhere to go, love, I'll fuck you, but it's got to be a quick one because I'm on price work.' This bizarre sex era ended with a near fatal plane crash. While I was having sex with an African girl in a friend's private plane, Cyril the pilot watching us in his mirror got so carried away he overshot the runway. Very shaken up we crawled out of the plane half naked into a nearby field.

As the months passed it got worse. Alone in the flat at night I became very lonely and was unable to sleep even on large doses of pills. Paranoia was setting in. I was convinced the world was out to get me. Ready for the end I'd bought ten 'escape cars' parked in various parts of London. Each car was equipped with reserves of everything and for this purpose I had thirty gallon cans of petrol stored at the flat. Desperate for some sleep I began injecting myself with sleeping drafts and one night passed out on my solid metal bed still smoking a cigarette. The burning fag-end set fire to the mattress and as the bed blazed around me I woke up. Semi-conscious I crawled into the hall where drugged to the hilt I just slept on, oblivious to the fire. I half woke up once again, hearing the porter banging on the front door, screaming, 'Fire, fire !' Rolling over I could see flames everywhere, the entire mattress was ablaze and crawling down the hall I unlocked the front door, mumbling, 'Quick, call the fire brigade !' 'They're already on their way,' the porter replied. Full to the brink with sleep injections I simply curled up at his feet and was soon fast asleep once more on the floor next to the lift.

When the firemen arrived they broke in via the third floor windows and ran their hoses through the lounge over my hidden petrol cans to put the fire out. Luckily the high metal bed frame had kept the fire from spreading throughout the flat. It would have blown up the entire block and half of Seymour Street with it.

Jack Erricson and his wife returning from a night-club at around 3 am saw fire engines outside the block and remarked to each other, 'That's got to be him !' They found me still asleep by the lift and carried me to their mews house nearby. I slept solid for the whole of the next day.

When I eventually woke I was very upset by this near catastrophe and spent a few days at the coast with Alen. Inspite of my lunacy he still loved me as much as ever.

Chapter 16

CLARA

Coming so close to death I became very frightened. Was I being punished by God? Desperately wanting his forgiveness I began all-night mercy trips to railway stations again, giving money away to tramps. I no longer considered myself Jesus, more a modern-day Robin Hood. Ironically, the more I gave away the more money flowed into the business each day, but at this stage I had fortunes stashed away anyhow and it all made no difference.

A bad famine had hit Biafra in Africa and emotionally overcome I decided to save the world single-handedly. Donating a thousand pounds to the disaster fund I halted normal business operations, making the entire office staff do nothing else but organise a mammoth fund-raising mailshot. Our efforts were extremely successful and along with a donation from B.B.C television we raised a considerable amount of money. Sadly, in return for my kindness all I got was one big kick in the teeth when I delivered the proceeds to the 'Save the Children Fund' head-office. The clerk merely said, 'Thank you,' and gave me a receipt. A fucking receipt? For me, an emotionally starved cripple this was no bloody good ! I wanted the adulation, the glory, not a bloody receipt ! Following this let-down I restricted all further Robin-Hood-work to winos. Tramps didn't write out receipts, they blessed me personally.

Around this time I began my love affair with Clara, daughter of a well known sports commentator.

I'd met her some months earlier when she worked for Jack and had found her an extremely attractive, interesting girl from the start. She was so different from the other women I'd known - highly intelligent, very sure of herself and great fun to be with, both in and out of bed. Without realising it I had fallen in love with Clara. She was the first person I actually enjoyed being with. I always called her 'George' which made me feel safer somehow, overcoming my deep mistrust of women. Tall and blond, Clara even looked different from my previous dark-haired girlfriends. She came from an upper-class family with a mother who regularly attended the Queen's garden parties at Buckingham Palace. For Clara, with her public school education and Hurrah-Henry-type friends, to have me as her 'Bank Robber' lover was a fascination of a new kind. Compared to a game of crochet with her Sloane-Ranger socialites nights out with me and my gangster associates were rather different.

If I was Robin, Clara made the perfect Maid Marion. We really liked each other and spent a great deal of time together, both at my flat or at her family's five storey home in Hamilton Terrace. Many weekends I was invited to stay with her parents at their weekend country house and inspite of our different backgrounds Clara's parents were always kind to me. Here was a mum and dad that loved their kids and looking at her brothers I got envious thinking they didn't have to snatch handbags for their parents attention. Clara was the nearest thing I found to true love and in fact, without my drug addiction, it might have become just that. Sadly, inspite of her wonderful influence my drugs made sure this semi-rational period didn't last long and soon the wild times returned.

It takes a certain type of person to want to become involved with a dangerous psychopath and full of drugs that person was me. On the day I met Brian Clifford it was like holding a red rag to a spaced out bull. I didn't need the money and it wasn't necessary for me to even speak to him but I did. Through him I was forced into so many more crimes and a load of headaches along with it. My entire life became sheer madness. With lorry loads of stolen perfume, cigarette's and wine etc. my flat became like Fagin's Den.

Brian Clifford was known as 'Little Legs' in the criminal underworld because he was short with fat little legs. He wore his wavy black hair combed back and was quite handsome, really. Brian, however, was a dangerous man and it was his psychopathic behaviour which was the turn-on for me. His uncontrollable temper made Ronnie Kray seem like a girl guide. Whereas the Krays, bless them, following the Cockney code of conduct only attacked fellow villains, Little Legs knew no code. He would have killed a bus load of nuns or the local church choir without batting an eyelid. He was not only an evil bastard but in the wrong mood was certifiable. I'd met him at the Jermyn Street Turkish Steam Baths through 'John the Cat', a burglar I knew, and after our first meeting Brian began picking me up every day to take me to Wheeler's for lunch. Watching me climb into Brian's Rolls Royce gay Martin, looking on, would always say, 'Mmm, rich friends, Duckie.'

Over the following months Little Legs and I socialised with our ladies in tow each evening. Clara, unaware of what was really going on or the dangers involved found the whole scene highly exciting and jolly good fun. One night after dinner Brian pulled up outside his offices in the Walworth Road and asked Clara to wait in the car while he took me and his girl upstairs to make a private phone call. He told us to sit down in the high-back leather chairs and while I talked to Joan Brian left the room. He returned unnoticed and without warning suddenly attacked this poor girl, punching her in the face. Like a monster he screamed, 'You cow, you shit pot,' pulling her head back and chopping off her long blonde hair, he left her looking like a war-camp victim. I sat there mortified, unable to move. 'We're going home, Steve,' Brian said, throwing the knife to the floor. He pulled me out of the room, leaving the girl frozen in terror staring at her hair all over the floor. A few minutes later in the car as we passed Battersea Power Station Clara asked innocently, 'Where's Joan?' 'Washing her hair', Little Legs replied, smirking at me in the rear view mirror. After dropping Clara off at Hamilton Terrace he took me to Regents Park and parked the car. With my head spinning round I listened as Brian opened his latest bag of tricks.

Little Legs knew exactly what he was doing and behind his display of lunacy was a calculating and highly intelligent brain. To frighten me he began to explain in intricate detail the look on peoples faces just before they die. I sat there in terror as he recounted his murders. 'Now for my piece de-la-resistance,' he said, giving me a wad of American hundred dollar bills. 'These are forged but can easily be cashed over the counter,' he explained, 'especially in the big foreign Banks.' The British Banks apparently were already on to them. 'That's where you come in,' he said, patting my knee. 'We're going to Switzerland tomorrow morning and you, my friend, are coming with us to change the dollars.' I was to be the scape-goat on offer to get caught if it all went wrong. Too shocked to reply and drugged as usual I agreed to join Brian and his side-kick on an early flight to Zurich.

An hour later when I got back to my flat the horrors set in. I panicked because I believed that once we'd cashed the forged bills Little Legs and his fellow lunatic would surely murder me. There was no way those greedy bastards would split the proceeds with me. I took more drugs to think clearer. With the amphetamine racing round my brain I soon found the answer of how to get back from Switzerland alive. I would take a small-time villain I knew along with me. My plan was to slip my accomplice the money by switching identical briefcases in the last bank so he could take the cash back to England. This way Brian would have to keep me alive at least till we got to London in order to get at the money. A few phone calls later I had employed my villain and secretly booked him an extra seat on our plane to Zurich.

Full of drugs the whole episode suddenly became very exciting cloak-and-dagger stuff. The following morning, like in a real-life James Bond Movie, I sat alongside Brian and partner with my accomplice two seats behind, carrying his identical case. After landing his taxi followed ours into central Zurich where I visited several banks, changing the forged dollars for pound notes and soon my briefcase was bursting with British money. Miraculously my two-bit villain was still in tow late that afternoon as we left the last bank.

Brian now took me to one of the best hotels and I believe it was here he planned to kill me. In the busy reception I put the briefcase down and winked at my accomplice who was now wearing a pathetic-looking fedora hat and sunglasses. He picked up my case, left and caught the next flight back to London.

It was all like a childish joke and high as a kite I was enjoying the drama - up to the time we reached our room that was. On hearing what I had done Brian didn't shout, he just went very quiet but the look in his eyes said it all. Breathing hard and ignoring me he turned to his evil-looking colleague, repeating over and over, 'Switched the case, switched the case.' I sat there watching his nostrils move, expecting the worst. Eventually he stood up, walked over to me and smiled, 'I would have done the same. Let's go to England and split the money four ways.' He wanted to give me a fraction of what I was due, kidding me half of the cash had to go to the forging gang. We spent a quiet night in Switzerland and caught the early morning flight to Heathrow. On the plane back, feeling very smug, I turned to Brian, saying, 'No, my little friend, two ways. We are dividing the money down the middle.' With my morning amphetamine in full swing I felt real good, especially in the safety of our Boeing 707, thinking, 'I call the shots now.' The pills inside me were.

Arriving at Heathrow I arrogantly told Brian to call at my flat at twelve noon the following day to collect his share. For my safety I arranged to have Moses and five other Jamaican minders up in the flat with me for moral and physical support. I collected the money from my apprentice hood later that evening and returned to Seymour Street to get one good nights sleep before the final round of my fight with Little Legs.

At twelve noon the next day the shit hit the fan. The Seymour Street flat was only small and the bedroom was packed with six large Jamaicans silently on guard when the doorbell rang. I was already charged up drug-wise but took one final handful of tablets for courage as I went down the hall. I opened the door, expecting to find Brian pointing a shotgun at me - but standing there was Camilla.

She looked more beautiful than ever, irresistible, just like a bag of heroin is to a junkie. Quickly I ushered her into the lounge, closing the door, saying, 'Wait in here, I've got an important visitor coming.' In panic I locked the doors of both rooms so now neither the Jamaicans nor Camilla could get out. Seconds later the bell rang again and this time it was my little Brain looking quite sweet but more vicious than ever. A row started over the amount of money I gave him and as he began to threaten me I opened the bedroom door to let out the Jamaicans brandishing knifes. Brian stood there unimpressed and argued for more cash. Should I let Camilla out on him, I wondered?

It was quite weird but at this stage I was only afraid of one thing, Camilla's reaction to it all. By now she was banging on the door, screaming from the inside, 'Open this door immediately.' 'You'd better go,' I said to Brian, nodding towards Camilla's locked door. 'Take this money for now, we'll talk another day.' He shook his head, shouting, 'I don't believe all this,' but amazingly with that he left. Camilla's banging was getting louder as I gave Moses a thousand pounds, sending him and his gang of cut-throats back to Nottinghill Gate. Closing the front door behind them I breathed a sigh of relief and unlocked the lounge to find Camilla looking rather annoyed. We talked for a while then, frightened that Clara might call round, I took Camilla to the Cumberland Hotel for a drink. True to my addictive nature I asked her to come to Ireland with me the following week.

A few days later Camilla and I caught the ferry from Fishguard. I was going to meet a well known safecracker whom I shall call O'Grady. I had recently acquired a building from which we were planning to tunnel into the neighbouring bank premises.

Arriving in Dun Laoghaire we booked into the Elfin Hotel where I left Camilla on her own, delaying our reconciliation talk, and travelled on to Dublin alone.

I wanted to see the Gresham Hotel again. This was where my gay jewel thief Gentleman George had left me when I was fourteen years old. Standing in O`Connell Street I stared at that big hotel and suddenly got very frightened as my mind swung from the past to the future. I began to see visions of what was going to happen to me over the next few years. The premonitions were horrifying.

That night I wanted to stop the drug train and get off, but I couldn't, it was all moving too fast now. I was locked on board, addicted, watching my life race by outside the window.

The next morning we met O'Grady and spent the day on his yacht in order to discuss things privately. Camilla was sunbathing on the top deck while we talked below. Sitting there as the sun shone in through the portholes I could already see so many future problems, especially with us two pathetic criminals. One couldn't stop swallowing pills while the other drank whisky non-stop. All in all we didn't make a very reliable pair but, inspite of that, our talks finished with everything drunkenly agreed. On the way back to shore the speed boat was going full throttle when O'Grady, now very sloshed, passed out across the wheel. Only twenty yards from a head-on crash into the harbour wall I threw myself over him and somehow turned the small boat back out to sea.

Back in the hotel Camilla and I, both a bit shaken, decided to stay an extra couple of days and it was that evening we agreed to give our relationship one more try. It was lunacy, doomed to failure. Knowing it could never work I delayed actually moving back together for as long as possible. Romantic dreams are easier to live with than life's reality.

At breakfast the following morning we met Rupert Croft-Cook, a well known crime writer. This was uncanny because I'd just read one of his books, 'Woolf from the Door.' I found this old man and his adventures with well known criminals very amusing. We sat up half the night talking and the following day Rupert announced he wanted to come back to London with me to write my life story. Stoned out of my head I agreed. Later that afternoon, after bidding my safecracker buddy goodbye and arranging to meet him in a months time, I boarded the ferry with Camilla and Rupert.

Arriving in England Camilla took a taxi home while I took Rupert to my flat where two senior members of the office staff were anxiously waiting for me. The news hit like a bombshell. Barclays Bank had announced the closing of our business accounts. This was a strange thing because they had always been in credit. Banks don't close down profitable accounts without good reason. Maybe they got wind of my criminal associations and were suspicious of a money laundering-operation. Ironically by then the business had generated a fortune in standing orders due to be processed over the following twelve months. This would have made me a legitimate millionaire. My 730 page drug-inspired Master Plan had become reality, but so was my acute addiction. My horrendous drug taking was now unstoppable.

Rupert stayed on for several days but with so much going on I had to cancel plans to tell him the story of my life. 'Come back when I've lived it,' I laughed as I drove him to Heathrow airport for his flight back to Dublin.

Chapter 17

THREE STONED ROBBERS

A month later I met O'Grady at the airport. He now looked very ill. I'd known this man for some years and even to my drugged eyes his mental and physical deterioration was obvious. He was shaking as he came through customs and headed straight for the bar where, several large scotches later, he steadied up. Driving into London he made me stop to buy two more bottles of whisky. The robbery we were about to carry out had been put together by a couple of very sick men but blinded by our addictions it was full steam ahead. After we looked at our premises I dropped him at his hotel so he could get some sleep.

For me there was no rest. My sick mind had gone from bad to worse. I intended to disguise myself as a down-and-out during the bank job and wheel away the loot in an old pram, reasoning the police would never associate a scruffy tramp with a robbery. This was no longer normal criminology, more like straight-jacket insanity. As usual I became totally obsessed with the idea and after putting on an old rag outfit, including a wig of matted hair, I walked around the Edgware Road near the bank to test the disguise. There I passed a neighbour and begged him for money - it worked, he didn't recognise me. Dressed in rags and chatting on the radio with my accomplices tunnelling below, I was ready for the funny farm, not a bank break-in. Like in a modern-day Laurel and Hardy film the third robber, making up our happy trio, chain smoked hash all day.

I wasn't doing the robbery for the money. For me it was a demented mockery of life itself, an extension of my childhood rebellion. Now totally engrossed with my tramp role I decided to sleep rough with the winos behind Paddington Station a day before the break-in. My plan was to establish a safe place to run to should things go wrong. Unchallenged I settled in with the local tramp community to experience something stronger than anything ever before. Granted, they mainly welcomed my new and plentiful supply of booze but for the first time in my life I was truly wanted. After a lifetime of loneliness I had found peace with societies drop-outs. Here I didn't feel a misfit with the wrong religion or school tie, anybody could join this mob. They had no worries, no responsibilities, nobody to upset them, nobody to love or hate them and apart from accidentally spilling the booze for them nothing could go wrong. For the first time I tasted 'fire water', methylated spirits. That night with the winos behind Paddington Station perhaps I was pre-booking my ticket into this emotionally safe world of oblivion.

The next day with all the necessary equipment now in our basement the lengthy process of tunnelling into the bank vaults began. During the noisy parts of the operation I sat outside the bank disguised as the tramp. When the police passed by I called on the radio down to my colleagues below to stop drilling. At first things seemed okay but the tunnel took far longer than we had estimated with O'Grady drinking more and more. His messages kept coming across the short wave, 'More liquid refreshment urgently required.' It was a strange sight as I, dressed in rags, bought two bottles of Scotch, paying from a wad of bank notes each time. Walking up and down with my pram I left the whisky in a brown paper bag by the basement door. This continued until late Sunday afternoon when, exasperated by it all, I decided to park the pram and check what was happening below. Here I found my worst premonitions had come true. The Irish safe-cracker was drunk as a skunk and part of the tunnel had collapsed. 'What an unholy, fucking mess,' I screamed. 'Relax,' said the third member of our team, 'You're taking too many of your pills again ! We've got till Tuesday before the banks re-open. Have a joint.'

So here we were, 'Drugs, Drink and Pot United', a pathetic trio of villains all nearing the end of their careers as they slipped deeper into their addictions. Even while robbing a bank we couldn't stop drinking, smoking dope or popping pills by the handful. Now we were settling down for our opium tea break.

The joint combined with all the amphetamine and acid hit me like a drug earthquake, making me so stoned I was unable to get off the floor. The walls began to move and my co-conspirators were now in chains. I was hallucinating but to me it all seemed to be actually happening. Laying on the ground I could hear barking coming from inside the half-finished tunnel and as the noise got louder dozens of huge dogs wearing policeman's hats leapt out. Unable to move I watched an even bigger dog follow them, wearing a judge's wig. He barked, 'Prison for you, boy ! We found this handbag under your bed !' Suddenly, thousands of birds flew out of the tunnel carrying handbags in their beaks. Trying to escape my horror trip I rolled into the tunnel and in the midst of my opium haze saw giant worms in policemen's uniforms coming towards me. My drug trip continued as I staggered out to the street to find everything had changed out there as well !

The cars, which had turned into giant prams with policemen sitting up in them were chasing me. I was cracking up. Running away still pushing my own precious pram I could hear screaming coming out of it. The walkie-talkie was still on. 'Come back with some booze, you little cunt,' O'Grady's distant voice blared out. I tried to switch it off but was too stoned to do it. In desperation I ran into a garage where I bought a can of petrol from the startled attendant. As if glued to the pram I carried on running through the busy London streets, finishing up at Chelsea Bridge. Here I soaked the pram in petrol and set fire to it. As I pushed the blazing pram into the river I could still hear, 'Come back you cunt ! Glug, Glug.....' as it sunk below.

My hallucinations continued for several hours before I passed out on the floor at Victoria Station. I never saw O'Grady again but many years later met the opium smoker in Winston Green Prison, Birmingham. A trifle more sober we walked round the exercise yard and laughed about that hazy weekend. 'Too many drugs, that was our problem,' he said. Was ? I thought. Still is, more like it.

Chapter 18

PARANOIA.

I woke up in a terrible state to find myself still dressed in rags lying on the platform at Victoria Station. It took quite a few uppers before I could gather my senses enough to return to my flat.

Over the next few weeks I became increasingly confused. The continued abuse of amphetamine was doing its damage, making me psychotic as I began to believe the world was out to get me. The acute feelings of persecution got worse and worse until I imagined everybody wanted to mislead me, even over what day of the week it was. One morning, waiting outside the bank at 9.30 am, I screamed at a passer-by, 'Why the fuck aren't they open?' 'It's Sunday mate,' he replied. I didn't believe him and very angry bought several newspapers to check. They were Sunday papers alright but still unconvinced, suspecting the newspaper vendor was in on the plot, I began to ask strangers in the street. Hearing them all say Sunday I got even more tormented by confusion. Still believing it was one giant conspiracy I headed home.

Convinced either the police would arrest me or villains would shoot me I continued with my plan to vanish off the face of the earth. I was behaving like Nazi criminals at the end of the war. First I parked ten second-hand cars in various locations all over London with spare clothes, drugs and cash hidden inside. A small red book contained coded information on the whereabouts of these vehicles. With my first line of escape in place I decided to hide the bulk of my money in as many places as possible, reasoning this way they would never find it all. In this psychotic mood I ordered one hundred fireproof boxes which practically filled two rooms of my Seymour Street flat. For several days I collected cash from all my old hiding places, taking a fortune back to my Marble Arch 'Berlin Bunker'.

In a state of panic in ten pound notes I put one thousand pounds in each of the hundred boxes plus the necessary medical supplies for war time survival. Along with the bank notes each box contained fifty Dexedrine tablets, fifty Valium, fifty Mandrax and five ready rolled joints. Locking and numbering each box I finished up with an enormous bunch of keys. While the war raged on outside my locked doors and blackened windows this mammoth task took over a week to complete. Working away night and day the only thing missing was the screaming of air-raid sirens.

Like a deranged lunatic I now began to hide the boxes in properties all over London. This took many more weeks during which my sanity began to disintegrate. To hide the money boxes I rented properties, stayed with friends or anybody who would have me just as long as I could gain access to an attic or unused basement. In my drugged head I figured when the war was over I would get the money back somehow. As I write today there must be many properties in London with hidden cash and drugs still in their lofts.

Dying my hair different colours I opened dozens of new bank accounts under false names to hide more cash. I was close to permanent insanity and compared to me Hitler in his bunker must have felt quite safe. When the task was finally completed I locked myself into the flat, waiting for the end to come.

For several days I sat alone in the darkness of my third floor 'Berlin Bunker' but nothing happened. Then I received a call. It was Little Legs threatening to kill my wife, children, Clara and Alen unless I gave him more money. Frightened for their safety I put half of Jamaica on twenty-four-hour watch outside Clara's home in Hamilton Terrace, Alen's flat at Gloucester Road and Camilla's place in Blackheath. Throughout the night drugged up to the eyeballs I drove past their houses to check on the cars full of black minders. Desperately confused I took even more drugs, if that was possible.

The following morning, afraid for the safety of my children, I decided to move them quickly and secretly out of London. Two weeks later I bought a large six bedroom house in Bray near Maidenhead where the entire family unaware of the dangers moved to.

Chapter 19

SLEEPING NAKED WITH THE WINOS

Leaving hardly any clothes in the flat I moved back with Camilla. Living together in the new house turned out to be the saddest four months of my entire life. My childhood sweetheart had grown into a cold, calculating woman. Her hysterical screaming had been replaced by a false smile and now our marriage was just an arrangement. I was mad to have returned to something that never was but like a true addict was back for more punishment, like a lemon being squeezed dry.

The new house was situated in a fashionable part of Berkshire, about fifty miles outside London. Our daughters along with Camilla's sisters now beautiful teenage girls all lived with us. Thoughout the years of drug abuse and lack of contact they'd become distant from me. We hardly ever talked and the only real conversation with Camilla was about money to decorate and furnish the new house. 'Good morning, how are you?' was replaced by, 'We need five hundred pounds more for carpets.' I often felt that it would be easier if we'd had a filing tray in the hall to leave memos, saving them all the aggravation of even looking at me. The winos behind Paddington Station had spoken more to me than all this family put together.

Clara, somebody who did care, someone I could have made a go of life with, was fifty miles down the road but I was unable to break my life-long Camilla addiction. Like all addicts I wanted to cheat on life and expected Clara to wait on the back-burner. All I had to do was to accept the Camilla dream was over and start again. But I couldn't.

Making everything even worse was that my business and gangster problems were getting bigger by the day back in London. During a drugged temper I'd sacked the remaining office staff and changed all the locks to stop anyone from entering the premises. In the middle of all this emotional turmoil I expected Little Legs to pop up at every street corner. He still hadn't found out where I'd moved to but was looking for me everywhere. Desperate and prepared to pay anything to get this madman off my back I went to see the Nesh Brothers who, like the Krays, were first division mobsters and feared all over London. A meeting was set up at my Seymour Street flat and two of the Neshes came to see me.

When I was in London I always saw Clara and she was in the kitchen the day they arrived. We sat down and I listened as the Nesh brothers explained that Clifford was no mug and it would therefore cost me plenty to warn him off. Why doesn't Prime Minister Ted Heath use this lot against Scargil and the miners', I thought to myself. The Neshes would soon solve the coal dispute ! While I continued negotiations with London's worst gangsters Clara came in with tea and cucumber sandwiches. Suddenly the lights went out as the miners' strike caused yet another blackout. Thanks to Clara our conference continued by candlelight. 'Looks cosy,' she said leaving the room.

When the two brothers left the thought of being beholden to the Neshes suddenly seemed far worse than Clifford had ever been. I was now the lead player in a never ending horror movie, swapping gangsters as others do used cars. With the deal completed I had part-exchanged one lunatic killer for an even worse mob. For Clara, however, London's top gangsters asking her, 'Any more sandwiches, sweetheart?' was all jolly hockey sticks. That evening I found her writing something in her diary. 'All action day. John called to bash Brian who has been naughty.'

Brian Clifford was verbally warned and fearing the power of the Neshes agreed to leave me alone and call everything even. This was good news but soon a fresh load of problems replaced Little Legs. The only cash I hadn't buried was a large quantity of Irish bank notes which I offered to the Neshes a day later to settle their first invoice. A row erupted over whether or not they were legal tender and after a lot of shouting I agreed to change the notes myself the following day.

This was the straw that broke the camel's back. After the Neshes left I cracked up. I'd had enough. I wanted out. All people ever wanted off me was money. Wives, parents, gangsters, that's all they were after. The only person who didn't want my money was Clara but that night she told me she was leaving soon to live in Australia. Her parents, concerned for their daughter's safety, had decided to send her as far away from me as possible. If she'd been my daughter I would have done the same, but for me at the time it was heartbreaking, another nail in my coffin.

The very next day I was to leave the flat, never to return again. The Seymour Street days were over. Walking towards Oxford Street I came across a tramp lying in a shop doorway. Mesmerised I stood there watching as he drunk his fire-water, oblivious to the world and oblivious to me.

Couldn't I become a tramp like him? Then nobody would ever bother me again. I thought smiling to myself.

Over in Paddington Martin, the gay antique dealer, was just closing as I arrived late that afternoon in Church Street. Giving him the 'I know you fancy me' smile I persuaded him to let me store some papers in his unused basement. Handing me the cellar key he left in a taxi, saying with a camp laugh, 'You owe me one, darling.'

I was about to close down my life. The tramp had given me the clue of how to get peace. My first job was to vanish the business. Looking round the ten offices I realised it would take forever on my own so I telephoned a staff agency who sent down four strong men. With me supervising they emptied the entire four story office building of every file, ledger and cheque book. Every last document went into a tunnel leading off Martin's main basement. My dream venture, the results of the Master Plan, were now being buried under the street - but I wasn't sad, I was free. When the last of about thirty suitcases was in place I bricked up the small hole that led to this tunnel, leaving a few boxes in the main basement. This way Martin would think that these cases were everything and remain unaware of the rest. The men now removed the facia from the front of the office building and after being paid they left. Fifteen minutes later a small second-hand furniture dealer arrived to clear every stick of furniture from the building leaving only green carpet. Mission completed I went to the pub opposite to celebrate my vanished empire. It had disappeared in under three hours.

With no business to milk the gangsters would leave me alone I laughed, boarding the train from Paddington to Maidenhead. Caught drunk-driving I could no longer use the car. Sitting on the train I pondered my last problem, Camilla and her never ending demands. Two hours later, arriving at the house, it all solved itself. Camilla had packed a case for me. With the lemon now not only looking dry but well past its sell-by date she wanted rid of me before the mould set in. There were no arguments or screaming fits that night, it had all been said so many times before. I merely picked up my suitcase to walk out the front door for what turned out to be the very last time.

All five children were in the front garden to say goodbye. It was very emotional. My own two daughters didn't fully realise what was happening but Camilla's sisters looked sad. I kissed them one by one and then, with mixed emotions of heartbreak and relief, walked away with my head held high. Don't look back, I said to myself as my eyes filled with tears, don't let them see you cry. At our street corner I put down my case and looked round one last time to see them still standing there in the distance. For a moment it all felt like Malta when I told three young girls that their mother was having eggs for breakfast with God in heaven.

With my family gone I was ready for solitary confinement on drug island.

Mixing acid and speed in my ever more desperate quest for happiness only God knows what combination I took that night at Maidenhead railway station. On the journey back to London I got into a terrible state, crying and as the train chugged through the Berkshire countryside I thought back over all those drug infested years. The first drug with Gay Dr. Newam, Gentleman

George, Alen, boatloads of drugs, suitcases of money. It was all spinning round in my mind. I was having a major breakdown. All my screws had finally come lose. Now I was really one card short of a full deck.

I became hysterical and opening the train window emptied the suitcase out of the moving train then, taking the money out of my pockets, I began to undress. Sobbing, 'You bastards won't get that now !' I threw my clothes out of the window one by one. By the time we arrived at Paddington Station I was totally naked and ran from the empty carriage past the shocked railway staff who were unable to get anywhere near me. Before anyone realised what was happening I'd vanished behind the station to where the winos sat. Even my drunken tramps were rather surprised at my naked arrival. With the money I was clutching I bought one wino's overcoat while his friend took the rest to buy booze. Suddenly I realised I had no more tablets, they'd gone out of the train window with my clothes but drinking myself into oblivion that night I soon felt safe again.

I was truly home at last as we fell asleep on top of each other without a care in the world.

Waking up the next morning I felt very confused and disorientated. Why was I wearing just a smelly overcoat? 'Oh fuck what happened last night?' I cried out, waking one or two of my snoring friends.

Desperate for my morning amphetamine fix I lay there in a state of panic. Suddenly I remembered drugs were still hidden in the basement of the empty office building in Church Street, only two miles away. There was only one small problem - the keys had also gone out of the train window. Unperturbed I decided to break in, after all it was my building. It was about four in the morning as I set off through the empty streets. Two policemen outside Paddington Police station hardly looked up at the bare-footed tramp shuffling by. Arriving at the empty office building I found it quite easy to break in from the rear and hidden in one of the back tunnels off the basement I found some cash along with pills of every description.

Trying to escape this nightmare I took a large dose of sedatives and quickly passed out on the floor.

A new era of my turmoiled life was about to begin.

Chapter 20

JUNK SHOP LANNA

I woke up in the empty four storey building feeling terrified. What had happened to me? Where were my clothes? Confused, seeing money and tablets of every description scattered all over the floor I swallowed several yellow pills, trying to stop shaking. Very frightened, laying there shivering inside that smelly overcoat, I could hear normal life going on outside. It was market day and looking through the grubby window I saw the stall-holders I knew so well - yet somehow they made me feel nervous. Crouching down on the floor so they couldn't see me I crawled down into the basement when suddenly I felt the buzz, the drugs were working. Getting higher by the second I became king again. But what was his majesty going to wear? I went from room to room looking for clothes but there was nothing, just green carpet. I sat down in dismay but soon, care of the drugs my bravado returned. I decided to simply walk out the front door and buy new clothes. What the fuck ! If anyone stopped me I would simply say, I lost my clothes last night. Big deal ! In this arrogant mood I went downstairs to discover the door was locked. I panicked ! Where were the keys ? How did I get in here? It took me quite some time before I remembered the small broken window at the back of the building through which I'd climbed in the day before. Climbing back out I cut my leg on the jagged glass and ran down the alley with blood dripping onto my naked feet. What difference ! With the drugs buzzing in my head and a pocket full of cash it was shopping time.

Twenty minutes later I was in Oxford Street outside Marks and Spencer's, a major British clothing store. There was a security guard just inside the door but fortunately I was still sane enough to realise that with my appearance he would evict me before I could buy anything. I had to be quick, grab and pay for at least a pair of trousers and a jumper then I'd be dressed enough to buy whatever else I needed.

Seeing my chance as he turned his back I darted in, grabbing, the first things I saw. As I waited to pay the security guard approached but he was too late. I'd got my trousers and was leaving the store. Outside in the busy street shoppers stopped dead in their tracks as in the middle of the pavement I discarded the smelly overcoat, proudly changing into a woman's pink jumper and a pair of trousers two sizes too small. Dressed like this I went into the nearest shoe shop and bought a pair of trainers from a somewhat frightened shop assistant. With shoes on my feet, feeling like an oil prince, I returned to Marks and Spencer's, smiling at the security guard who stared at me in disbelief. 'It's okay, I'm a film star,' I said on passing him. 'All this is being filmed for a TV documentary.' Inside, going into top drug gear, I bought two hundred pounds worth of clothes and then went for a shave at the Cumberland Hotel. Changed, shaved and looking a million dollars I returned to the store for my final revenge on the guard, giving him plenty of abuse. He merely replied, 'Fuck off , Mr. Junkie !' How did he know I was taking drugs? I never told him, I thought to myself leaving the store. Outside I hailed a black taxi and pulling away in the Saturday morning traffic I saw the discarded overcoat still laying in the gutter. I shuddered as once more nightmare visions of the future flashed into my mind.

Looking back again I was horrified to see myself lying inside the coat.

An hour or so later, with remarkably little damage, a locksmith broke into the building and fitted new locks. I really mustn't get upset and throw these away, I laughed to myself as he handed me the keys. Soon I was strutting up and down Church Street like a peacock in my new clothes, buying lots of imitation jewellery, old paintings and other cheap antiques which I spread all over the empty showroom. Within one hour I had created my own junk-shop. It wasn't the money I was after. I didn't need it. I wanted peace and something to do while I took my drugs. Here was my own thing that my wife and all the gangsters wouldn't even look at, let alone want off me.

Right ! Somewhere to live now I smiled, buying a second-hand bed in the shop opposite. With the help of a stall holder I carried it up to my old executive office on the top floor. This is my new home, I thought, shaking my head as I took more pills to block out my pain. In a few short hours I'd transformed myself from a tramp in a smelly overcoat to the proprietor of a junk-antique-shop with sleeping quarters above.

Drugs now enabled me to become totally engrossed in my new, carefree life, allowing me to blank out all the misery from those last few months. Instantly open for business I put a huge notice outside the shop which read, 'We buy anything up to one hundred thousand pounds. Cash waiting on premises. No questions asked.' Oh boy, did this start some fun and games ! Over the next few weeks every Tom, Dick and Harry came in with things to sell, most of which were stolen. Without me even trying the business was flourishing and more bloody money poured in. I couldn't get away from the stuff. Nobody bothered me now. One night, however, I did see familiar faces in a big car parked opposite but obviously those gangsters now believed I'd gone mad and never came again.

Meanwhile Clara, who often visited me, was sad seeing what I was doing to myself. It was tragic, we both felt so hopeless. Here were two people who loved each other, one was shortly leaving for an island on the other side of the world while the other had already left for another island years before. Drug island.

That April Clara drove me to the funeral of Alen's mother. Looking at her and Alen I recognised the love I'd chosen to throw away in exchange for instant karma drug karma. Seeing the old lady's coffin I reflected on her words at the time of the Kray mobsters blackmail, 'If someone loves you they're worth dying for.' Sadly for me not even worth stopping drugs for.

Put off by my erratic drugged mood swings Clara visited me less and less over the following months but it made no difference now. Everyday, everything, and everybody was meaningless. My life had become one cheap B movie.

With no particular place to go I was always in my shop till late, smoking joints, happily poncing about in drugged euphoria. One night I saw a very pretty girl bounce by. She was slim with long black curly hair and watching her go into the flat above Martin's shop I thought, I must find out more about that one. The next day I asked David, Martin's live-in lover boy, who she was. 'She's the tenant upstairs, American,' he told me. 'Nice bit of stuff,' I mused. Later that morning when I went to buy some cigarettes I couldn't believe my eyes. There were dozens of magazines with this girl on the front cover, posing semi-nude under an umbrella. Now even more eager to meet my pretty American neighbour I bought every copy of that magazine. Tearing off the front pages I plastered them across the window of the shop. As she passed late that evening she stopped in amazement and laughed. Coming out of my shop I joked, 'Didn't know we had such famous neighbours.' I introduced myself and we talked for a while in the street. Her name was Lanna and full of bravado I invited myself up to her flat for a drink. I tried to have sex with her but when she was down to her knickers she refused to go further, saying we should get to know each other first. Full sex had to wait till the following night.

While Lanna, who wanted to be a rock and roll singer, waited for global fame she supported herself with photo sessions or the buying and selling of cheap jewellery. My wheeler-dealer ways impressed this go-getting but naive young girl and we talked till the early hours with me going into my usual drug fantasy. I told her about my friendship with Elvis's manager, Colonel Tom Parker. 'Known him for years, I'll ring him tomorrow for you,' I said, still trying to get inside her knickers. I never did get through to Elvis or his manager but the following day I moved in with Lanna who joined me as a partner in the junk business. I'd never cared about what was coming in or out money-wise and now just left it all to Lanna. To me it was just a game to escape reality which hurt too much.

Deep down I was very sad but to some degree succeeded in blocking out my feelings simply by staying stoned all the time. Medically speaking, however, I began to notice a big change in the way I reacted to the drugs. For many years I stayed high for days on end but now, regardless of how many pills I took, the buzz only lasted a few hours. My metabolism had developed a tolerance towards the substances. I began to lose track of what I was doing from hour to hour and was in a much worse mental state than I appeared. Often I started doing something to forget what I was doing or found myself in a shop not knowing what I'd come to buy.

One day I rediscovered some stolen jewellery which I'd hidden a year or so before in the basement during one of my drug-highs to only forget it existed. Out of my crust I stuffed the gems in my pockets to only forget them again.

To attract the passing crowd Lanna had started putting costume jewellery on a table outside the shop which she sold for small change. That Saturday morning hundreds of people seemed to appear from nowhere. Like a football crowd going mad people punched each other, fighting to sift through the costume earrings and necklaces. In my stoned mind I'd mixed priceless pieces of stolen jewellery with the imitation rubbish. Total chaos ensued with everything selling rather faster than usual. It was entitled to - diamond rings at twenty pence were super value. Ironically this crazy interlude boosted our business beyond belief because word got around and our shop was always mobbed from then on.

Many people wondered whether my behaviour was one big act to camouflage something or merely a drugged game to amuse myself. Here was a disturbed man with access to huge amounts of money, seemingly hell-bent on giving or throwing it all away. How can anyone assess a man who behaved as I did? One minute he was sitting around drunk with the winos wearing a tattered overcoat, then, a few hours later was leaving a clothing store by taxi. Playing mad had started as a game to rid myself of the mobsters. Had the act gone terribly wrong? It had and it hadn't. I was taking so many drugs it's impossible even today to say where the act ended and insanity began.

Clara, leaving for Australia that weekend, had come to say goodbye. We knew it was all over and standing outside my shop eating icecreams were saying our final farewells when suddenly Camilla arrived unannounced. Ranting and raving she demanded more money for unfinished interior decorations at the house in Maidenhead. In the middle of the argument Clara, who'd looked on in disbelief, suddenly had one big cornet squashed into her face. What did I do? Tell Camilla to fuck off? No, I gave her money. This was madness but perhaps, like Alen, I was unable to wake up from my fantasy and paid, wanting to keep the elusive dream alive. It was time not to have my head certified, but chopped off altogether.

I was out of touch with reality as the drugs once more brought on paranoid fear. I believed the whole world was out to get me but who should I be most afraid of? Ronnie Kray, climbing over the prison wall to attack me? The police, the Neshes, Little Legs or perhaps my wife, returning in an armoured icecream van? It was a living nightmare from which I couldn't wake up.

One morning the years of drug taking simply caught up with me and I collapsed in the street, crying for hours. The shop and the entire building closed down and somehow the remaining antique-junk stock just vanished, like everything else in my life. On the final day I got drunk and left a big notice on the window which read, 'Goodbye forever. Gone to the moon with

Apollo 11.' It was the American's last day on the moon and my last day of sanity.

Both physically and mentally I broke down with one major screw lost for good and for several days hid inside a cupboard in Lanna's flat.

The end was getting closer day by day.

Chapter 21

GOD'S FACE INSIDE THE LIGHTNING

Now, as the years of drug abuse took their toll, the first major change in me took place. For the next month or so with Lanna mostly out, all I did was stay in bed, too scared to even answer the front door. Everything seemed to have vanished around me, houses, flats, cars, businesses. Somehow it had all just gone. Even my new clothes were missing. All I had left were bottles of drugs and they didn't work like they used to. I couldn't get high or happy anymore. I was unable to face people. Once when Martin called to see Lanna I was so frightened I hid under the bed.

One morning I answered the phone thinking it was Lanna to find myself talking with a thief I knew from the old days. A big robbery was due to take place the following day and some months before, high on drugs, I'd agreed to take part in it. 'Pick you up at eleven tonight, Stevie boy,' he said. Before I could reply the line went dead. Oh my God ! What was I going to do? I had to pull myself together and spent the rest of the day trying to climb out of my mental collapse.

Looking into the mirror I couldn't believe this snivelling wreck was actually me. The drugs had killed my mind, leaving just a wet brain. I had become a twenty-eight-year-old geriatric. That's the price I had to pay. All addicts pay it. The hammer has to fall eventually. Throughout that day I took more and more amphetamine pills, still expecting the confident drug-high to return. A kettle must boil when it's switched on I thought, but hours passed, nothing. I couldn't even get

208

out of bed. These drugs were not cheap black-market ones but Smith Kliene and French Dexedrine pills on private prescription. Something was radically wrong - not with the drugs but with my battered mind.

Just before eleven that evening I climbed up onto the roof of the building and watched in silence as the two thieves arrived. Lanna, under strict instructions, opened the door and told them I was out. 'We'll wait,' they said. 'He knows we're coming.' Hiding high above I watched the men pacing up and down in the yard. I was too frightened not only to do the robbery but even to go down and tell them. Very annoyed eventually they left.

As time passed I didn't get much better but started to watch TV with Lanna. She was pleased to see that America was pulling out of Vietnam and her cousin would be coming home. It wasn't all good news, however. Lyndon B. Johnson, the ex-president, had died.

Another week or so later Lanna persuaded me to get out of bed and with the help of even larger quantities of drugs I managed to go out. At first it was mostly at night when the streets were empty but one day I went to see Terry Marvin at his Highheat offices. Why I went there I don't know, perhaps I was hoping it would help me find myself again.

Tel greeted me with open arms which had always been his fashion, regardless of any rows we might have had. That morning he introduced me to Jack Contel, the future world champion boxer, who at that time was still under his control. Waiting for Terry I chatted with Jack about the recent Frazier and Foreman fight in Jamaica and like many he was surprised Frazier had lost. Walking round the offices I met many other well known underworld figures. The reception had become like a gangster's social club. Terry's Al Capone fantasy had caught up with him and without him realising it was him working for the gangsters now. Replacing normal staff on normal wages, mobsters of various standing were paid fortunes for doing nothing but hang about. Regardless of the cost Terry, with his gangster complex, had to have his daily injection of excitement to feel 'one of the boys'. In his private office he proudly showed me a painting sent by 'Ronnie Kray' from prison. Whether it was a genuine Kray water-colour was irrelevant as long as we all believed it was.

Sitting down Terry smiled and said, 'I've got a super job for you.' He went on to offer me two hundred pounds a week for doing next to nothing, or so I thought. What I didn't realise was that Terry had something up his sleeve.

At the time he was being investigated by the 'News of the World', a well known British tabloid. The story was very juicy, unmasking the man whose company acted as the front for many of the Kray Twin ventures and those of another prominent gangster family. The scandal was Terry's own private 'Watergate'. Nixon might have thought he had problems but in Golders Green, North London trouble was really brewing. It read like a criminal 'Who's Who.' Murder, fraud, vicious beatings, crooked mortgages, bent policemen and blackmail, it went on and on, like a criminal soap opera. I agreed to start, hoping that being around old familiar faces would make me feel better.

A day or so later someone spotted a car parked opposite with 'News of the World' photographers busy taking pictures of everyone coming in and out. With the release of the exposure expected that Sunday Terry called an emergency meeting with several dubious characters. None of those gangsters could afford this story to hit the front pages. Terry had many local police officers on the bung but this type of scandal would precipitate police action from much higher up. It didn't take long for Tel and his grizzly gang to come up with a cunning way to stop the story. Someone would approach the paper, offering to sell documents sneaked out of Terry's personal file and in getting the 'News of the World' to accept these stolen papers both parties would be committing a felony. The document thief would now confess all to the police who'd charge him with theft, automatically implicating the newspaper for receiving stolen goods. This would prevent the newspaper from publishing the story until after the theft and receiving charges were heard in court. To print before would have been a sub-judice act.

All Terry and Co. needed now was someone stupid enough to actually admit to theft and conspiracy charges, a complete zombie. To find such an idiot they didn't have to look further than the office toilet where I was taking my umpteenth pill of the day. Stoned out of my head, without even considering the consequences, I happily agreed to deceive the newspaper. With pills rattling in my pockets I crossed the Finchley Road and waved to the photographers who followed me round the corner. I showed them various documents to wet their appetite. They fell for the scam and took me to meet their editor at his offices. At the 'News of the World' building I produced several incriminating documents and a price was settled. The editor foolishly agreed to give me a sum of money on account and I was taken to the cashiers office where I was paid. With my copy of the signed receipt Terry and his gangster friend's now had all they needed to stop the story being printed. Outside the newspaper building a car with a rather large-looking gentleman was waiting and without speaking he drove me back to Terry's. In the office I waited with several more heavy characters while someone went opposite to Golders Green police, arranging for me to be arrested. Five minutes later I was taken over to the station where I signed a confession, implicating the 'News of the World'. The police kept me in custody overnight then released me on bail. The youngest brother of a well known criminal family collected me from the police cells and took me back to Lanna's. Dropping me off he said, 'Just you keep away from everything and everybody.' I didn't need telling twice. I was too ill and simply went back to bed where I stayed for several weeks.

My mother and brother Paul now became very concerned about my health, having received a letter from Australia in which Clara explained how ill I really was. On their invitation Lanna and I gave up the flat above Martin's to stay with my mother who'd sold our old family house and was now living in a small flat in Hendon Lane, Finchley.

By now I needed to be urgently hospitalised. A sanatorium would have been the only safe place for me. My mind was deteriorating. It wasn't just drugs now. I was mad. Suspicious of everybody I thought perhaps moving me to the flat was a plot. Maybe my mother and Lanna were in collaboration with the six-inch people coming through the letter box each morning. They were all trying to steal my little red book. It was in this special diary I'd meticulously listed all the places where I still remembered cash was hidden. Some of the properties had by now changed hands with the new owners unaware of the treasure above their heads. As my mistrust grew I even slept with the red book stuffed

212

down my underpants but one night, fed up with the book crushing my dick, I came up with a more comfortable idea. Devise a coded poem listing all the cash hiding places. It read like this:

> Up in the morning with the lark
>
> It's all hidden in the park.
>
> Let's all play and have some fun
>
> It's all hidden at Church 1
>
> Altogether pick up sticks
>
> It's all hidden at no. 76

And so the poem went on and on for two pages...........................

The park referred to Hyde Park Avenue at our family house, Church was Church Street at Martin's, no 76 referred to Norfolk Avenue, my grandparent's house and so it continued. Memorising the poem all day, every day my poor battered mind was trying to salvage something from those drug-infested years of lunacy. Weeks later, when I was able to write the poem down backwards, I ceremoniously burnt the book, putting the ashes in a small jam-jar on which the label read, 'Red Book Jam'. 'Operation Tramp' going according to new master plan, I smiled. Now nobody could ever get my cash boxes, only I knew the poem. Three times every day I wrote it out, each time burning what I'd written, putting the ashes in the jar. Finally, at the end of each poem session, I ticked the 'Poem Remembered' chart which I carried at all times.

Already quite insane I got worse by the day. Towards the end I started running down the busy Hendon Lane, shouting, 'It will take a ten ton truck to kill me now, you bastards !' Many vehicles swerved to avoid running me over, one of which was a police car. This led me to be seen by one of London's most prominent psychiatrists, Dr. John Randall. I had seen many shrinks before, acting mad to get drugs, but now it was for real. I was mad.

Through Dr. Randall I got proper medical help for the first time in my life. He was a credit to his profession, a genuine man for whom the welfare of his patients was more important than his wallet. 'You must be admitted today,' he told me, 'I'm sending you immediately to Temple Hill House, a psychiatric Hospital in Hampstead.' He continued, 'I can't let you leave this surgery, you're a danger to yourself and others.' An hour later I arrived at Temple Hill, a large detached mansion on Hampstead Heath which had been converted into a hospital of about thirty rooms. As the ambulance pulled through the big gates I saw Jack Contel run by, training on the heath opposite. He was preparing for his world title challenge shortly to take place at Wembley. I waved but he didn't see me.

The hospital reception was full of strange-looking customers, men dressed up as women. Apart from his usual in-patients Doctor Randall held clinics there twice a week for disturbed transvestites. Waiting to be admitted I wrote out my poem and after burning it repeated out loud, 'Up in the morning with the lark........' when a beautiful blonde came over and said, 'And you'll get eaten by a shark !' He-she smiled, 'That's a better poem, duckie.' I started to cry. Another transvestite put his-her arm round me, saying, 'Take no notice of Jean, she's a bitch.' A nurse came in and took

214

me to a ward upstairs where I was given a strong sedative.

The following day I was interviewed by a woman doctor for the entire morning but without admitting to my horrendous drug habit it was impossible for her to diagnose me. After several hours of talk she wrote on my hospital card, 'Acute schizophrenia, predisposed to paranoid fears.' This was the closest anybody could get to the real problem, amphetamine addiction.

Initially I was put under deep sleep treatment and kept unconscious twenty hours a day for several weeks. I was woken only to eat and go to the toilet. Each waking period lasted thirty minutes, then it was back to sleep with another injection. Every time I woke I repeated my poem, drifting off still mumbling it. There was no more writing it down, my pad and ashes jam-jar were in a locker somewhere. Weeks later when the treatment ended I was allowed to mix with other patients and given back my possessions. Once again I could burn my poems.

In occupational therapy we often painted and I always drew poem scenes, larks, churches etc. I laughed when I saw them on the wall, thinking, nobody on this whole planet knows the secrets those pictures contain. One nurse always joked, 'You'll be the new Picasso.' The old artist had died a month or so earlier.

Taking only the hospital medication I seemed to settle but as the weeks went by I got bored and decided it was time for additional treatment. I telephoned Lanna to bring me a pre-packed suitcase of clothes. The bag had a false bottom in which I'd hidden a secret supply of drugs for emergencies. On the morning Lanna delivered the bag I couldn't end the visit quick enough and as she waved goodbye I rushed into the toilet to

215

take about thirty Dexedrine tablets. This was more than I had ever swallowed in one go before and following the restful period in hospital my brainbox was ready for one almighty buzz. Sitting amongst the other half-dead patients I began to feel wonderful, cured, my head was exploding. I ran all over the hospital laughing, telling the nurses I was leaving. I looked for my coat and in another second I would have been gone when suddenly a big male nurse grabbed me. 'There you are !' he shouted. In what seemed like a flash he pulled me into a side ward and with the help of another strapped me to a bed. I struggled but couldn't move as he gave me an injection. It should have put me out but with the Dexedrine now working full-blast I was wide awake. Instinctively I closed my eyes, pretending to be unconscious to avoid further injections. I felt pads being attached to my head. I imagined I was about to have a brain scan but thinking they can't read my poem through a machine felt quite relaxed. Suddenly flashes of lightening lit up my head as my body leapt into the air.

God's face was staring at me.

A few seconds silence. Then the earthquake erupted again, lighting up the cells of my brain like exploding fireworks.

This time God was laughing at me.

I groaned in pain as it all repeated itself several times. Then nothing. Silence.

My head was throbbing. I opened my eyes but the wires were gone. I was alone. Nearby I could hear people groaning. Were we all dead? Was I in a real life 'Exorcist' movie? Where was the priest? Had he cut the devil out me? Suddenly a nurse appeared, not with a cross of Jesus but a clipboard. He led me into a strange room where I sat with a crowd of disturbed-looking individuals, staring into space as they drunk their tea. Minutes later I realised I couldn't remember how we had got into that room or where the bloody tea had come from.

I had been given electric shock therapy which takes away your memory for a while, in some cases for ever. The degree of memory loss varies from one patient to the next but in my case it was complete. The previous ten years of my life were totally wiped out. I was no longer aware I was in a hospital. An hour later a nurse took me back to the day room. I just sat there in a cloud of contented mystery, wondering where the fuck I was. While the Dexedrine spun round in my empty brain a nurse came by and gave me a peanut butter sandwich.

I felt something in my pocket and pulled out a chart which read, Poem written, ashes in jar. There were ticks under each column and the last entry was Thursday morning. A nurse passed and I asked her what day it was. 'Thursday afternoon,' she replied. 'Where am I ?' 'You're in hospital. You've just had electric shock treatment, it makes you forget things for a while,' she explained. Looking at my chart she smiled, asking what the poem referred to. 'I don't know any stupid poems !' I shouted, throwing the chart into the waste bin. 'Come with me,' she said, leading me into the occupational therapy room. She pointed to a jam-jar full of ashes on the shelf. 'Is this yours?' 'Don't be so fucking stupid. What ever next?' I screamed. 'What is this, a nuthouse?' Getting exasperated I walked away and sat back down in the day room very confused. A whole section of my life was no longer there. All the faces and places that I'd seen were gone as if they never existed. In my case my memory took over twenty years to come back and even today who is to say what did not.

I was to have many more electric shock sessions but under sedation so I didn't see God's face again. Eventually I was discharged from Temple Hill House, not depressed anymore, not anything anymore. With an empty mind I couldn't even remember where I met Lanna.

We moved into a new flat Lanna had found in Alba Gardens, Golders Green. From there I quickly resumed my amphetamine addiction. Drugs were the one thing I hadn't forgotten. When Lanna began quizzing me about hidden cash I got amused, not having a clue of what she was talking about. I thought it was some type of a joke that I couldn't see the funny side of. A few weeks later, however, Lanna was delighted when we found a bank book with about a thousand pounds in it at my mother's flat. I was puzzled, having no recollection of ever opening the account, but the money came in handy. Predictably very soon the drugs stopped working again and I went back to bed where I stayed for the next month. Lanna became increasingly aggravated and eventually had me readmitted to Temple Hill for more memory erasure with my head becoming like the local power station.

For a considerable time I stayed at that house on Hampstead Hill, forgetting now that even Lanna was around. Apart from the patients and nurses nobody outside the hospital existed anymore. One day Lanna came to visit with a very nice young man. Smiling

Lanna explained she was now living with this chap who'd moved into our flat. Empty minds don't get upset and wishing them luck I thought, nice couple, why did they come to see me? Mystified I stood in the gravel drive waving goodbye and went inside to get my head plugged back in.

Some weeks later my mother came to collect the empty shell that was once her son. With a head like a burnt out light-bulb I followed mum to her car. Sit here, follow me, eat this - like a robot with all my fuses blown I just obeyed.

After several weeks at my mother's, doing and thinking nothing, I received a telephone call from Camilla. I knew who she was but couldn't properly recall when we'd last met or how things had been left between us. 'Super, I look forward to it,' I replied when she invited me down to stay that weekend. Boarding the train that Friday afternoon at Paddington Station I thought, why did she move out of London?

Camilla, looking more beautiful than ever, met me in her new car at the local station. It was weird. I couldn't remember ever buying that house, let alone living there. With the whole family round the table for Saturday lunch the weekend started carefree. Looking at Camilla's sisters I could picture myself bringing them back from Malta but after that? When I tried to think about the past I got violent headaches. My own daughters Tessa and Antonia were smiling at me. It felt so strange. Where had I been since I last sat here? After dinner the hospitality ended when Camilla took me for a drive, showing me a house she wanted me to buy her.

The electric shocks must have fused the stupidity valve inside my head. Quite quietly I replied, 'No, my days of giving you money are over. I'm afraid your mission of 'be nice to Stephen' has failed. I don't want to buy your love anymore. I'd rather go without.'

In silence I was driven directly to the local station not even going back to say goodbye to the kids. There were no rows, I just got out the car and walked away. On the train I read Princess Anne and Mark Philips were getting married. I hope they make a better go of it I smiled to myself, taking more of my not so happy pills.

About a week later I received notice of the divorce hearing to be heard at a County Court in Berkshire. On the actual day, however, very upset and stoned out of my head I travelled down to the court. When our case was called I jumped up and ran towards the judge, screaming, 'Stop, stop, the case !' I created such a fuss officials removed me from the court after which the hearing went ahead and we were officially divorced.

I was very upset but what was the difference? In all those years following that first kiss in the car it had been just my fantasy. A non-existent dream.

As I left the Court building Josephina, the eldest sister, told me that Camilla was pregnant, shortly getting re-married. The pain I felt that day as I watched Camilla drive off with her husband-to-be was intense.

That cut was the deepest.

Back at my mother's flat I sunk into an even lower state, getting the horrors again with the six inch people climbing through the letter box. To me it was very real as those little bastards ran all over the hall, laughing at me. Towards the end of this zombie-period something predictable happened - Lanna called. Having tired of the new man and still hopeful of unearthing hidden cash boxes she wanted me back.

True to form, following my usual self-destructive lifestyle, I said yes.

Chapter 22

TWO LOST CHILDREN BOARD A SINKING SHIP

Lanna, who was now living in a smart one-room service flat in Hendon, collected me at my mother's and once again we set up home. It was around this time I started to suffer from violent headaches and began adding large doses of painkillers to my already massive intake of amphetamine. Without even counting I just took a few of each every hour or so. The pain was unbearable but I got no real sympathy from Lanna who, determined not to leave me empty handed, was only waiting for the missing cash boxes to re-appear.

Meanwhile the divorce courts had granted me access rights to my daughters and they were due to stay with me for two weeks before that Christmas. Camilla, herself now remarried, had bought a big house in Wellington with her new husband Barry. For this guy, who was broke when they met, Camilla, an attractive woman with money, had been like a lottery win, taking him overnight from rented digs to a fashionable house. I'd only met him briefly at the courts but he was one pompous son-of-a-bitch who, having fallen on his feet, smiled arrogantly every time he saw me. Collecting my daughters from their new home I was stunned to find them living in an enormous white house with a garden extending down to the river. Seeing all this splendour made me feel very hurt.

Tessa and Antonia, however, were pleased to stay with me. They had great fun over those two weeks but for me it was somehow quite sad. Being with those two kids made me realise more than ever what I'd lost. Of course it was too late now but I wanted desperately to be a dad for them, at least during their stay. Like all children on access visits they enjoyed the undiluted overdose of attention from me the missing parent as I agreed to all their childish demands. It's easy to be the best dad in the world for two weeks at a time. Some nights, seeing them cuddled up in bed together, I cried, wanting so much to turn back the clock.

They were due to return to Camilla two days before Christmas but on the morning of their departure they refused to leave. Tessa, now eleven and still besotted with her dad, had manipulated little Antonia's mind. 'It's more fun to live with daddy,' she said over and over again, brainwashing her younger sister. I rang Camilla, who regarded this as a temporary Christmas problem, and agreed to let them stay on until New Year's Day. For me and my two little girls it was a wonderful few days as we fed the pigeons at Trafalgar Square and saw the lights in Oxford Street. Everything remained peaceful until Tessa phoned her mother at the end of that week, saying they were never coming back because they wanted to live with dad forever. Now the shit hit the fan. Camilla went totally berserk. The social services, however, refused to exercise emergency powers and until the matter went back to court bar kidnap the children there was nothing she could do. Wild with anger she informed the authorities of my addiction but they refused to intervene, leaving the children in the care of a sick man, incapable of looking after himself, let alone two kids. It was like giving a homicidal killer parole with a loaded machine gun ! An exaggeration? Not really when you consider I'd just left a lock-up psychiatric ward after receiving electric shock treatment and was still as addicted to drugs as ever.

Lanna's one room service flat was far to small to bring up two kids so we had to find a bigger place immediately. It was my mother who came up with the answer. The four room maisonette above my late father's shop had just become empty after the long term tenants had suddenly been given a council house. This Tottenham flat was very primitive and in need of repair but with only a nominal ground rent we could live there for next to nothing. In typical drugged quick-quick fashion we all moved in that very day. I bought some bright red carpet for two of the rooms and using all the old beds along with the other tatty furniture left behind my children now had their new home.

Tessa and Antonia started to go to rough neighbourhood schools pending the initial custody case. Amazingly, three weeks later a hopeless drug addict, taking swigs of brandy in the court toilets, was granted interim custody. The temporary order was pending the main high court hearing where full social reports would be heard.

The weeks that followed were a very emotional period for me as I desperately tried to care of my daughters, which was not easy. My latest drug cocktail of anti-depressant tablets, amphetamine, and booze made me increasingly disorientated and not exactly the best of dads. I just couldn't stop taking the drugs but inspite of my addiction I loved my little girls. Somehow I made sure they had clean clothes to wear for school each morning. At night I washed out their dirty underwear, often drying it in the heated oven since they'd brought so few things down with them. Every morning, although very unsteady on my feet, I walked them round the corner to their schools. From behind my drugged haze I somehow managed to keep our leaky boat afloat but at night, once the kids were asleep, I

224

drank myself into oblivion. I was very much on my own because Lanna, only hanging on for a pay day, showed no interest in the children whatsoever and was either out or asleep.

One morning the school rang, saying someone was trying to snatch Antonia from the playground. The day before Patricia Hearst, the US millionaire's daughter, had been kidnapped. With this spinning round in my mind I ran round in a frenzy to the school only to find a very beautiful, very pregnant Camilla screaming outside the locked playground gates. When she saw me she went mad, 'You bastard, I'll make sure you won't get away with this. You'll soon be locked up just like Ronnie Biggs. Sooner or later you all get caught.' She screamed and screamed. Biggs, one of the Great Train Robbers, had just been arrested in Brazil and was awaiting extradition. Camilla's husband Barry, meanwhile, just stood around stroking his overgrown moustache. He looked very bored, having already got all he wanted out of the new marriage in the shape of bricks and mortar. The police were called to the school but powerless to intervene in a civil dispute ordered Camilla to keep the peace and the matter was simply referred back to court. To ensure Antonia was not snatched again I took her away from school for the remainder of the week.

This lunatic situation continued until the half-term holiday when, under court instructions, Antonia and Tessa had to return for a two-week access visit to their mother's in Wellington. Camilla's pompous new husband with his usual stuck on smile came to pick the girls up. As he drove off Antonia was looking out of the back window and seeing her little round face I began to cry. I knew it was goodbye for good. I was never to see her again.

Predictably, during the access visit this confused six-year-old was brainwashed into believing I might try to kill her and now it was me she wouldn't return to. For Tessa, however, it was a different proposition. Nobody could convince her that I was dangerous and she refused to say she was afraid of the father she doted on. The bond we'd built during those years up in my library in that Totteridge house was too strong to break. Now she returned to a dad who was getting sicker by the day. Making matters worse was an even more desperate, treasure-hunting Lanna still living with her spaced-out father.

Tessa on her own was easier to look after and in many ways she began to look after me. Around this time I received ten thousand pounds, my share from the sale of the house in Maidenhead, but trusting nobody, not even the banks, I cashed the cheque to keep all the money stuffed in my pockets. As fate would have it when I left the bank I bumped into Sammy, a character from the old days. He was a typical second-rate wheeler dealer and during the mid-seventies when property was on the rise he bought and sold houses. Sammy showed me photographs of his latest acquisition, a mansion called Lynford Hall, which he'd recently let to film stars on location. Set in its own ten acres of Buckinghamshire countryside the huge building had its own trout lake and an indoor Olympic size swimming pool. As per usual, Sammy was in heavy debt and needed money quickly to keep the wolves from the door. Hearing about my windfall was his gift from heaven as, stoned out of my mind, I agreed a deal with him. Our arrangement was concluded in the street outside the bank. I would give him two thousand pounds in return for a lease, making me into a sitting tenant of sorts even if the banks repossessed. High as a kite I followed him to his friend's office in Green Street where the lease was typed up.

With the keys to a mansion I now imagined myself as a millionaire pop star, and needing to look the part I bought the appropriate clothes - a plain white suit along with matching white shoes and tie. Returning from the posh streets of Mayfair to working class Tottenham I looked a cross between a washing powder advert and a local Elvis gone horribly wrong. With me constantly falling over in the street the new white suit didn't stay white for very long.

Feeling worse by the day I was relieved to wave goodbye to Tessa as she left for her end-of-term access visit to Wellington a few days later.

Desperately trying to reduce my drug intake before the custody hearing I booked myself into Champney's, the exclusive health farm near Tring in Hertfordshire. In anticipation of the cold turkey withdrawal I opted for one last drug binge before checking in and finished up in an all-night joint with all the usual pill-heads. At 3am, having swallowed samples of every bloody substance on offer, I climbed on stage, grabbed the D.J.'s microphone and screamed, 'Drug intermission for a custody case ! It's rest time ! No more pills !' 'Fuck off and put the music back on !' someone shouted up from the crowded floor.

How I found the car let alone drove, the thirty odd miles out to Tring early that morning was a miracle ! As dawn broke, I skidded to a halt in front of the big wooden doors of Champney House. My noisy arrival woke many of the residents in this secluded building and several members of staff came rushing out to investigate. Quickly I was ushered into the medical office. Seeing the state I was in, the majority of the staff were against me staying. I was lucky because after many promises to be quiet they accepted two weeks advance payment and I was shown to a beautiful room looking out onto park like grounds. For the next hour or so I somehow managed to keep quiet as I waited for the millionaire Arabs and other wealthy residents to get up. Over the next couple of weeks I actually managed to reduce my drug intake considerably and felt quite peaceful until, predictably, towards the end of my stay Lanna arrived.

Not believing my memory loss was genuine she became increasingly annoyed at my refusal to tell her where the cash boxes were hidden. 'Only nutcases bury money. It'll go mouldy, the worms will eat it and then nobody can spend it !' she shouted. Watching her leave I wondered what the fuck she was on about.

A day or so later as I left Champney's, a wealthy supermarket owner who I'd become friendly with, invited me to his silver wedding celebration. The following weekend Lanna and I drove up to a village outside Manchester where our host had booked us into a local hotel to stay after the party. This would turn out to be Lanna's night of reckoning. It was an amazing evening and I was quite drunk when we finally got back to our hotel. Before going to bed I counted the money in my pockets. I was shocked when I discovered there was only about a thousand pounds left following the months of reckless spending. Lanna's face dropped as she watched. It now looked like she would get nothing for staying with me. That night there was something strange going on. She kept going downstairs to reception in the early hours to make phone calls but when I quizzed her she claimed she was ringing America.

The following morning we joined our hosts for lunch after which we left for London. As we drove down the motorway Lanna suddenly insisted we stayed the night at Lyndford Hall, claiming she'd left some clothes there. Reluctantly I agreed but only for one night because Tessa was returning to Tottenham from Wellington the following day.

It was around midnight when we arrived in the huge grounds and Lanna seemed very nervous, as if something was about to happen. Even in my drugged-up state I could sense things weren't quite right. From the master bedroom she kept looking out the window. 'Are we expecting guests?' I asked as she left the room to supposedly get something from the car. While she was gone I took my usual mega-dose of sleepers and was beginning to drift off as she returned. 'Oh no, you've taken your sleeping pills already. Don't go to sleep !' she shouted with panic in her voice. The drugs started to take effect and as I half opened my eyes I saw her leave the room again.

Minutes later I heard a car stopping outside in the gravel drive. There were voices and doors being slammed. 'He's here and we're definitely on our own,' I heard Lanna say. I tried to get up to look who it was but couldn't move. I was too drugged to get off the bed. Footsteps were coming up the main staircase. 'How long ago did he take his pills?' a man's voice was asking. 'Let's inject him anyway, then the bastard will talk !' another man was saying. The voices were getting closer and then three hazy faces were looking down on me !

Through the mist I suddenly recognised Brian Clifford's piercing eyes as I felt a sharp needle in my arm. Was this real? I thought, beginning to feel nice, floating, just like in Dr. Newam's surgery all those years ago. Then Little Legs started shouting, 'Where's the fucking money boxes, you cunt? We know you've buried them in the woods here somewhere !' What was happening? What bloody boxes? Why does everybody keep on about buried money? I mumbled something incoherent and closed my eyes. 'You fucking stupid bitch,' I heard him scream. 'This cunt's too drugged to know his own name. Put the dog to sleep. Kill the bastard.' The dog he meant was me but what could I do? Too stoned I just passed out into nothingness.

When I woke it was daylight and it all seemed like a bad dream but looking at my arm I could see bruising where I'd been injected. This was no imaginary trip, this was real life. Everything was quiet but I was too groggy to get off the bed and just lay there staring at the trees beyond the lake. Eventually I rolled off to crawl into the bathroom where I found my Dexedrine pills and swallowed the lot. As the pills took effect I looked out of the window but my car had gone, leaving only tyre marks in the gravel. Nervously I went downstairs, expecting the worst, but I was alone.

Down at the swimming pool all the poolside furniture had been thrown in the water. Was there a body floating amongst the cushions? 'Oh God no !' I cried and horrified, unable to look, ran to the kitchen to ring for a cab but the phone had been ripped off the wall. Thinking, these people will soon be back to kill me next, I ran out of the house, up the drive and through the big metal gates. I just kept on running until I reached the safety of the nearby village. Here I rang for a taxi which took me to a local railway station from where I caught a train to London.

Back in Tottenham I found Lanna's clothes but no Lanna. I bought myself a bottle of brandy and paying for it discovered there was only ten pounds left in my pocket. The rest had gone. Throughout that day, very confused and frightened of what was going on, I took more and more drugs.

At around 5 pm Tessa's stepfather was banging on the street door. Outside I found Tessa smiling from ear to ear. 'Hello Daddy. I'm home,' she said, putting her arms round me. I didn't speak with her stepfather as he carried in about five large boxes and left. Tessa was so excited, telling me all her news as she unpacked, unaware of the horror story unfolding around her. This innocent child had brought down everything she owned, every toy, book and item of clothing. Here she was, committed to make her new life with the dad she loved so much.

Late that night after Tessa was fast asleep a middle-aged woman called to collect Lanna's clothes but by then I was too drunk to ask who'd sent her. When I came to the next day I realised all Lanna's things had gone. It was as if she had never existed and I never saw or heard of her again.

Moneywise she left empty handed, never to find her elusive cash boxes. They stayed buried for many years to come.

Tessa and I were now quite alone.

The nightmare story so far had been merely the preview. Now the main feature was about to begin.

Chapter 23

THE MAIN HORROR SHOW BEGINS

As Tessa woke the following morning her first words to me were, 'Win the custody case for me, Dad. I want to grow up with you !' Here was my innocent daughter, too naive to realise just how addicted I was, as she clung on to her childhood image of dad. To her I'd always been the hero coming home with lots of toys when in reality I'd been off on yet another drug binge. Even now her fantasy continued, inspite of us living in four shabby rooms.

Throughout that first day Tessa excitedly put her things out round the flat. She was especially proud of the four butterfly pictures she'd drawn for me and stuck them to the wall in our living room. The woman living opposite had promised her a puppy and it was late that night when she eventually got to bed. 'We'll call it Snoopy,' she said, closing her eyes. I sat at the end of her bed watching her asleep and felt so hopeless. I was a lost cause, the drugs had captured me, I couldn't stop. Listening to the rats running under the floorboards I decided when she woke I would tell her she had to return to her mother. I had to get her off my fast sinking boat while there was still time.

Early next morning when she opened her eyes it was as if she already sensed what I was about to say. 'Tessa, I'm too ill to fight this custody case. You must go back to your mother.' There was a lump in my throat, the words hardly came out. She began to cry, 'Don't send me away, Daddy. Don't do it. You can win this case if you want to, if you really love me !' How was I to

232

tell my little girl that her father was a pathetic drug addict that couldn't live without his pills? Tired and confused I lay on the bed, wondering what to do next.

Tessa now got up and assumed the mother role, changing from a helpless child to a capable nurse. 'Daddy, have a rest. I'll make us both a hot breakfast,' she said, proudly breaking into her piggy bank before going to buy some eggs. Eating her breakfast my tears kept falling onto the plate. 'Why are you crying Daddy? Don't you like my food?' she asked. 'I love it,' I replied, forcing it down. A little while later as she left for school she waved goodbye, shouting, 'Win it for me Dad !' I got up to look from the window to see her walk off with the girl from across the road. It was then I decided that whatever it took, whatever the future held, I had to win that case ! To lose it would have been kicking her love in the teeth.

Pulling what was left of myself together I realised first I had to get hold of some cash. Suddenly I remembered Andy, a Greek silver dealer I'd been friendly with for many years. I'd seen him drive by our flat in his van a week or so before. He was a kind man, one of the last people with a little time for me. That afternoon I went to see him at his factory. Seeing the state I was in he took pity giving me twenty silver fruit bowls to sell, not really expecting to be paid for them. This was his way of saying goodbye. 'You're killing yourself with those drugs,' he said looking sad. 'Why don't you get help?' After loading the bowls into my car we shook hands and I went to pick my daughter up from school.

On my way back I got lost in a deserted factory estate and beginning to panic crashed into a rubbish skip. Nobody witnessed the accident. I remember the

233

bang but then nothing. Eventually I came to slumped across the steering wheel with my head bleeding. In great pain I managed to climb from the wreck to discover the front of the car was totally smashed in. Staggering around I found a call box and rang for a mini cab who took me back to the wreck where he loaded the silver bowls into his car. I'd been unconscious for some considerable time because it was pitch dark when we finally pulled up outside our flat. Tessa was standing in the open window and rushed down as she saw the driver help me out. While I sat on the stairs she helped unload the silver bowls into our passageway. I had no money to pay the fare but the driver accepted two silver bowls, giving Tessa some cash in exchange. Before leaving he helped me up the creaky stairs and offered to get help but I refused so he left me on my bed.

The following morning Tessa stayed home from school and phoned the social officer dealing with our case. Soon after the senior inspector Mr. Parry arrived and seeing me immediately called an ambulance. I must have passed out as they carried me downstairs and remembered nothing more until I came to again a day or so later in hospital.

Imagining Tessa was still alone in the flat I rang her from the bedside phone but got no answer. With nightmare visions in my mind I rang the social worker who told me my daughter was safe in an orphans' home and that I'd been in hospital for two days. I was shocked, realising that Tessa living in a children's home could seriously jeopardise the custody case.

Although still badly concussed I took my clothes from under the bed and slipped out of the hospital without the nurses noticing. I couldn't even walk straight and falling all over the street it took me ages to get back to the flat. Before going upstairs I got some more drugs which were hidden in an old car on the wasteland behind our building. In my sick, addicted mind I thought that with these pills everything would somehow turn out okay. It was scandalous when later that day an obviously sick and drugged man was allowed to collect an eleven-year-old child from an orphanage to take her home.

Back at our flat I realised I had to reduce the drug intake once again if there was to be any chance of winning custody. With nobody in the world to turn to I telephoned Champney's Health Farm. I had little money but figured since they knew me I could pay by cheque at the end of our stay and although it would bounce after we'd left I was beyond caring. The following morning I rang Tessa's school to say she was ill and we set off for Tring. Somehow we arrived there in one piece and were allowed to stay in a chalet at the side of the main house. With me falling all over the place and Tessa crying, 'My dad's ill,' them letting me stay there was nothing short of a miracle. Very relieved I got into bed, knowing Tessa was safe amongst the rich and famous. Over the first few days I slept all the time, getting the rest I so desperately needed. As time passed I felt stronger and joined the other guests to eat in the main house. Hilda Baker, the television actress, often had dinner at our table and we always talked for hours after our meal. Hilda was an outspoken Lancashire lass, older than me, and after hearing only a fraction of my sorrowful story she insisted I returned Tessa to her mother immediately. 'Get Tessa out of your miserable life before it's too late,' Hilda told me every evening as we said goodnight.

Meanwhile Tottenham social services had got to know of our whereabouts. They knew Tessa had taken time off school but with the actual custody hearing imminent they let the status quo continue, waiting for the high court to decide what was to happen. I think everyone at the local Child Welfare Office had a bellyful of it. I couldn't make up my mind how long to stay at Champneys but the owners, Mr. and Mrs. Wheeler, decided for me when they refused us further credit. That afternoon we left the celebrities and strawberries to return to the rats of Tottenham.

I now sold the remaining silver bowls which at least gave us enough cash to eat with. A day or so later the postman handed me a letter from the High Court in Chancery Lane, giving notice that the case for the custody of Tessa Maria was to be heard in a months time. After my three-week rest I was thinking clearer and realised I needed a winning long-term solution, something that would look stable in the eyes of the court. With that in mind I advertised for a housekeeper, offering free accommodation in exchange.

The next day two eighteen year old Irish girls, Mary and Grace who'd just arrived in England, came to see me. They were naive kids with no relatives in London and were easily taken in by all my drugged ramblings. In return for rent-free digs Grace, a plump dark haired girl, agreed to say she was our part-time house keeper. Mary, a good looking girl with short red hair would claim to have known me for some considerable time, saying we were engaged to be married. It was the perfect image for the courts, a cosy little household. To complete the picture of respectability it needed to look as though I had regular employment. To fix this I went to see an old acquaintance who gave me a reference, stating I'd

236

worked for him for the past year as office manager. It now looked very lovey-dovey, especially the bowls of fruit and fresh flowers on show every time the local social services visited us.

Even the rats seemed to behave.

A week or so before the actual hearing Tessa, myself and the Irish girls were interviewed by court officials. Sticking to our well rehearsed stories we looked a stable group. Mary and I even held hands. I could sense they were more than happy with our make-believe set-up and we'd won the case. What really clinched it was my sweet and self assured eleven-year-old who insisted on growing up with dad. In those days it was rare for any father to win a contested custody case, let alone a hopelessly addicted criminal.

Driving home from the courts we passed Lisson Grove and Martin's antique business. It felt strange to look at those familiar sights and I stopped for several moments. Unable to answer my own questions as to what I was looking for I got back in the car and drove home. The following morning after Tessa left for school the memories suddenly came flooding back. I could picture myself burying lots of suitcases in Martin's basement but my mind was very jumbled and I couldn't put together the details. Grace was out working so I took Mary to Church Street to investigate. On route with Abba singing 'Waterloo' I excitedly told her about the buried treasure. Arriving in Paddington I was surprised to find Martin no longer owned the premises and was now trading from a small shop down the road. The manager of the new business told us the basement rooms were empty and that he'd cleared out all the rubbish himself when he took over. I still insisted on just one look and somehow he reluctantly let us go down while he served a customer who'd entered his shop. My brickwork was untouched but with one big shove I pushed it through and within seconds Mary and I were carrying the first of about twenty suitcases into the yard above. Quickly I hailed two black cabs and we lifted the cases over the gates, loading both taxis to capacity. The manager stood there dumbfounded, seeing this strange couple who'd arrived just five minutes ago pull away in a convoy of taxis. It had all happened so quickly he never had the chance to react.

Back in Tottenham the cases were carried up to the lounge and with the last of Mary's savings we paid for the taxis. Grace came home shortly after and was shell-shocked when she saw the twenty odd suitcases. I tried in vain to undo the locks but getting more and more excited cut the cases open with a large carving knife.

I was too drugged to appreciate the implications of what I had unearthed. The memory loss following the electric shock treatment made it impossible for me to make sense of it all. I was like a child rediscovering long lost toys but the contents of all those cases triggered off a flood of recollections, sending me mad. It was now 1974 but seeing all the papers convinced me it was still 1970 and the people around me had come out of some Dr. Who time machine. I couldn't understand it all. Why was I living with the rats of Tottenham when I had dozens of bank accounts all over the world? There were keys to many cars and properties, lists of hidden money boxes, it was all too much for me to take in. Finding an envelope with a thousand pounds in cash blew my mind altogether and I screamed, 'We're

238

millionaires !' Both Irish girls rushed in and seeing all those bank notes were now also convinced I'd found my missing millions. In a frenzy all three of us ripped open the other cases to uncover surprise after surprise.

With some of my new-found cash I bought an electric typewriter and began to dictate totally useless letters over matters finished with five years ago. I wound up having a terrible argument with Grace over which date to put on my letters. She'd put 1974 but I was furious, insisting it was 1970. When she returned with a newspaper, showing me the date I got very upset. 'A fucking forgery !' I screamed, but getting more confused I put an end to letter-writing.

By the time Tessa returned from school that afternoon I was drunk, having consumed several bottles of champagne to celebrate the treasure. Mary and Grace were also a bit tipsy and a puzzled looking schoolgirl sat down on the couch, trying to make sense of the scene unfolding in her grubby Tottenham home. 'You've always wanted parrots !' I shouted rather drunkenly as I kissed Tessa on the forehead. I gave Grace a handful of notes and an hour later she returned in a taxi with Tessa, carrying two noisy birds. The parrots in their enormous cages were proudly positioned in the middle of the floor, surrounded by bank notes, car keys and God knows what else. We called one of the birds Charlie, after a robber friend of mine, and the other one Swievie, the Maltese word for luck.

The flat became like a scene from the mad hatter's tea party as we let both birds out of the cage to fly and flutter round the room. With the Rolling Stones 'It's only Rock and Roll but I Like it' blasting away in the background the only one not drunk was Tessa who, like a confused Alice, eventually fell asleep on the floor. A while later Mary and Grace passed out on the couch with their arms round each other, leaving only me wide awake. The inquisitive parrots went in and out of their cages, investigating their strange new surroundings as I spent the night swallowing pills and re-examining the papers.

By morning I'd decided to live in the 'Sammy' mansion at Lynford Hall, convinced that I'd be able to think clearer in better surroundings. Getting carried away I woke all three girls, screaming like a drugged pied piper, 'We're millionaires and we're going to live like royalty. Follow me !'

I borrowed the old fruit lorry from a market-stall holder down the road and two bleary eyed Irish girls helped one very happy schoolgirl load up. They put twenty suitcases, two parrots and a few blankets in the back of the open truck. The old battered lorry broke down several times on the way. We looked like local hillbillies, gypsies on the move. Quite late that night we finally rattled through the gates of Lynford Hall. The mansion lay in total darkness as we stood there on the steps under the full moon. Going inside I was shocked to find the electricity and phones, in fact everything, had been disconnected. Since I was last there the entire house had been stripped of carpets and light fittings. Everything had gone, even the sinks and toilets had been pulled up. I got very upset and began to scream, behaving like some kind of monster. With only floor-boards to sleep on the Irish girls insisted I took them and Tessa to a local hotel.

Leaving three tired girls sleeping in the village guest house I drove the fruit lorry back to the deserted mansion where I went even madder, running all over the empty house, screaming, 'I'll burn the missing millions then no cunt will ever get them !' In a state of near insanity that's exactly what I did creating a massive bonfire on the terrace at the back of the house. Setting fire to the contents of all twenty cases I destroyed the details of all hidden money. I will never know exactly how much I lost but it sure was one hell of a lot of dosh. I got drunk on the last bottle of bubbly and started to sing as I watched the flames leap into the sky. It was a windy night and only good fortune prevented the fire from spreading to the nearby woods or setting light to the house itself.

Someone must have alerted the police because in the middle of all this mayhem a local squad car arrived. The two country bobbie's eyes popped out when they saw the scene. They asked many questions and one of them kept repeating, 'What are you burning?' Charlie the parrot on the back of the fruit lorry started imitating him. 'Shut that fucking bird up and stop laughing,' the officer said, getting very irritated. As he spoke the parrot continued calling out, 'What you burning, what you burning?'

Eventually I calmed down enough to show them the keys to the property and my so-called tenancy agreement. I had committed no crime. Just having a bonfire was not breaking the law and by now the fire had burnt out anyhow. The policeman was fuming as he got back in the car, saying he would check with the local authorities on the ownership of the mansion. 'I'll definitely be seeing you later,' he said, wagging his finger at me. (see foot note 1)

After they left I drove off, leaving the ashes to burn out on their own. With the exhaust sounding like a tank I went back to the hotel to wake the poor girls. It was 4 am as we began our long drive back to the rats of Tottenham we'd left only fourteen hours earlier.

Back at the flat I collapsed on the floor and when I woke up later that evening I realised I'd spent, lost or possibly burnt all the cash. With my head spinning round I decided on more death-defying feats of madness. The custody case was being heard that Wednesday and I felt apprehensive. Inspite of everything we'd done, there was still a chance we might lose. In case this happened I wanted Tessa to leave me in style. Wanting to give her one last treat I took more drugs for the courage to steal more money.

Our flat was directly above my father's old tailor shop which was now leased to an upmarket Indian Jeweller. The premises had an alarm system but I knew that I could break in through the inside corridor wall without activating the bell. In the middle of the night, completely stoned out of my mind, I made a hole in the wall while the girls slept upstairs. Soon I found myself inside the shop and stole a large quantity of ornate jewellery, not even contemplating the problems when the shopkeeper reopened on Monday.

On Sunday morning two bemused Irish girls and Tessa accompanied me to Petticoat Lane street market where we sold the stolen jewellery for quite a lot of money. We bought a new outfit of clothes each and looking very smart, carrying a third parrot called Sparkles, went to the Great Eastern Hotel for an expensive champagne dinner. Toasting our hopeful victory at the custody hearing, even the waiter had a glass as he wished us luck. At home we continued to drink more and more while I waited for the police to call.

Mr. Patel opened his shop early the next morning. I could hear him call out, 'Oh my goodness gracious me. A hole in the wall !' Soon the police called at our flat to question us. In order to make it look as if someone had broken in from the outside I had already smashed in the street door. We claimed that returning late the previous evening we had been shocked to find the robbery committed but were all too drunk to ring the police. The officers didn't fully believe the story but went away for the time being. This was all I needed with the custody case being heard in two days.

That Wednesday in Chancery Lane High Court, inspite of serious accusations from my ex-wife regarding crime, drugs and a host of other things, I was given permanent custody of an eleven-year-old child. Even in court during the long case I constantly took more drugs. I was close to insanity and had no money that I knew of. Making matters even worse I had no future and a home infested with rats but I still won. This was disgusting. Something stinks when a system allows this to happen. After all, my child's life was at stake.

Following this epic case I collapsed and spent the next week or so in bed while Mary and Grace looked after Tessa.

Soon things went from bad to worse. The police were threatening to charge me and the Irish girls, possibly even my daughter, with the robbery. To protect the girls I had no choice but to confess to it, saying I did it while drunk. I was charged but soon released on bail. A few days later Mary and Grace were collected by their worried parents and taken back to Ireland. They left my life as quickly as they had entered it, two innocents unlucky enough to get trapped in the cobwebs of an addicts misery.

The senior social worker had always turned a blind eye to many things and knew I'd never been working in the first place. Ironically it was him that now helped me to claim social security. We got about twenty pounds a week and receiving our first weeks allowance Tessa took charge of the money. 'We'll ration it out, dad,' she said proudly. 'Half for food and the rest for your headache pills.' This is what my amphetamine drugs were in the innocent eyes of that sweet child ! We lived for several weeks like this with Tessa becoming a schoolgirl mum as the drugs inflicted worse damage by the day. Tessa, however, was happy because she had her dad at home and 'Snoopy', our new puppy sleeping at the bottom of her bed.

A storm had to break and break it did. One day as Tessa and I returned from school we found Sweivie the parrot head down in a goldfish bowl. Seconds later the door opened and Brian Clifford walked in. With him was a huge man, over six foot tall, accompanied by an older woman with short blonde hair and cold eyes. 'Nasty these accidents,' Clifford said, nodding towards the dead parrot.

Tessa started to cry, throwing her arms round me. The big man pointed a gun at me. This was bad news. Alone with my precious daughter I was again confronted by this dangerous psychopath. For Little Legs your wife, kids and parents were all fair game if he'd got out the wrong side of bed that morning. Trembling with fear I held Tessa close, expecting the very worst. Obviously Clifford still believed I'd cheated him but at that time it was all quite irrelevant because I remembered nothing. All Little Legs represented was a character from my past and apart from the recent horror night at Lynford Hall everything was vague. The men grabbed me and I had to watch as the blonde took Tessa from the flat. I was tied up but kept pleading with them to bring my daughter back. 'I'm a sick drug addict,' I cried. 'I've forgotten everything. I've had electric shock treatment.' While the other man searched the flat Clifford, came towards me with a carving knife, screaming, 'Perhaps a little facial surgery will jog your bad memory.' I felt the cold blade cut the side of my face and warm blood started to run down my neck. He pushed me up against the wall and with my hands tied behind my back I watched blood drip onto my tee-shirt. I closed my eyes, preparing to die, when the other man came back into the room. He was impatient and began to argue with Clifford, 'All this is still a waste of fucking time. Let's go.' he shouted.

'He's got the money, I know it,' Clifford insisted as he started kicking me. I collapsed. Laying there feeling his boot I wished I'd killed him years ago. But I couldn't kill him or anyone. I was never a mobster, just a pathetic drug addict whose Robin Hood fantasies had taken him into real life situations way out of his league. 'We'll take your kid if you don't talk !' he screamed. At this suggestion the bigger man exploded and began shouting, 'I don't want a fucking kidnapping charge. This cunt is too ill to talk. Lets fuck off.' Screaming, 'I'll be back one day !' Clifford spat in my face and followed the big man out of the flat. (see footnote 2)

Oh fuck, what's happening to me? Unable to release myself I lay trussed up on the floor. Where was my daughter? Horrific thoughts paralysed my mind. Clifford had thrown my tablets all over the room and with my hands locked behind me I began to roll over on my side, sucking up and chewing the tablets - an addict to the bitter end. The drugs had just began to work when the door opened and Tessa rushed in. She didn't cry and remained remarkably calm inspite of finding her father trussed up and covered in blood. As she untied my hands Snoopy the puppy started licking the blood off me. Tessa washed me and tearing a sheet into strips bandaged my face stopping the bleeding.

Soon my whole body started trembling as the worst ever drug-induced panic set in. Locking Snoopy into Tessa's bedroom I dragged my daughter out into the busy shopping street. The woman from across the road looked shocked to see us both running away in such a frenzy. We caught a train to London airport where Tessa slept all night with her head on my lap. Instead of feeling safe amongst the crowds the reverse happened. I started to believe everybody in the terminal building was spying on us and imagined each flight announcement was a coded message about our whereabouts. Sitting there spaced on amphetamine was sheer torment and around 7 am, no longer able to contain my panic, I woke Tessa to begin an eight hour escape from nobody. I dragged that poor child around London on and off buses, convinced we were being followed. We spent hours down in the subway system, riding two stops on a train then leaping off to travel back in the opposite direction. My sick head was re-enacting a film scene from 'The French Connection'. Throughout the day my panic increased as I kept refuelling it with pills. Eventually we left the subway at Hampstead Station. Outside I saw a helicopter hovering above and fully believed it was looking for us. Now the chase was on ! We ran as fast as we could up Hampstead Hill, pushing past the shocked shoppers. Near the pond by Jack Straws Castle I heard the motor of the helicopter getting louder and louder. Convinced they were going to shoot at any moment I dived for cover, pushing Tessa over onto the grassy bank opposite the pond. We rolled down and hid under some bushes. There I held my child close. She was crying. 'Daddy, what's wrong? Who's after us?' she stammered. Pointing at the helicopter I shouted, 'It's them !'

Suddenly Tessa resumed her adult role and crawled out from underneath the bush. 'It's going away Daddy !' she said with tears streaming down her grubby, tired face. Standing there in her torn school dress she sternly said, 'Daddy, I'm hungry. You must slow down. Take some of your blue night-time pills.' The look in her face shocked me back to reality. Oh God, what had I done to my child !

I'd taken my precious daughter to live in my own sick world of drug induced paranoia.

It was me who had kidnapped her - onto drug island.

Footnote:

1. - The officer did see me again when several

   years later he arrested me for armed

   robbery and kidnapping.

2. - Brian Clifford died with a bullet in his

   head on the 28.9.1985.

Chapter 24

FAREWELL TESSA

I chewed a handful of blue valium tablets as I hid
from the enemy under that bush on Hampstead Green.
Ten minutes later as the tranquillisers took effect the
monsters were gone and I'd calmed down enough to
take Tessa off the heath. She was hungry and tired as
we walked to the offices of a solicitor I knew in nearby
Golders Green. I'd known this man for many years and
he was shocked to see me with a bandaged face,
dragging my tearful little daughter behind. After
hearing just part of our incoherent story he interrupted
and instructed his secretary to take Tessa to a nearby
cafe to feed her. Then he sat me down for a lecture.
'Nobody is after you apart from crooks you owe money
to !' he shouted. 'It's the drugs sending you mad. You
have been on them for so many years they're affecting
your brain. You urgently need help. If you don't send
that child back to her mother's I'll report you to the
welfare authorities. I assure you they will believe me !'

The valium had calmed me down and slowly it
dawned on me I had to let my child go. Everything he
said was true. 'Stephen, you had it all once,' he calmly
continued. 'Can't you see what you've lost through
your addiction? You still have Tessa. Please send that
precious child back to normality while there's still time!'

Tears of shame streamed down my face as he
phoned Camilla, arranging for Tessa to be picked up
the following morning. Putting down the phone he
looked at me and said, 'Steve, it's not the police that
will lock you up, its those pills ! Carry on with that

cheating game and you soon will either be dead or living with the winos on skid row !' He shook his head. Tessa came back into the office and he sat her down saying, 'Tessa your Dad is very ill. He can't look after you anymore. Try to understand. We have phoned your mother. Your stepfather will pick you up tomorrow.' With those words he left us alone. Tessa threw her arms round me and cried, 'Oh Daddy, why? We've only just won the custody case !' I couldn't speak but just shook my head. Later Tessa and I were driven back to the flat in Tottenham. It was our final night together and probably the last time we would see each other for a long, long time. There was so much to say, we talked nearly all night. Somehow we both felt relieved now the inevitable had finally happened. Even Snoopy the dog seemed more at peace. Holding each other we just cried, neither of us could stop. By the early hours Tessa was tired and went to bed while I sat and continued talking with her. The puppy slept under the bed as I told her of my own lonely childhood, Violet and the Robin Hood stories. Tessa put her arms round me, allowing herself to become an eleven-year-old girl and in those final hours I became her dad. I spoke about Antonia who'd never had a father because my drug addiction was out of control by the time she was born. Taking a picture of Antonia from my pocket I said, 'Look at that sweet child. Why did I throw it all away?'

Tessa suddenly sat up in bed. 'Daddy, I have a deal for you,' she said. 'If I go back will you promise to stop taking your pills?' With tears streaming down my face I replied. 'Perhaps one day I will find real love. Perhaps I will meet my princess and perhaps then I will be able to stop. Perhaps.' Falling asleep Tessa said, 'I hope she comes soon Daddy.'

Sadly for me, she didn't.

Chapter 25

SLIPPING INTO DARKNESS

It was quite late when we woke hearing Tessa's stepfather banging on the door. As we waited in the lounge for my daughter to finish packing he turned towards me and condescendingly said, 'Sorry how things turned out for you in life !' I wanted to kill the bastard sneering at me as if saying - well, I've got your wife and kids now - you stay here and take your drugs !

Tessa first brought in her bags then reappeared with Snoopy on her arm. 'No Tessa, can't take the dog !' Terry said firmly. She pleaded with him but he kept repeating over and over, 'We've already got a dog.' It was a lost cause and with tears in her eyes she turned to me and said, 'You keep him, dad. He'll remind you of me.' Crying she put the puppy back in her room and closed the door so he wouldn't follow her into the busy street.

Several moments later Tessa came back down and hugged me, sobbing, 'Daddy, I wanted so much to stay with you !' I felt terrible but not wanting to give that mother-fucker any extra pleasure somehow held back my own tears. As Tessa and I held each other Barry, getting impatient, said, 'Come on now, Tessa. We've a long drive ahead of us.' He was one cold-hearted bastard, totally indifferent to father and daughter saying their last goodbyes. Without speaking we all went downstairs where he pushed her into his car saying, 'No dramas now. You two will see each other again one day.'

Watching the car pull away I could see Tessa crying and knew my sanity was going with her. Moments later as they turned the corner I broke down in the street and cried unashamedly. Back in the flat amongst that squalor I shook my head. What the fuck had happened to me? How had I wound up so alone and destitute? The answer was laying at my feet, an empty bottle of Dexedrine pills. Having sunk to that desolate level I was more powerless now over my addiction than ever before.

The four rooms with their creaky floors were full of memories from Tessa's past year there with pictures she'd drawn still pinned to the walls. The brave child who had breathed life into this flat was gone. Everything looked deserted and still crying I climbed up the broken stairs to her bedroom to let Snoopy out. The small brown mongrel waggled his tail as I walked in, making me feel a little better - I wasn't completely alone. In the corner was a bowl of milk left for him. On my daughter's bed I found a note saying, 'Surprises for you under the pillow.' I lifted it up to find twenty pounds in cash, twenty amphetamine pills and a letter which read, 'Daddy, here are my savings for you. I stole some of your medicine pills so you would have plenty on the day I left!'

Seeing the drugs my heart lit up with joy. It was like a lottery win and immediately my sadness vanished. Elated I took ten pills and sat on the bed, waiting for the high. As the drugs hit my brain I came alive with excitement, realising that her money could get even more pills from Dr. Lando. Quickly I changed into my blue doctor's suit. I called it that because I only ever wore it to get my prescriptions, worrying if I looked too scruffy the doctor wouldn't give me my pills. Rubbish ! If I'd gone in naked he wouldn't have

251

even noticed as he wrote out yet another prescription. Now down to ten stone the suit was so massive on me I needed string to keep up the trousers. Since the only money I got was Monday's social payment Tessa's cash windfall for extra drugs was heaven ! I was so happy. Leaving five tablets in the flat as a reserve I swallowed the remainder and rushed out of the door. One hundred yards down the road, like a true addict, I turned and ran back to down the reserve pills. Now even more stoned I continued my journey to the doctor, feeling on top of the world.

On the train the buzz from the last pills hit me and I began reading a discarded newspaper where holidays were advertised. A cruise ! I thought. That's what I need ! A world cruise to have a rest and engrossed in selecting the right boat trip I overshot my station and had to travel back.

Dr. Lando had his one room surgery in Harley Street where he shared the elegant waiting facilities with several other, normal doctors. Lando's patients, mostly there for drug prescriptions, stood out from the rest. If someone was nervously pacing up and down you could be sure he was one of Lando's mob waiting for fresh drug supplies. To the addict the doctor is God with the power to give or deny a few days bliss. It was first come, first served as Lando, a tall grey-haired man of about sixty hardly looked up as he saw up to fifteen patients an hour. His consultation consisted of, 'Well, what's the problem?' To which the patient replied, 'I need more Dexedrine and Mandrax'. Scribble, scribble, doctor hands prescription to patient who pays and leaves with doctor calling out, 'Send the next one up !' If nobody sneezed it took three-minutes, twenty-eight seconds before each and every one of us was sprinting round to 'John Bell Croydon' in Wigmore Street to cash our prescriptions. Here, waiting for drugs was the same crowd that had been in front of you in the surgery. This chemist always carried large enough quantities of all the goodies Lando and numerous other private doctors so freely dished out. Occasionally there was a query by the pharmacist which sent the waiting addict berserk, especially if he had to go back to the doctor for something extra to be written on the prescription. Those precious moments are a life-time to an addict. As soon as I was handed my tablets I always ripped open the packet and took my first pills while still standing in the chemists. This didn't surprise the staff, they were used to it.

For the next six months, once my prescription was cashed, I headed straight back to Tottenham, arriving there very stoned. Under the influence of drugs those rooms and their shabby contents took on a new meaning. I felt safe there, it was my escape from the world that had hurt me so much. Sitting amongst the squalor full of self-pity I would ask myself, why has everybody thrown me on the rubbish heap? Surely someone could come to see if I was still alive ! My mother, Isabella's girls, did none of them care? Was it only my money they had been after? Easing away the hurt and pain I retreated more and more into my own world of drugs. Each day, as the stimulants took effect I became engrossed once again in the ritual of rearranging the broken furniture. For hours I would be busy moving the old beds from one room to another. I was making a home that nobody would ever want to take off me.

While Tessa was living there I had, on occasions, still talked with local people in that busy street. Now as the drugs inflicted more damage, I became totally withdrawn. Apart from saying, 'I need more Dexedrine and Mandrax', to Dr. Lando once a week now I never spoke with anybody. It was now I started deteriorating mentally and physically quicker than at any other period in my life. Drugs prevented me from suffering the nervous breakdown I was going through because when you're permanently stoned you can't feel heartache, let alone cry over it. At night with powerful sedatives putting me into unconscious, dreamless sleep I never lay awake feeling sad. On such high quantities of uppers and downers your feelings are shut away inside your mind like in a pressure cooker waiting to explode into insanity.

Completely unable to control the amount of tablets I took I usually ran out of uppers by Thursday of each week when my perception of things instantly changed. The come-down hit me like a severe fever attack. With no amphetamine racing round in my brain the regular weekly horror movie began with everything starting to look as bad as it really was. To counter this sudden doom I kept myself unconscious with high doses of sleeping pills throughout Friday, Saturday and Sunday. Often, having slept for thirty hours, I knew if it was Monday because then the shops were open and the street was noisier. If it was quiet I had another day to sleep away before collecting the social money for more drugs. I now never opened the door to anyone and only went out in the middle of the night to get food from dustbins or steal the bread delivered outside local foodstores.

My mother had still one year's paid lease to run on those rooms and it was costing her nothing to leave her sick son there. It was a cheap way to ease her conscience and kept me out of the way. She never came round to see me. Everything around me crumbled with the electricity, gas, and phone being cut off. Only the

254

water was somehow left on. Snoopy the dog never once left those rooms and like me got crazier and thinner each day. We were living like inmates of Nazi Belsen but in peacetime London. As the weeks turned into months I slipped further down towards the gutter.

One day in a drug induced fit I stripped the flat of all the furniture and carpets and burnt everything in the back yard. This left me living like a wild animal on floor-boards with my half-starved dog and the rats running round us. Awake for days on drugs I began crawling from room to room, holding long conversations with imaginary people. I even offered them drugs but they always refused saying it was okay, however, if I took them. Crumbs from the little food I ate dropped all over the floor, leaving the dog and the rats to fight for the leftovers. As Snoopy got weaker the rats ate better. As time went on I stopped washing and having smashed up the toilet system I now weed and shit on the floor alongside my dog. The entire flat stunk. Losing consciousness one night I ate my own shit, becoming violently sick.

Confused and deranged I began to go out in the middle of the night to bring back more broken furniture from rubbish skips. There were chairs with three legs, broken televisions, tables that wouldn't stand up, all junk. Quickly all four rooms were filled to capacity with useless jumble which I believed were priceless antiques.

Arranging the chairs in circles I held imaginary show-downs with groups of non-existent people. 'You cow, you never loved me,' I screamed at the chair supposed to be my wife, 'you two just abandoned me,' at the mum and dad chairs. Sometimes, believing Tessa was still with me, I said good-night to a pile of rags in her bedroom. When my imaginary guests were staying the night I told them to keep quiet and not to disturb my sleeping daughter. Perhaps this pretence life acted as a safety valve which saved me from admitting what had actually happened. Facing reality I would have gone insane for ever or thrown myself under a bus.

Things got worse as the drugs now brought on acute symptoms of schizophrenia. I became convinced there would be a police raid on my flat and nailed up the street door to keep them out, leaving just a small rear window for me to climb in and out of. Thinking every passing car was checking if I was up there alone, I made models of what I thought looked like people, using old coats and rags drooped over broken chairs piled on top of each other. Crawling on my belly I moved my scarecrow images across the floor in front of the windows to resemble men walking round the flat. Out of view I whispered to my starving dog, 'This will stop the enemy.'

As the paranoia got worse I began shouting out of the windows, 'Come and get me, you bastards,' to passers-by. It wasn't just drug addiction, I was crossing over the border line to permanent insanity. Summer, winter, spring, it all blended into one, it didn't matter. Throughout the year or so I was up in that hellhole my only comfort was talking to Snoopy, my fellow prisoner. The starving dog only ate the food scraps I brought home. He never once went out. During my sleeping periods I always cuddled him under the rags.

That winter I came back from the doctor's one day to find Snoopy had died, having never seen the light of day. I was inconsolable. Getting hysterical and wanting to keep part of my dog I cut his eyes out and kept them in silver paper in my pockets for days. Wrapping Snoopy in a blanket with some bricks I walked to London Bridge and held a sea-burial for my only friend. I lit candles and threw him into the river as the shocked morning rush-hour crowd looked on. Watching my dog sink beneath the murky Thames waters I felt more alone than ever.

Back at the flat my drug routine continued but without Snoopy to react to me I became increasingly inward until in the middle of one drug trip I found the answer. Death, suicide. Why hadn't I thought of this before? This wasn't a cry for help. I was simply going to leave on death's secret journey and finally be able to say, 'Fuck you,' to the world that had hurt me so much.

For two weeks I saved all the sleeping pills from Lando until I had sufficient stock to ensure I reached my holiday home in the sky with no stomach-pump interruptions. During that fortnight everything seemed different, temporary, like I was already looking down on it all. I didn't feel depressed, quite the opposite. I was happy, thinking we are all only passing through anyhow. I was merely catching an early bus while the others struggled on.

The day before my flight to heaven I went to the casualty of a local hospital and faking chest pains was admitted for observation. Throughout that night I talked non-stop to the young night nurse, telling her my entire life story. She listened intently and I was only occasionally interrupted by a patient needing attention. All my pent-up emotions came out. How I was unloved as a child, how a gay psychiatrist had abused me, how I was frightened of the mobsters, the wife who didn't love me, the pathetic saga went on and on but there was never a hint of suicide. By morning, with my last rights duly heard. I discharged myself, declaring the chest pains had gone.

On my way back to the rooms I bought milk to take the sleeping pills with, proudly thinking - no water, I'm not dying like a bum. Laying down on my rags in Tessa's old room I took the first handful of sleeping pills. As they took effect I wondered whether I'd forgotten something, just like a traveller checks his passport on the way to the airport. I got up to look out of the window for the last time, thinking, I'm leaving all these traffic jams behind. A few minutes later I began to feel frightened. Don't be a fucking coward, be a man for once in your life ! I told myself as I swallowed the last bottle of pills. I waited but began to panic again. Should I break a window and scream for help? Was there any point? With so many pills inside me I was going to die anyhow. Very scared I could see God smiling at me as I closed my eyes to meet my death.

The next thing I knew was that I was looking down on my own body laying on the rags. I was dead? I was free, all my troubles lay behind me. For a while it was wonderful but suddenly I felt myself being pulled down towards the dead body below. I tried desperately to resist and just managed to prevent myself from re-entering the body. But the force kept getting stronger. Again and again I resisted but it eventually overcame me and I was forced back inside my body to meet all my hurt and pain once more.

Staggering out into the street I cried, still not sure whether I was dead or alive. Everything looked so detached, like I couldn't touch it. After an hour or so of wandering around I went into a baker's, begging for some bread. As the man gave me a loaf I knew I was alive. I had been cheated once again, but this time by God himself. Even he had double-crossed me like all the other bastards !

After my suicide bid I became even more morose and believing I was now living in hell started to talk to the rats. Soon on intimate terms I was calling them by their first names which was all okay until one day I became convinced that even the rats had betrayed me. They'd stolen my drugs. I went berserk, ripping up the floor-boards to look for the missing pills and finished up falling through the ceiling, getting stuck for the rest of the weekend. On the Monday Mr. Patel, the shopkeeper below, heard my screams and called the council. I was taken into St. Anne's Psychiatric Hospital and kept under sedation for a week. As soon as I came to I ran away but to my dismay discovered my slum-base had been completely boarded up. My last semblance of a home had gone forever.

Twenty years later I still wake in the night hearing Snoopy cry for me.

Chapter 26

CHRISTMAS DINNER WITH THE TRAMPS

I was now living on the streets and life became much more precarious because with no fixed address my social payments were stopped. This left me paying for drug prescriptions from petty theft. While on the drug high I would steal leather gloves, wallets and other small items from big stores which I sold to small second-hand shops. As a result of the stolen income my drug intake doubled. After the isolation of the rooms this was a different life but the despair was the same. Instead of rearranging broken furniture all day I now aimlessly roamed the streets. On the amphetamine come-down I still took knock-out sleeping pills but now did so wherever I happened to be, passing out in public toilets, park benches, or in shop doorways. It all made no difference. The heavy drug consumption blocked out the pain of accepting I was now a tramp.

Occasionally on a high I thought clearer and started stealing clothes, becoming the best dressed hobo London ever knew. In the big stores I picked up what I wanted but instead of going to the cash desk I simply ran out of the store and kept running until I was miles away. Even if the store detectives spotted me they couldn't catch me as I vanished into the distance at the speed of light. I also stole my food using the same routine. I was no longer a getaway driver, more a getaway runner. Amazingly I was only outrun and caught on three occasions by fit store detectives. One security officer, an Australian girl and marathon runner, chased me for nearly three miles before catching me. This might seem like I was having a bit of naughty fun but it was quite the opposite. It was a very lonely and painful existence, living like a wild animal in the concrete jungle of London.

Often I slept all day going round on the circle line of London's underground. Having passed out in the crowded morning rush hour train I woke up that evening with the same mob coming home from work. At other times I slept on the last train going to various towns outside London, like for example Liverpool. On arrival I simply told the station staff that I got on the wrong train drunk but had lost my money and needed to get back to London urgently. This story often enabled me to sleep on in the warmth of the waiting room before being put on the first morning train back. Sometimes I even got a hot breakfast, courtesy of British Rail. One night in Glasgow I was greeted with, 'What the fuck's going on? You were here last week !' and following this incident, unable to remember which rail routes I'd travelled, the sleep trains ended.

To get more drug money I began nicking pictures from the corridor walls of hotels and on such a stealing trip discovered the Grosvenor, a busy five star hotel next to Victoria Station. On the quiet third floor I came across the linen room. Inside were about thirty mattresses piled on top of each other and rearranging them I created my own private bed, hidden from view. It became quite easy to get in and out of my new home by using the back entrance of the hotel, avoiding the main porter's desk. Once inside the busy foyer I slipped up the elegant stairway to vanish along the corridor into the linen room where I slept for days. It was a perfect tramp's pied-a-terre just down the road from the Queen at Buckingham Palace. My hideaway behind the mattresses became home from home for me with spare drugs and fresh stolen clothes left there. I lived like this for months until one morning, feeling a bit cocky, I went into the hotel dining room where I ordered a hot breakfast, giving a false room number for the bill. That evening two porters were waiting for me at the top of the stairs and my Grosvenor Hotel days ended abruptly.

With my hotel-home gone I was on the streets again and winter had arrived. I knew it was around Christmas because the shops were full of trees and decorations and over a year had passed since I lost the Tottenham slum base.

It was now my feelings of hurt surfaced with a vengeance. I was no longer just an addict but a homeless tramp living in the streets with nothing. It was the season of goodwill but alone on a park bench I pictured my ex-wife, her new husband and all her sisters eating turkey and pulling their crackers in that big house. At least Tessa and Antonia were there with them. Life had discarded me like old wrapping paper. It was the drugs that had put me where I was but I felt used by everybody. I was angry and hurt but probably no more than Alen had been when he realised I wasn't gay and just a pack of lies.

Perhaps God had given me a dose of my own medicine.

In the gutter I realised more and more the value of true love and from a park bench, in a rare moment of sanity, I wrote to Alen, begging him for forgiveness. Throughout my life I had bought artificial love, but on skid row the love shops were closed. Living in this harsh reality I needed even more pills just to bear the pain of being alive.

Over the next few days I shoplifted various items which to my deranged mind were Christmas presents for my own family. I carried these gifts around, feeling secure in thinking that strangers passing me believed I was on my way home. I couldn't bear to think of them seeing me as a tramp in the street. That evening I got into St. James Park to sleep somewhere near the lake. As the drug-high wore off I cried bitterly, knowing, as I did on each drug come-down, I had no-one, nothing. With a huge dose of sedatives I passed out still clutching my bottles of wine and other stolen goodies.

Waking up I felt numb with the cold. It was snowing and only after taking a large dose of amphetamine was I able to get up and function again. I thought it was Christmas morning. Whether it actually was or not I will never know but to me alone on my park bench it was Christmas day.

Desperate to find somebody to have Christmas lunch with I began roaming around until I came across three winos asleep in a shop doorway. Showing them some wine they all eagerly followed me into the middle of the park which was now covered in thick snow. Sitting them down on a bench I announced, 'It's Christmas dinner-time and you are my new family.' They began to pester me for a drink but getting angry I shouted, 'Either be my family or fuck off.' With big eyes on the booze they obeyed my demands. Pointing to them one by one I shouted, 'You be my brother and you be my wife. No you be my daughter, no my mother !' Getting confused I screamed hysterically, 'Oh fuck ! Just be anybody who loves me, just fucking love me !' The Scottish tramp laughed, 'I'll be who you fooking well want for a drink !' Soon we were all quite drunk and I vanished behind a tree, reappearing with a paper hat on and bribing them with more drinks we sang Christmas carols together.

The more drugged and drunk I got the more obsessed I became with making this a family Christmas. Through the haze I could imagine us all sitting at home in a living room. But where was our tree? Scraping together a pile of snow about four feet high into what I thought looked like a snowman I stuck in two empty bottles to represent the eyes. 'This is our Christmas tree ! It's story time !' I screamed. Making them all listen I went through my usual long monologue of self pity. How from all my wealth I had wound up a tramp on the street. I had the drinks so they obediently listened. The Scottish tramp, a short stocky man with a red woollen hat, commiserated, saying, 'I worked in a library in Glasgow, could have been in charge but was always off sick through drink so someone else got promotion'. He went on to tell us how he left in a fit of rage and drunk himself silly, winding up on the streets of London many years ago. The older man wearing a tatty raincoat tied with string never spoke.

Suddenly the old lady of the trio appeared to sober up and taking centre stage she proudly stated, 'I was a barrister once and I lived here in Westminster.' Aged between sixty and seventy, a gaunt woman, she somehow looked commanding as she related her alcoholic slide. She told us how once she'd been taken off a case after returning from the lunch recess drunk. The others laughed but I shut them up. Her story was obviously true. As she was speaking in her refined accent I could picture her wearing her barrister's robes.

Overcome by the whole scene, saying I would return with more booze, I ran to Alen's home nearby to beg for money. For some time now he had wanted nothing more to do with me following previous drugged scenes and was very irate when he opened the door. 'Can't come in, I've got guests, we're having a meal,' he said curtly. 'Having a fucking meal? Don't want me anymore? Give me some money or I'll force my way in !' I screamed. 'Wait here,' he nervously replied, closing the front door. Shortly he returned and gave me one hundred pounds, saying it was the very last money ever. 'If you ever come back I will call the police, regardless of the embarrassment it causes,' he said sternly. His words upset me, he really meant it this time and after so many years this was yet another of the last goodbyes. I went back to the three tramps still sitting in the park where I'd left them and bundling them all into a taxi I screamed, 'It's beds tonight ! No park benches this Christmas for us lot !'

Shortly after three bewildered tramps waited in a taxi outside a small hotel in Victoria while I paid for four rooms in advance. With our room keys safely in my pocket we sat down for our evening dinner in the crowded bar. Halfway through the meal I realised we were sticking out like sore thumbs and afraid we might get slung out I took them up to their rooms. In clean beds, each with a bottle, my new family soon fell asleep.

I, myself, tried to sleep but was too high and began roaming up and down the corridors. After a while I decided to leave the hotel but before going wanted to put 'Happy Christmas' notes under each door.

When I reached the old lady's room her door opened. She asked me inside and we sat down to share her bottle. Showing me her father's gold crested signet-ring which she wore with string round her neck she spoke of his suicide. Her father had found her mother in bed with his own brother. The old lady cried bitterly as she related the tale. I gave her two pills, saying, 'These will make you happy !' Ten minutes later she actually seemed to cheer up. 'Give me more !' she said starting to cry again. Taken in by her grief I threw several pills on the floor, shouting, 'Take my happiness, I'm losing the taste for it !' Picking up the tablets she offered me the signet ring she'd kept so safe through all her years in the gutter. Overcome with emotion I refused, running out into the streets and after roaming round all night I found myself back in the park where our party had been. Our family snowman was still there staring at me with his green winebottle eyes. Out of my head I slumped down and began to sing Christmas songs.

As the morning sun came up the weather got warmer and the snowman began to melt, vanishing like everything else in my life.

Taking a handful of sleepers I passed out, watching the winebottle eyes drop in a puddle of melted snow.

Chapter 27

LIVING IN THE GUTTER

When I woke many hours later all the snow had gone, leaving only green fields of emptiness. Taking my amphetamine I waited, stiff and cold, for the chemical buzz to enable me not to live, but merely exist through the pain of another empty day.

And so my life on the streets continued, interrupted by many periods of short prison remands. The most stupid thing I ever did to get arrested was up in Birmingham. How or why I wound up there I don't know, possibly a sleep-train gone wrong. With a stranger I'd met in the street I broke into a departmental store. He stole some watches and left while I had far bigger ideas. The alarm system was out of action so I had all night in the store alone. I helped myself to a clipboard from the stationery department with the intention of going from floor to floor to make an inventory of what I would steal. Sadly, it was the liquor department I came across first and here the police found me the next day as the store opened. I'd passed out on the floor, surrounded by empty bottles. With one almighty hangover I was remanded for three weeks in Winston Green Prison to sober up. Amazingly, in court I was only given a fine and time to pay !

Often when I was found unconscious on a park bench I was taken to lock-up psychiatric asylums but completely disorientated most times I didn't know anymore whether I was in hospital or back in prison. I just knew I was somewhere. I was in so many institutions I lost count but into some I smuggled drugs, mostly up my arse.

Once in Brixton prison on remand the cheap back-street drugs I'd sneaked in gave me horrific hallucinations, like acid tablets. I imagined the cell walls were getting bigger and smaller like in a scene from Alice in Wonderland. When the cell got smaller it felt like my head was being crushed against the ceiling then suddenly, everything reversed itself and the cell became enormous with my top bunk rising twenty feet above the ground. These hallucinations were bad enough but there was worse to come. I had swapped some tobacco for a cup of liquid soap to wash my prison clothes but my new cell mate thought it was a green alcoholic liquor and drunk the bloody lot. A short while later, with my drug cycle shrinking me, he became violently sick, shitting himself at the same time. As he took his trousers off shit gushed out of his bum all over the cell floor. It felt like I was an ant in a horror movie as I imagined myself about to drown in a sea of shit and sick. The man was groaning, doubled up in pain, but we were left like this until the cell was unlocked the next day.

Still hallucinating I was put into the prison's hospital section, a big locked ward with about fifteen prisoners sharing. All these men, unknown to me, were convicted murderers under observation. Laying spaced out on my bunk I listened to the conversation of two inmates on their beds either side of me. 'Mine didn't die right away. Did your one?' They were calmly discussing how they'd killed their wives, as if it was last Saturday's football match. 'No,' answered the other. 'Mine kept breathing, staring at me, giving me sarcastic looks. Bloody grinning she was, so I stabbed her in the heart and cut her throat from ear to ear. That stopped her looking at me. What about your one Fred?' 'Murmuring, weren't she, wouldn't stop. I kept hitting her on the head with a hammer but she just would not stop whining. I couldn't take it because I was late for my darts match so I tied her up and put her under the bed. I threw terrible darts all night. I lost ! I couldn't sleep either with the bloody groaning under me so I went downstairs and slept on the couch to get some peace. In the morning I popped up before going to work but she had stopped, it was all quiet. Not easy, is it, this killing your wife business. Especially on your first go. They take so long to die, don't they'? Then he calmly continued, 'Tea's round soon Fred. Pass the paper. Fuck me ! Look Spurs football team got beat again ! Chelsea drew.' That night I had horrific dreams of them killing me, arguing over whose murder method was better. The following morning in the showers another prisoner boasted to me about how he'd stabbed another man in that very shower, demonstrating it to me as if he had a knife. Horrified I ran back to the safety of the wife killers, now discussing the problems of cleaning up the blood. 'Just wouldn't come out, new carpet as well !'

A few months later, in another institution, I woke up actually believing I had died and was now in hell's department for dead drug addicts. The chart at the end of my bed read, 'drug overdose'. A few feet away a crowd of monsters with long noses were eating at a table. They laughed at me, saying, 'We took drugs like you !' I touched my own nose to see if it was now long like theirs. A monster wearing a big black witches hat and blowing a trumpet came over to my bed. 'Hello,' he said, 'come and eat with us !' Was this the ultimate horror show? 'Go away !' I screamed. Now all the monsters came over, blowing their trumpets, shouting,

'Welcome Mr. Overdose, you're one of us now.' Closing my eyes I waited for the devil himself to arrive.

Suddenly I was drifting off to sleep again into the heavy white clouds. Had God forgiven me? Was the devil too busy that day? I found myself in a beautiful park with my daughters.

Someone was calling, 'Stephen, come and have some dinner. It's Christmas day.' I opened my eyes to see a woman in blue standing at my bedside. The nurse told me in a soft Irish voice that I'd been transferred here from a general hospital after being found unconscious in the street following an overdose. I got up and joined the other patients wearing their party hats and joke noses for my Christmas dinner in a locked psychiatric ward.

Later, laying on my bed I vaguely remembered being in a busy street with all the shoppers, feeling so lost. Another Christmas had arrived and I had nowhere to go. Again I'd carried an empty box around all day, pretending I was going to a family Christmas. As the drug high wore off I sat on a bench in the busy Kings Road, Chelsea and finding reality too painful swallowed a handful of sleepers to escape. As they took effect the street noise drifted into the background, I was floating away..... no more people, no more cars, just white clouds.

Then, suddenly, monsters all around me. Where is my nose, my trumpet? Nurse, where am I?

I woke up properly a day or so later with reality cutting like a surgeon's knife. I was broke and alone. I had lost all hope. Outside the asylum I had absolutely nothing. Worse than all this, I was a addict? with no drugs to take !

From my bed I could see the locked door open every now and again as someone came in or out. I stood up and waited by the door. When my chance came I slipped out into the busy corridor. It was full of nurses and doctors rushing about. Further down that long passageway my eyes lit up as I came across the window-counter of the hospital pharmacy. A nurse was just pushing her trolley out and watching her lock the bottom door I realised she'd left the top glass section open. I waited till she was out of sight then jumped in to find myself standing amongst shelves stacked with pills. An addicts paradise ! Frantically I searched for amphetamine but knowing the nurse could return any second grabbed three bottles and jumped back into the busy corridor. Seconds later I was in a toilet, taking my first handful of pills, not knowing or caring what the tablets actually were. I just craved for some type of buzz, regardless whether it was up or down. A short while later, feeling dizzy, I stumbled back into the corridor and out into the hospital grounds where a security guard found me. After trying several wards he reunited me with my fellow monsters, all looking quite tame now without their hats and funny noses.

Soon I fell asleep on my bed, waking every few hours to go to the ward toilet where I swallowed more of the stolen sedatives. There a fellow monster saw me and blackmailed me for some pills. Reluctantly I gave him some and went back to sleep but soon I was woken by the head nurse who confiscated my remaining tranquillisers. The monster who'd been caught taking his tablets had informed on me.

It was always easy to get discharged from those hospitals if you convinced the doctors you weren't a danger to yourself or others. After playing my usual everything's okay act I was due to leave on January the fifth. That day, providence in the shape of a little Irish nurse, saved me from a certain twenty-year-prison sentence. That woman recognised how the years of drug abuse had affected me, sensing that I was just a lost soul living from one bottle of pills to the next. Trying to reverse the doctor's decision she delayed my departure by five precious hours.

Cowboys, Russian spies, kings of distant lands and a glutton of Jesus's were amongst the many characters I met in the lock-up wards. Was I myself Robin Hood, Jesus or just sad Stephen? Probably by now a drugged mixture of them all.

As time went on I became even more schizophrenic through the continued drug abuse. Once, after walking non stop for ten hours, I arrived in the Kent countryside at dawn. As I stood at the edge of a field a black horse came over and spoke to me, explaining he was God and black people, being more holy, were shortly to rule the world. Although I was white it had been decided in heaven I was getting Jesus's old job. Feeling very honoured I discussed the details of my new position with the Godly horse until a passing police car picked me up. Unable to appreciate my new job offer they took me to their local station but since I'd committed no offence I was released with the kind words, 'Fuck off back to London and be Jesus there !'

After many more police cells, prisons, park benches and shop doorways I left yet another loony-bin, but this time there was a difference. For somewhere to sleep I had been given a letter of introduction to Pound Lane Resettlement Unit in North London. This was a mission, the first of many I was to live in. In a very low state mentally I arrived in a long narrow alley leading up to the main doors. Either side was high wire-fencing, enclosing an old Jewish cemetery which made the brick-built Victorian mansion beyond seem even more sinister. I hesitated at the main door but an old man wobbling towards me pointed his finger and showed me the way in. Even on this warm spring day he was wearing a thick overcoat, his hands were swollen and his bloodshot face looked empty and sad.

At the reception we were stopped by an unfriendly man who ordered us to wait. He was exceptionally tall and looking down on me as I handed him my letter barked, 'Well, what's this?' Having read it he laughed, 'Sending them from everywhere these days.' 'Sending who?' I asked. 'Down and outs, tramps like you !'

It shook me. Before I had always been too drugged to think of myself as a tramp. 'Get in there !' he ordered, pointing at a door. 'Take all your clothes off. We must get rid of the lice.' 'I haven't got any lice,' I exclaimed, showing him my empty pockets, thinking he meant drugs. 'Flees, bugs !' he shouted, pulling my hair. 'You are smothered in them !' He pushed me naked into the shower room where I was hosed down by a man wearing wellington boots, rubber gloves and a surgical mask. I began to cry. Here I was, a discarded wreck about to enter a leper colony ! Another man covered me in white powder as I cried out, 'Give me my clothes back !' 'Clothes? Filthy rags, more like it, must be burnt !' he smirked. Thinking he meant I should be burnt I panicked and tried to run but slipped on the floor. 'Oh my God !' I cried out. 'What's happening to me !'

This Robin Hood jewel thief had taken one drug too many.

The old man I'd met earlier came in. He, too, was naked and covered in white powder. Holding me close he said, 'Don't cry'. This was the first act of kindness I'd been shown in years. With my arms round him we stood there, still naked, as I sobbed my heart out. The wardens were looking on, laughing, 'Here, you two lovers, get these clothes on.' They handed us a set of very basic clothes. 'You can sell these tonight in the pub over the road,' whispered the old man. 'Get yourself some hooch. That will take away those tears.' 'Hooch?' I queried. 'Booze !' he replied. 'Nice underpants, eh?'

Soon we were pushed through another door which I half expected to be a gas chamber. 'Here's two odd ones,' commented the shower man, handing us over to another attendant who led us down a dark corridor and said, 'Room three, end two bunks on the left.'

Room three was a large, smelly dormitory with about forty beds in it, twenty on either side all filled with down and out men. I began to cry again, seeing so many people squeezed together, social lepers set aside from the human race. Worse still, I was now one of them. 'Shut up you little cunt or I'll kick your fucking head in,' someone shouted at me. 'Get the bastard out of here,' screamed another. They all had the same lost and meaningless look on their faces. Their eyes were blank, devoid of hope and looking in the toilet mirror I saw the same look in my own reflection. Even when I forced a smile the lost look wouldn't go.

On the bed I quietly cried myself to sleep but after only a couple of hours I woke to hear forty men farting and snoring the night away. I'd been in many psychiatric hospitals over the years but they'd been so different with male and female patients, nurses and visitors. Even in prison you only lost your freedom, not your dignity.

Pound Lane wasn't like other institutions ! Nobody had forced me there, I was here of my own choice, unable to live in the outside world. Even in Britain where social security paid for your rent and food without having to work, I couldn't survive life in its most simple form. I had joined life's losers. This mission wasn't a locked institution. I was free to leave that den of smells at any time but I just couldn't. I was beaten.

Over the years I had lost my marriage, children, houses, cars, everything. But all that was nothing compared with this ! Here I lost my spirit, my will to carry on. I was grovelling for charity handouts just to stay alive. Day after day I sat there totally dejected, seeing no escape from this leper colony. The whole building was dark with plain grey walls. With the dormitories locked we were forced to spend the day in the dismal day room on hard chairs where we smoked each others dog-ends. In the afternoon they opened a television room with about twenty chairs in it. This was the highlight of the day and always caused a wild rush, with all available places quickly taken. If you got up to go to the toilet you lost your place like in a game of musical chairs. Night times were much more lively as many of the inmates returned drunk to wet their beds. God only knows where their drink money came from.

The pain I felt during those months was so deep it never completely left me. It was an isolated feeling of despair, of impending doom where you believe the absolute worst is about to happen. For me, having fallen from all my wealth and confidence to that dosshouse of despair, it had.

As the months passed I didn't recover but woke up just enough to think of drugs and the world outside again. Drugs to me represented the only hope of leaving this place. Even roaming the streets seemed a better form of life compared to that slow death. One day I mustered up the courage and after selling most of my clothes walked away, leaving the lepers still sitting on the hard chairs of Pound Lane. With that little money I went straight to Dr. Lando's surgery where I got the usual prescription, rejoining the drug roller-coaster, roaming around and sleeping rough. On my first night back on the streets I sat awake all night on a bench near Westminster Bridge where I'd thrown Snoopy into the river.

The next morning I found an entrance to an unused basement in Parson's Green and on going inside was confronted by two rough-looking men busy drinking their meths. They accepted me in but one of them warned me not to sleep on the right hand side, 'That's my side. I'm the boss here !' That night or possibly the next, after taking a large dose of sleeping pills, I returned. All the rag-beds were still there but no winos. Falling over empty bottles I passed out. I remember gaining semi-consciousness to see one of the winos standing over me. He screamed something and hit me on the head with a bottle, cutting my forehead, but I just passed back out. After a while I woke again to find him laughing as he urinated over my face but still too heavily sedated to get up I simply closed my eyes and slept on. Some time later he or another man fell on top of me. I couldn't move and lay there for an eternity until I found the strength to roll over and push him off. Laying side by side with the man I suddenly realised he was dead ! I was terrified but even after taking uppers my bones were too stiff to stand up.

I crawled out of the basement into the street and began to panic. Should I tell the police there was a dead man down there? Had he been murdered or had I killed him in my drugged haze without remembering it? Oh my God, what had I done ! Kneeling on the sidewalk I began to pray. I hobbled into a nearby church and stayed for hours until I had calmed down. I felt like a trapped fox with visions of thousands of winos closing in for the kill, looking to hang me from the nearest lamppost. From that day on, paranoid of being executed, I only slept in shop doorways where I felt safer.

Wearing four layers of clothes I never felt the cold as I slept rough. My hair became long and matted and I stunk, having long stopped washing. Ironically I finished up on the benches behind Euston Railway station where all those years ago I'd given away fortunes in cash. Alas, now there was no drugged-up Jesus or Robin Hood giving away money. The next year or so just vanished with me drunk most of the time on cheap booze and when I wasn't drunk I was asleep.

Living rough you tend to stay on the same bench for weeks on end, sharing meths with other local down and outs who become your family. Then, for no reason, you suddenly move all your dirty carrier bags to another park as if emigrating, looking for new hope. Seasons become irrelevant, you only know what time of year it is by the hot or cold weather.

It all makes no difference in the world of the winos.

One day I sat in a park opposite a woman with two children. Seeing me sit down she moved to another bench further down. I felt uneasy myself and moved back to where the winos sat. Here I felt safer with my own kind, at home in the gutter.

As time passed my will to survive was quickly evaporating. I'd given up. Losing all desire to steal new clothes I even found it pointless to get more amphetamine. I just wanted to sleep. Whereas before I had cared what passer-byes thought of me I was now oblivious to their existence. It was as if there was a glass screen separating me from the rest of the world.

One woman in whose shop doorway I regularly slept always brought a child in a pram as she opened up. Moving me on each morning she often gave me old rolls to eat from her small food shop. One day I realised that her child was now walking. I had seen her grow out of nappies while I lived in the gutter.

Towards the end of the lost years I began sleeping in the same doorway every night with another tramp. We never once spoke but always moved closer till our feet touched. Just to feel another human being moving made us feel safer. It reassured us we were not already in a coffin.

Dead, buried, and forgotten.

One morning after a long time like this I woke up to see two schoolchildren dropping coins by my side saying, 'Look at this poor old man. He's been there forever ! Could be our grandfather !'

Grandfather?

It shook me.

I was only thirty-something and had become a geriatric street vagrant.

Chapter 28

PHOENIX HOUSE

During the cold weather I was sleeping in a boiler room at Heathrow airport and like all tramps now carried my worldly possessions around in carrier bags. They were full of useless rubbish but carrying something which was still mine made me somehow feel better.

The schoolchildren calling me 'grandpa' had shocked me into action and after a long period of just dossing on park benches I went back on amphetamine. Although I was going nowhere at least I was moving, about which was better than being blotto all day with the winos. One night, while sheltering in the warmth of the boiler room, the police found me and although I hadn't committed any crime they took me along to their local station. Having been awake for days on drugs I was in such an incoherent state that the only information they got out of me was that I'd been born in Barnet. The two policemen, however, were genuinely concerned for my safety and somehow arranged for me to be taken the twenty odd miles to Barnet General Hospital. It was as if they were trying to find an owner for the damaged human suitcase found on their own doorstep. They hadn't the heart to just throw me away.

On arrival at the hospital I was put behind a screen in casualty and examined. There was nothing physically wrong with me and several puzzled doctors looked in before one of them realised I'd overdosed on amphetamine. He kept me in that cubical for several hours, allowing the drugs to wear off.

The psychotic hallucinations I suffered that day show the serious side-effects of amphetamine abuse. Laying there, wearing only a paper gown, I started to believe I'd been taken to planet Mars. I got extremely frightened as nurses popped their heads round the curtain, looking at me as if I was an alien. Convinced I could only return to earth by eating the disposable paper gown I proceeded to do so, chewing chunks at a time. Gradually, as the effect of the drugs wore off and having eaten more of the hospital gown, I returned to earth. I was beamed down to casualty just as the staff shift changed, which convinced me even more the new nurses coming on duty were earthlings welcoming me back.

Later I was interviewed by a psychiatrist who knew of my case from old hospital records dating back many years. There was only one thing wrong with me - I was a hopeless, long-term addict. What was the point in keeping me again for a couple of weeks just to release me back to the next bottle of pills? I was discharged and given the fare money to go to a drug shelter at Charing Cross. It was just up the road from where I'd recently been sleeping with the winos. My journey to Mars had frightened me and I now desperately wanted to stop taking drugs.

Arriving at the charity shelter complete with my old carrier bags I was welcomed by a friendly man with a long beard and asked inside. While we chatted he showed me a great deal of understanding, explaining he had once been an addict himself. After talking for about an hour he asked me the ultimate, soul-searching question - would I rather he gave me a hundred pills or get me into a place to treat my addiction? 'Think carefully. Your answer must be honest, from the heart,' he said, giving me half an hour on my own to consider the alternatives. Obviously he hadn't got a hundred tablets, but at the time I believed he had. The choice was agonising, because to an addict in the middle of a comedown one hundred tablets are like gold dust.

I thought back over the years of misery on skid row and with all the sincerity I was capable of decided for the first ever time to come off drugs. This was a monumental decision for me after twenty years of swallowing amphetamine pills all day, every day. When I told him he telephoned Phoenix House, one of the best drug rehabilitation centres in England. Putting down the phone he explained that two people were on their way to see me. 'I can't promise anything,' he said. 'But they might take you back with them.'

An hour or so later a man and woman in their late twenties arrived, both former addicts in their final phase of treatment. They questioned me about my drug habit and quizzed me why I wanted to stop. I told them about the pain I'd lived through and satisfied with my answers they agreed to take me back to Phoenix House. First they searched me for drugs, then we thanked the man in charge of the shelter and left. Outside in the street one of the recovering addicts asked me, 'Do you really need those old carrier bags?' I silently shook my head. 'Let's throw them away,' he suggested, pointing towards a bin. Somewhat hesitantly I obeyed throwing both bags in. As we waited at the bus stop opposite Trafalgar Square they bought me some chocolate and cigarettes. Boarding the bus for Herne Hill I turned back to the bin and saw the wino who I'd often slept next to. He was rummaging through my old bags. It seemed so strange.

Sitting upstairs on the bus I felt safe, as if I was with old friends. This was a miracle after so many years alone on the streets. Seeing my companions laugh together I found it hard to believe they once had been addicts like me.

Phoenix House was a thirty-roomed mansion in South London in a private road on a hill. It was a drug-free oasis, detached in every way from London life. That day I began the eighteen-month recovery programme. As a newcomer I was strictly supervised by established inmates throughout each intensive day. Old-timers who had been there longer, had progressed up the ladder and now gave out the same harsh orders they'd once received. The programme emulated real life, teaching you first to accept being told what to do and as time passed taking on responsibility. Towards the end of treatment addicts were moved into a rehabilitation section from where they could find an outside job and a place to live. This enabled them to re-enter the outside world whilst still enjoying the security of the unit. All the staff, including the director, were recovered addicts. To break old habits newcomers lost all contact with the outside world for the first year.

I was taken into a huge day room where about twenty addicts, aged between seventeen and thirty, were lined up to meet me. They were all at different stages of recovery and greeting them was a terrifying experience. This group of people were to be my new family whom I would have to eat, work, and mix with. To do this without drugs represented the highest mountain I ever had to climb. From the age of fourteen my only contact with the world had been through drugs. I'd never mixed with anybody unless I was stoned out of my mind or full of alcohol. The drink-drug crutches had been an integral part of my daily life. Making matters worse was that for many years now I'd only spoken with nurses, doctors or policemen. My only other conversations had been with a starving dog or God in the shape of a black horse. Now real people, twenty strange faces, were looking at me. I was so frightened that day I wanted the floor to swallow me up as the leader said, 'This is Stephen.'

I was allocated to one of the five teams, each consisting of six people. Our team leader, Peter, was a man of about thirty, tall with short black hair and tattoos on both hands. He was in Pheonix House on court licence as an alternative to a custodial prison sentence and seemed very confident as he showed me round our sleeping quarters. The two of us shared this large room with Tom, a young Irish heroin addict who reminded me of John Lennon with his small round glasses. That evening Peter explained I was allowed to write only one letter out in the first six months. I chose to write to my mother and ironically it was this fateful letter which was to become my undoing. Writing away at the table I was petrified listening to Peter and Tom chatting so normally and prayed the lights would go out so I could be alone under the sheets. That first night at Pheonix House I really felt like a fish on the sand.

Early the next morning Tom showed me how to make my bed to perfection, without a crease. Soon after it was inspected by two senior recovering addicts carrying clipboards. They looked at my perfect bed - and pulled the sheets to the floor, saying it must be made again ! I could have cried as they did this twice more before finally accepting my work.

In the dining room before breakfast the same anxious feeling of being with people started to boil up again. Everybody seemed to be looking at me. After our morning meal it was meeting time and I was given my own packet of tobacco with some cigarette papers. The tobacco had to last a week and was a lesson in teaching you to ration things out.

On my first day I was assigned to work in the kitchen where, as the new boy, I had to wash everything, including the floors, to absolute perfection. There were only two others working with me, a tall gay boy called Ashley and Jenny, an attractive, self-assured girl with red hair. Working alone with these two I felt slightly less threatened than when I was with everybody.

Phoenix was entirely self-sufficient with people moving round all day like busy bees, carrying out numerous tasks in the house and grounds. The inmates ran everything, the catering, cleaning, maintenance, gardening and laundry. Living, eating and sleeping together we created our own small drug-free world. Whether you were cutting grass with scissors or cleaning large floor areas with a toothbrush you were very much a part of this community. For me it meant washing dishes all day until after our evening meal when the worst part of the day began - group therapy.

Group therapy consisted of ten people sitting in a circle. On the first night I started crying as I could see myself talking with the broken chairs in the Tottenham hell-hole after Snoopy died. Sensing my distress the leader took me to the kitchen for a drink of water so I could calm down. After we returned I watched as everybody spoke in turn with absolute honesty of what they thought of others in relationship to day to day events. If accused you had a chance to answer all allegations against you. It always got very heated with lots of cursing but never became physical. When screaming at others we had to hold on to the seat of our chairs so we would never threaten with hand gestures. I found the whole thing horrendous and in a cowardly fashion always managed to avoid direct confrontations.

After therapy each evening there was an hour's free time with hot milk drinks and it was in this period I began to get friendly with Pierre, a French heroin addict. His father, a rich Paris banker, was paying privately to have his wayward son treated there. This French guy was a good-looking boy with blond hair who wore designer clothes. Somehow he was a cut above the rest of us. He impressed me with tales of his playboy adventures with top gangsters in France. His similar background drew me closer to him. Pierre, determined to quit drugs, took Phoenix House very seriously and just being with him each evening was beginning to get me slightly more involved with the others.

I still found it daunting to mix but as the weeks turned into months it was changing for the better. Now there were rare occasions when I chatted with other addicts about my drug-taking and during therapy I even began to stand up to abuse thrown at me.

After several months when I was put to work in the garden things really improved. It couldn't have been planned better, perhaps it was, but working with me in the garden were Pierre and Tom. Pierre in charge was very relaxed about everything and he allowed Tom and myself long periods just to talk. Although the work was designed to keep us busy all day you can only cut the lawn or prune the trees so many times. Often we emptied the sheds to clean the already spotless tools. It was Pierre's duty to inspect all we'd done but even when he rejected something he did so with a smile. One day we had to burn a lot of rubbish, including piles of old newspapers. Looking at these papers I realised I'd lost so many years in the oblivion of the gutter.

In November 1974 Ali had become heavyweight champion again, in February 75 Onassis had died in Paris, in October 75 Liz Taylor had remarried Richard Burton, in January 76 Concorde had it's first flight, in September 76 Mao Tse-Tung had died, in January 77 Jimmy Carter had become President, in May 78 Princess Margaret divorced Tony Armstrong. One of the last papers read in August 77 Elvis, the King, had died. I shook my head. Elvis was dead ? Where the fuck had I been when all this had happened? 'Do you remember any of this , Tom?' I asked. 'No mate, I was too busy injecting myself !' he smiled.

As more time passed I began to look on Tom and Pierre as friends. Confiding in them over what scared me about a future without drugs. It helped me enormously to hear they had similar fears and I actually found myself looking forward to each day's work.

Occasionally we celebrated birthdays with huge cakes made especially by the kitchen staff. All the tables would be pushed together like for a king's banquet. On Pierre's birthday, instead of sitting at the very end as usual, I bravely opted to sit in the middle with the birthday boy.

Twice a week we played organised football matches on the lawns of the big back garden and it was during one of these I had a heavy confrontation with a long-term inmate. That evening this guy was put into my therapy group and being the more confident of the two of us soon shouted me down, saying I knew nothing about football. When it was their turn to speak Pierre and Tom individually spoke up against this man. It felt wonderful having friends sticking up for me.

Inspite of these heated arguments all of us, including the enemy, were not taking drugs. Pheonix House was working its miracle. The longer I stayed off drugs, which by now was about five months, the more I became involved with everyone. It was slow but it was happening.

One afternoon when I was raking the leaves I looked up to see Jenny, the kitchen girl, standing at the window. She didn't see me watching her as she looked out over London, smiling. It was as if she was imagining her new, drug-free life which was shortly to begin. Spotting me she called out, 'Not so long and we can all live out there again !' She held up a small placard. It was the one I'd made in art class and read, 'Phoenix People Proudly Progress'.

At breakfast the next day we all said goodbye to Pierre and Ginger who were going to visit Paris. Ginger, an old-timer, had been chosen to go with Pierre to help him on his final home visit before he was to return to France for good.

After a lifetime on drugs my own recovery, however, was still like walking on thin ice. A further uninterrupted period in Phoenix House would have allowed me time to grow, teaching me to express myself and become an equal amongst the others. Sadly, that precious time was cruelly cut short. Waiting to talk to me were two police officers from Scotland Yard who'd traced me through the letter I wrote my mother. I was devastated. Here I was, desperately trying to get off drugs after years of living on skid row, and now this ! What did they want? Officers from England's main police station don't investigate petty crime. Whether those officers had the right to take me out of a treatment centre I don't know, but mentally confused I agreed to go with them the following morning.

With the other addicts asking, 'What's going on?' I was suddenly catapulted into the hall of fame inside the enclosed world of Phoenix House. I'd become the special junkie wanted by Scotland Yard, which not only distanced me from the others but also them from me. The precariously thin ice of my recovery now had one bloody great crack in it. From an ex-vagrant I had become a criminal superstar !

In bed that night I agonised about whether I should run away. This police enquiry was no parking ticket, a skeleton from my past had come back to bite. With Tom and Peter asleep I looked out of the bedroom window, considering my escape. But where was I to run to? All roads only led back to a life-sentence on drug island. I thought back to the wino looking through my old bags and the misery of being hosed down like a leper at Pound Lane. I've got to stay, I must face it, I decided. Unable to sleep and laying awake in bed all night I cursed - Why the fuck couldn't they have left me alone? Especially now !

During breakfast the following morning the police arrived and with everybody watching I was taken away. The rule of Pheonix House was that nobody ever left, even on court appearances, without a senior member of staff accompanying them. Yet nobody came with me. I think many senior staff were now more than dubious as to whether I had ever been a tramp, suspecting my amphetamine addiction was just an act to evade justice. On our way to headquarters the officers were super friendly, 'Have a cigarette, some chocolate,' all the usual rubbish to soften someone up.

After being signed in I was taken to a long narrow room with about thirty filing cabinets full of photographs and incriminating documents dating back many years. As the many hours of questioning began it soon became clear it was heavy stuff they were investigating. Their enquiry involved the jailed crime-bosses the Kray twins and other leading London crime families, including the American Alan Cooper and his Mafia connections.

The police were looking to find out how small companies like Highheat had suddenly acquired betting shops, night clubs and so much more. Where had all their money suddenly appeared from? What made everything look even more ominous was that Terry Marvin, my ex-partner with his dream of being Al Capone had befriended every well-known London Gangster. Scotland Yard was dealing with fact and fantasy so mixed up that it all looked far more sinister than it was. The police produced certificates showing me as half-partner in the main company. With documents and photographs dating back to 1962 I was looking at the high times of my life through which I'd drifted on a cloud of drugs.

Off amphetamine it all looked so different, quite unreal, like it had never happened. Sitting there I began to wonder whether we were talking about the same person. This can't be me, I've just come from the shop doorways ! Perhaps they wanted my identical twin? Even the police seemed confused as to whether they were interviewing the right person as I stood there in my simple clothes from the drug hostel. The longer the questioning continued the more lost I felt and without the bravado drugs gave me I just wanted to get back to the safety of Phoenix House.

After about six hours the police saw they were getting nowhere and I was asked to make a written statement which I did, incriminating nobody, explaining my memory had gone. Relieved it was finally over I expected to be driven back to Pheonix House but instead I was taken down a long corridor and locked into a cell.

I shouted, banging on the door but it was two hours before the hatch opened and a policeman's face appeared. 'Let me out,' I screamed, 'I'm only in here as a witness.' 'No, you're not,' he replied. 'You're under arrest on a serious charge. Shotguns involved !' 'What charge?' I asked, beginning to panic. He couldn't tell me, explaining that another police district from outside London was involved and a car was on it's way to take me there. The hatch closed.

Paralysed with fear I wondered what the police had uncovered now. Shotguns, oh my God ! What hadn't I burnt? My mind began to race from one old crime to the next. In seconds I had been transformed from an addicted ex-tramp to someone in at the deep end of his criminal past. Later one of the original detectives looked through the hatch and sneeringly said, 'We are sorry. It was just by chance we saw your photo on the wanted board.' 'You lying cunt,' I screamed, 'You knew I was wanted when you collected me from the drug hostel.' 'I forgot. We all get bad memories, just like you,' he grinned and closed the hatch.

Alone in that cell, very mixed up after having my past so dramatically brought back, I now began to remember much more. Not in any chronological order, just bits and pieces of everything. It made no sense. Did I really once own a night club and drive a new white

Jaguar? How could all this be when I'd been starving for years in the streets? As the night went on I began to realise for the first time the damage amphetamine had caused.

From immense wealth to skid row, from champagne to cheap wine - momentarily I could see clearly where I had once been in life.

Early the next morning the cell door opened and in handcuffs I was taken to a waiting police car. As we drove through the morning rush hour past Euston Station I got very distraught, having been awake all night with worry. Seeing the winos asleep on the benches I began wishing I had stayed with them. As our car stopped at some traffic lights I saw a tramp asleep on the same bench where I'd always slept myself. He turned towards me. I was horrified. He had my face. I was looking at myself ! 'Better off on the benches than in prison,' my identical twin shouted. Yanking at the handcuffs I screamed, 'Let me out, my home is here with the tramps.' 'Keep quiet, you will only make matters worse,' the officer I was locked to sternly replied.

A couple of hours later we arrived at a small village police station outside Bedford and I was put into a cell. For hours I sat there bewildered until the door opened and standing in front of me was the police officer who'd investigated the burning papers at Lyndford Hall. 'Hello,' he said smirkingly, 'Nice to see you again after all this time.'

A robbery had taken place some years before and the culprit, who was never caught had escaped, kidnapping a car and driver at gun-point. This officer, harbouring a long-term grudge, had encouraged witnesses to pick me out from police mugshots.

Offering me a reduced short sentence he tried to persuade me to sign a confession but when I refused he became irate and shouted, 'Then you'll be put in an identification parade. You're going down for a long time !'

Back in my cell I began to wonder. Had I actually done this robbery while high on drugs and forgotten all about it? I could recall parts about guns and hold-ups but never kidnapping anyone. Again a confession statement was put in front of me but this time I read it and noticed the crime had taken place at 12 noon on the 5th of January some years before. Why the 5th of January struck something in my mind I don't know, but it did. Suddenly I remembered the monster hospital. If by some miracle it was the same year the little Irish nurse had kept me till 12 noon - I was a free man.

I had been in custody now for about thirty hours and once again demanded to see a solicitor, refusing to take part in any identification parades. I told the policeman about the hospital, saying, 'If I was a drugged-up zombie roaming the streets on the day of the kidnapping you can make the charge stick but if I was in that hospital you can fuck yourself.' Waiting in the cell I began to feel cocky, feeling I was going to beat this charge. Unfortunately this new found arrogance re-enforced my ever-growing inner rebellion against the regime of Phoenix House.

The crack in the thin ice was getting bigger.

I was drifting back towards drug island.

A day later the cell door opened and waiting to meet me was Peter from Phoenix House. That little Irish nurse had really saved me and the police had to let me go. On the train back to London I felt the big shot, so much better than Peter, this run-of-the-mill junkie sitting next to me. I was first division again. I was a star. I was the hero, returning to the adulation of the lower-class addicts of Phoenix House. I'd beaten a kidnapping charge !

Back at the hostel I got furious when I found no special dinner had been arranged to welcome me back. Even Tom didn't make any special fuss of me ! Hurt, I began to isolate myself again, thinking, 'These idiots. They've never dealt with Scotland Yard or big time criminals.'

Initially the good that Pheonix House had done outweighed the rebellion but as time passed the scales tilted in the other direction. By the time Pierre and Ginger returned from Paris my attitude towards Phoenix House had already changed. Even Pierre, with his mind on Paris, wasn't impressed with my Scotland Yard adventures. To make matters worse I was transferred from the garden to work in the laundry with a sultry-looking girl who hardly ever spoke. The making of the beds, group therapy, in fact everything now seemed stupid. Over the weeks which followed the rot got worse and I began to steal food at night, putting on a lot of weight. When one of the leaders mentioned how fat I'd become I resented it, convinced they were all against me. The only time I felt okay was after lights out when I could be alone with my thoughts.

On one of these nights under the sheets I began to think of the bright lights of London and the wild times I had back in the money days. The familiar tape inside my head began to play again, reasoning against all reason. Money? I could steal it ! All I needed was confidence ! All I needed was bravery ! All I needed was drugs !

Early the very next morning I ran away from Phoenix House. The police, without realising it, had helped to condemn me to carry on serving the worst sentence of all.

A life sentence on drug island.

I pray that other addicts in treatment don't run away as I did and suffer anything like the horrendous consequences I was about to. My suffering so far had been just the first course. Now I was about to get the bloody main meal !

Chapter 29

THE LIVING DEAD

As I ran through the garden a much younger boy, only there a week, came up behind me calling, 'I'm coming with you !' At first we couldn't open the back gate and struggling with it I heard more shouting, 'Stephen, don't go. Wait, let me talk to you !' It was Jenny looking out of her window. Seconds later as she rushed across the lawn, the big gate swung open and we vanished round the corner. Within five minutes we were on a train to Central London. The boy, whose name I never really knew, suggested we stuck together, collected his old car and got some cash off his mother.

Early that afternoon with money in his pocket, we were parking outside Dr. Landos surgery in Harley Street. Fifteen minutes later we'd cashed our prescriptions for large quantities of amphetamine and mandrax. Together in his car we began swallowing handfuls of tablets and with his remaining money now in my pocket we were on our way to another doctor, when our problems really started.

As he stopped at some traffic lights my companion suddenly passed out and slumped against the wheel. He had taken sleepers by mistake. I pulled him into the passenger seat and took over the driving. My groggy passenger now lay motionless beside me as out of my head I began driving round in circles, trying to find the other doctor. Suddenly I realised the boy was breathing very strangely and had slipped to the floor. I stopped the car to find him in a coma and panicking, thinking he was about to die, took him to a nearby hospital. He was admitted as an emergency to have his stomach pumped out. In a state of terror, refusing to give my name, I left the car keys with the nurse and grabbing the remaining drugs ran away.

After my long stay in Phoenix House the effect of the drugs frightened me. Once again I was alone in the streets of London. Clutching my pills I aimlessly ran about as the horror whirlwind gathered speed. What was going on? What was I doing? In desperation I bought some cheap brandy and with the last of the money paid for two nights in a sleazy hotel. I was shown to a small, dark basement room, furnished only with a bed and a gas fire with a wooden shelf above. It was a dismal room with one tiny window looking out to the street above. Trying to compose myself I poured the pills onto the shelf in two piles, uppers to the right, downers to the left. Proudly placing a bottle of brandy at either end I stared at my chemicals on display thinking, surely this lot will get me going and back to where I once belonged !

Alone in that room with my mountain of drugs I kept taking more and more uppers, expecting the inspiration of the glory days to return. I waited and waited for the bliss to arrive but instead of getting happy I only got tense and frightened.

A day later, having taken drugs non-stop for thirty hours, I finally gave up. Desperate to stop the horror movie inside my head I reached for the unopened brandy and swallowed my first handful of sleepers. Laying back I waited for relief from this nightmare. Through the window I could see lots of feet hurrying along the street above in the morning rush hour. In the next room someone was coughing, now they were talking and a while later I could hear their groans of sexual pleasure.

Suddenly the sleepers and brandy took effect and a thousand violins began to play a victory march inside my head. I felt good again, wheezy. The room was moving round. Everything looked great. I could hear the couple in the next room, they had started again. Should I join them for a threesome, I thought, stuffing sleeping pills into my pockets.

Carrying the last of the brandy I staggered out of the hotel and from Argyle Square crossed over into the busy Kings Cross Station. In my mind the morning travellers were cheering for me, the 'Druggie champ of the world' as I slumped down on a bench to drink on.

Eventually, sinking into a drugged stupor, I locked myself inside a toilet cubical where I slept on the floor amongst the puddles of urine. Later that day I woke, cold and stiff, as I was kicked under the door. 'Can't sleep here,' said a loud voice. With one final swig of brandy I crawled out of the toilet to climb into the warmth of a train just as it was leaving the station.

Many hours later I was woken to find myself in Newcastle, three hundred miles from London.

So ended one of the worst pill taking sessions in my life.

This lunatic drug episode had wiped out all the good Phoenix House had done as if I'd never been there. My addiction had reached rock-bottom. I was now progressing into another twilight zone, a place even darker and more hopeless than being blotto in skid row. All addicts and alcoholics eventually enter this basement level when their chemical intake no longer works. The lift stops here. Drowning rats live with more hope.

Falling all over the streets outside Newcastle station I was picked up by the police. They dropped me off outside the local Salvation Army Mission, saying, 'Go and sleep it off in there.' I rang the bell and as the door opened I practically fell inside. It would be nearly a year before I was to see the light of day again. Someone gave me some sweet tea with which I swallowed more sleeping pills to escape my horror. I passed out on the floor. As I slipped into yet another oblivion I imagined giant ants coming across the floor to eat me.

A day or so later I was woken by the boss man wearing his Salvation Army uniform. He was furious and sternly said, 'Don't do that again. Can't have no dead bodies in here !' Like a lost child I reached into my pockets and handed him my last few pills. Now there were no more drugs, just me, dressed in dirty jeans, trainers and a green tee shirt.

'Its prayer time,' the boss said as he lead me to the communal lounge where three rows of battered old chairs had been lined up to face a platform. On the stage was an old upright piano which until now had been covered with a grey blanket. Six Salvation Army Staff in immaculate uniforms began to sing 'Glory Glory Hallelujah !' The room came alive. Every one of the thirty old tramps making up the compulsory congregation began to sing in full voice. At the end of each song an old man with white hair lifted both arms in the air and screamed, 'Praise be the Lord !' In the middle of it all the music stopped and the pianist, a thin woman with horn-rimmed glasses, took centre stage, preaching to the now silent audience. 'God is here, he is our saviour !' she exclaimed at the end of the service. Now the old man shouted even louder, 'Praise be the Lord !' to which all the Salvation officers answered, 'May the Lord be with you, Kenneth,' ending the prayers. With the service finished God left the room. The blanket went back over the piano and an old television was wheeled out, leaving us all to stare at the screen, whether it was on or off.

On the other side of this large room, in front of the serving hatch, was the dining section, about ten tables with red plastic chairs. When the bell rang thirty tired old men shuffled across to the tables to eat a meal, consisting of two slices of bread, a piece of old cheese and tea served in white tin mugs. Then it was back to the softer chairs on God's side of the room till bed time.

From 7 pm in the evening every hour a bell rang and the dormitory door was unlocked for five minutes. Once you decided to go to bed you couldn't come back out, you were there till morning. Thirty-odd metal beds each with a thin grey blanket and a rock hard pillow were squeezed into capacity. The indentation on my cushion from the last tramp's head was like his empty mind was still there for me to climb into.

In the mornings we silently shuffled out to the tables and the red chairs again for the usual breakfast - one shrivelled sausage and about twenty baked beans on the far side of the plate. Two bread slices made up the meal along with the customary tin mug of lukewarm tea. After that we sat till lunch, till tea, till bed. The only break in the emptiness was God's time at 3 pm when for half an hour the entire room came alive. God was never late as he popped in each day and as time passed I, too, was singing my hallelujahs. Nobody, including me, ever went out or even spoke. We all just sat there in God's chairs all day, every day half asleep, thinking nothing.

This mission was ten leagues below Pound Lane, which in comparison seemed like a luxury holiday club. Here there were no free clothes and the lice were very much part of the congregation. Because Newcastle is a quiet town on route to nowhere most inhabitants there were local old men with no hope of ever leaving, simply waiting to die.

At first I could smell these decrepit old men but very soon I became part of the smell. Like the others, for security reasons I never took my clothes off. Once when I washed my socks they were stolen and I went for days without until I was given a grey pair by the boss man. 'Don't lose these,' he said, 'You won't get any more. Keep them on at all times !' The men who did take off their shoes in bed slept holding them. Cleaning teeth, combing hair and baths were history, nothing mattered in the world of the living dead.

One fat tramp who looked like Billy Bunter had terrible pains in his legs and took ages just to walk the twenty feet from God's chairs to the dining section. Like the others he never spoke but after a few months asked if he could lean on me when he crossed the room.

Us lost souls were held together by our common void. We all had nothing to do, nobody to write to, nobody to phone, nothing to be late for or even get up for. None of us had sunk to that level overnight, we hadn't been born tramps. Every one of us had come from someplace, with mums, dads, perhaps even a wife and children. For me it was the end station after years of drug abuse. I was tired all the time as if watching my own funeral without being allowed to climb into the coffin. There was no end to the tunnel, let alone light, just a void. With my spirit broken I'd given up and no longer wanted anything, even drugs. At the end of each day Bunter used to say to me, 'Well, that's another day out the way, one less to live.'

One morning all the uniformed staff hovered round Kenneth's bed. The frail old man with his white hair had died in the night. He was laying on his back, his hands above his head on the pillow. Every tramp gathered round and raising our arms together we shouted in a chorus, 'Praise be The Lord !' Without another word we turned away and shuffled in for another sausage and twenty beans. Like Kenneth, if anybody died in the night he was not moved until the following morning well after rigor mortis had set in. Another pitiful body for an unmarked grave with no mourners to even acknowledge his death, let alone cry over it. Dying meant simply moving from the living dead to the actual dead. That day at God's time everybody sang louder than usual but there were no more cries of 'Praise be the Lord !' Like Kenneth they were now history.

His death stirred me from just sitting around half asleep like a zombie. After ten months I began to think of life outside the mission again. Each morning I started to look in the toilet mirror, repeating to myself, 'You must go out, go out !' The self hypnosis somehow worked and after several days I left the building for the first time.

It was a crisp spring morning and walking up the coast line I felt strange seeing so many new faces after the battered men of the previous year. I watched a group of fishermen laughing together as one of them landed a fish. That fish wriggling in the sunlight was more alive than all of those old tramps put together !

Suddenly I got frightened and ran back, getting there just as God's time was beginning. I sat down for a while but then, with the piano and hallelujahs going full blast, my courage returned. I left them all still singing to go back out, but this time I went past the fishermen and on towards the town half a mile away.

The city centre was a different world with its shops, banks, libraries and clean people hurrying about. They all had somewhere to go, someone to love, someone to hate, something to think about. I was looking at the world of the living. In my head was a faint glimmer of hope as I began picking up cigarette butts. I begged for money to buy rolling papers and was soon lighting my first fag. I was coming alive again after ten dark months with the living dead.

In the mission life continued as usual but I now made regular trips to the city centre. I started to live in the outside world for the first time ever off drugs. Apart from being blotto with the winos and Phoenix House my only other drug free periods had been enforced ones in prison or lock up asylums. One night Bunter, the fat tramp, told me of Whitney Bay, a seaside resort ten miles away suggesting that perhaps I could get a casual job at the funfair. It sounded good but I was afraid to leave the security of the mission. Again I began self-hypnosis sessions in front of the toilet mirror, repeating, 'Whitney Bay,' over and over. As I got more determined my words got louder until the boss man came in to investigate the noise, thinking I was drunk. Once more the magic mirror worked and a week later I walked the ten miles to Whitney Bay.

Every step of the way my hopes and dreams increased but they were all quickly shattered when I arrived to find an out of season resort with all funfairs closed. It started to rain and I cried all the way back to the mission, arriving soaking wet, too late for tea.

The next day, with some of my fighting spirit back, I spoke again to the fat tramp who told me of Leeds, a big town with lots of action - but it was a hundred miles away. I wanted to go but was afraid if things didn't work out I wouldn't be able to get back to my Newcastle base. For a few more days I repeated, 'Go to Leeds' to my image in the toilet mirror before I plucked up the courage to leave. Leaving forever was an emotional decision and I wanted to say goodbye properly to my 'Hallelujah Men'. First I went out begging in the city centre and returned with about fifty rolled cigarettes and several bars of chocolate. After God's time that day I jumped onto the stage, shouting, 'I'm going to Leeds. Goodbye everybody !' I gave them all a rolled cigarette along with several squares of chocolate. When I shook hands with each one of them some replied, but most just stared back in their usual silence. As I was about to make my final exit the tubby tramp called me back and putting his arms round me said, 'Good luck, son. You must move on, can't stay here and die with us lot. Wish I could join you, but these old legs don't work anymore.' He pulled up his trousers, showing me his swollen, red raw legs. 'Help me over to the street door. I want to watch you go,' he said. Leaning on me he slowly moved across the room and down the corridor to the main door.

Outside in the street I left him holding on to a wall as I walked away, still wearing the same old jeans and green tee shirt I'd arrived in a year ago. Reaching the corner I turned to wave and saw he had been joined by several of the old men, waving and shouting, 'Good luck. Thanks for the chocolate !' I waved back and with tears in my eyes turned the corner. Feeling the sea breeze in my face I was crying - but they were tears of hope. Goodbye Newcastle, goodbye 'Hallelujah Men', goodbye wriggling fish !

Only destiny saved me from staying there forever, still sitting today amongst some of the same men singing hallelujah with God at 3 pm.

Hitch-hiking and walking the journey to Leeds took until the following morning. Every step brought new fears as I wondered if I could stay off drugs and re-join the human race. This was my Alabama walk to freedom after twenty years on drug island. Arriving there I found another Salvation Army mission to live in but Leeds was a bigger town with constant changes even in the tramp community. Life inside the bigger mission was far more lively, there were many different levels of dropouts.

The lowest thirty percent, which I called the 'Living Dead', were the same as the old men of Newcastle. They were the long term institutionalised, too weak to go out looking for drink and they hardly ever moved or spoke.

Next came the 'Moving Tramps' who made up a further thirty percent. These men were still strong enough to beg or steal for drink and would go out for short periods only to return drunk and sleep it off. They were noisier than all the others and communicated, but only amongst themselves.

Twenty percent were 'Druggies', mostly younger, disturbed types, dressed slightly better. They were quiet, keeping very much to themselves. Unlike the 'Moving Tramps' or 'Living Dead', who only had the clothes on their back, this group still had a few possessions in carrier bags or battered cases.

Another ten percent had only been homeless for a few months. Members of this group had that new-boy look, as if they were saying, 'I'm not staying long'. They still got drunk but in a much quieter way.

The final ten percent were the high rollers. Most still had part-time, casual cash-in-hand jobs, washing-up in hotels or selling evening papers. With all their income spent on drink they were the worst, drunk every night. Many of these, although filthy, wore shirts, sometimes even a tie. During their first weeks at the mission they occasionally took off some clothes, washing an item or two. Sneaking in cans of beer to drink together in the mission toilets before bedtime they still regarded themselves as success stories compared to the other groups below them. They couldn't recognise how far down societies ladder they themselves had already slipped and inevitably, as time passed, they fell into the lower groups. Some, within a few short years, joined the 'Living Dead'. Many dropouts at the higher levels could still be saved, and returned to society. But sadly it's society itself that doesn't give a fuck whether they return or not.

Life in that Leeds mission was terrifying for me. I had never lived anywhere off drugs. It was like locking up a fourteen-year-old boy caught handbag-snatching for twenty-three years on drug island to then release him in Leeds with nothing and nobody. For me, the released prisoner, still emotionally fourteen years old, Leeds was a very awe-inspiring, frightening place.

One day as I was begging near the railway station I saw a notice which offered help to alcoholics in a new unit. That afternoon I went for an interview but I only talked of my drink problems, thinking if I mentioned drugs they would reject me. The interviewers, suspecting I was only after more comfortable accommodation, insisted that I attended Alcoholics Anonymous meetings for a month before I returned. I did so, going to a meeting every night, but mainly to eat biscuits and scrounge cigarettes. I never spoke and unfortunately was still too far gone mentally to respond to the message.

A month later I was admitted to a new-type of alcoholic unit in a village hospital outside Leeds where I was to live for the next ten weeks.

Chapter 30

RECOVERY, HOPE AND RELAPSE

Living in the unit was like staying at the Hilton Hotel after the previous year in the mission. The alcoholic ward occupied the entire first floor of a large village hospital which, set in huge grounds, had the atmosphere of a country health farm. The ten-week programme enforced a detox-type abstinence and to help patients open up everyone in turn had to tell his or her life's history. Throughout the story nobody was allowed to interrupt but after it was finished both staff and fellow patients expressed their opinions. The unit didn't have the intensity of Phoenix House and this, along with the fact I had been off drugs for a year, helped me to settle in quickly. With a guaranteed roof over my head, beautiful surroundings and good food I was getting stronger each day.

After a couple of weeks they gave me a job making beds in the geriatric ward of the main hospital, easy work for which I was paid a few pounds pocket money. It was there I met an old man of ninety who was dying of both liver cirrhosis and old age. Every morning as I made his bed we talked and he gradually told me the story of his life. He had spent seventy years getting drunk every night after returning on unexpected leave from the navy to find his wife in bed with a local man. 'Should have killed them both that day,' he said with a far-away look in his eyes. He went on to tell me how, heartbroken, he had lived his life in bar rooms. 'Never once in my entire life went to bed sober before they got me in here,' he proudly boasted. Most mornings I wheeled him on to the patio so he could look out at the lawns with their huge oak trees. 'Look at those birds,' he would say, 'I never noticed them before.' 'Amazing,' he continued, 'they fly without petrol. Clever little things.' As we got more friendly he introduced himself, saying, 'My name's Sidney. What's your's, kid?' 'Stephen,' I replied. 'You could be my grandson,' he smiled. 'Those bastards had ten grandchildren. They're both dead now. She died last year.' He looked lost as he whispered, 'Go and watch the birds fly, watch the wind blow, don't throw it all away like I did.'

A few days later I came down to find his bed was empty and had been stripped. 'Where's Sidney?' I asked another old man. 'Taken the box ride,' he said. 'Box ride?' I queried. 'Coffin, dead,' came back the reply. Leaving my bed-making I sat in the grounds, feeling quite sad. A bird landed near me. 'Clever little things,' I thought.

As the weeks passed the good food began to show it's effect and putting some weight back on I was looking well. After about six weeks I began to notice an attractive nurse from the general hospital who always sat on a bench outside the geriatric ward to have her tea. One day she offered me some extra money to help her on her clothes stall at the annual jumble sale. I was more than pleased to help and we arranged I would start the next day in order to get things ready. Taking me over to the other side of the hospital she showed me a huge room packed with stuff donated by the affluent village community. There were dozens of boxes full of quality second-hand clothes and asking me to sort through them told me I could take whatever I wanted. For me, dressed for the last year in the same old jeans and green tee shirt, this was like opening Aladdin's Clothes Cave. Greedily I filled two enormous suitcases.

She laughed, saying, 'You will never wear that lot if you live to be a hundred !' Not that she cared. There was enough clothes for twenty sales. Besides, all the jumble came from the locals so you would only wind up on the day of the sale with one villager saying to another, 'That's my old coat I gave away. Looks nice on you.'

On the day of the sale I looked a million dollars in my new outfit and with my bed-making money I bought a bedside lamp and a big old radio. Later, back in the alcoholic unit, I felt very proud as I put the radio and lamp either side of my bed. Laying back listening to my music I was beginning to feel almost human. Sadly the next morning, my new found peace quickly vanished when the head nurse popped his head round the door and said, 'Don't get too comfortable. You're leaving soon. Your treatment's over next Thursday.'

I had been addicted for over twenty years and now my treatment was over next Thursday ! This was sheer madness ! It was like telling a child of ten to leave home and fend for himself ! Your time's up number three, you're better. Good luck, good bye !

With only a week to go I panicked but that morning luck smiled on me when in the local paper I found a live-in hotel job in a town nearby. A week later the attractive nurse drove me, with my suitcases, bedside lamp and radio, to the local railway station. I felt good as she kissed me goodbye, it was more of a kiss than a peck. Arriving at Ilkley station with all my luggage I took a short cab ride to the hotel. This is progress, I thought, sitting back in the taxi. Progress ! Oh fuck ! If only I'd known that morning what life still had in store for me !

As I arrived at the hotel the manager met me in the foyer and showed me to my room. 'Welcome

Stephen,' he said, 'I hope you will be happy working here and your stay with us will be a long one.' He was a nice, friendly man who spoke with a London accent. This luxury hotel, situated on the edge of the Yorkshire Moors, had an exclusive clientele and even Prince Charles had once stayed there. I was given a large room overlooking the gardens and that night, listening to my radio, felt like a rich tourist.

The following morning I started washing dishes. I was the only washer-up, so you could say I was in charge of my department. It was a busy kitchen and throughout the day an endless stream of dirty plates arrived on a conveyor belt. During my break periods someone else took the dishes off but just piled them up, leaving a new mountain of work to greet me when I returned.

For the first time I was living in a normal environment but inspite of the pleasant surroundings I soon became very nervous, missing the security of the hospital. Whereas before I had mixed with fellow alcoholics and was treated gently by the nursing staff here it was all so different. I was on my own amongst everyday working people, expected to fit in and become one of them. Nobody took my temperature or concerned themselves about my health anymore. This was the real world. I was just another brick in the wall. Scared stiff I withdrew into myself, unable to speak a single word with my fellow workers. To them I must have appeared the silent weirdo who'd suddenly arrived out of nowhere. Perhaps a serial killer on the move?

As time passed I began to face the reality of where the drugs had taken me. It stunned me. How the fuck had I wound up washing dishes when once I had so much money? Where did it all go? What had happened to me all those years ago? Each day as I stood there working away a poem I once knew started to come back to me - 'Up in the morning with the Lark.....' More and more of my past life started to flash back. Things like buried cash floated in and out of my mind. It was like a jigsaw puzzle slowly coming together.

This avalanche of memories flooding back after so many years terrified me. The electric shock treatment had wiped out so much and now I was remembering things that I never knew existed. How I'd once lived like a king in big houses, driving the best cars. I now could face up to the fact that I hadn't always been a tramp. As the weeks passed it all became clearer. Yes, I could picture myself hiding money, but where? When I tried to concentrate on specific things it all got too much and gave me severe headaches. Never throughout Pound Lane, Phoenix House or Newcastle had I remembered things as clearly as this. During those years my past had ceased to exist. It was as if I was becoming a different person, someone I once knew.

I began to think about my daughters Tessa and Antonia again for the first time in ages. It was like a door in my mind had opened with an inner voice saying - it's okay, you can handle these thoughts now, regardless of the pain. There seemed little prospect of seeing them again but one day I found enough courage to ask a young waitress for help. Remembering the street where my ex-wife had lived I figured if we could trace the number this girl could ring, pretending to be Tessa's friend. Sadly my ex-wife had long moved with no forwarding address. After this the waitress often smiled at me but I always looked away and we never spoke again.

As the months and the dirty dishes passed by I started to walk across the Yorkshire Moors on my days off strolling around for hours in the deserted hills. One afternoon I discovered a small stream in the hillside which ran down to the main brook below. Collecting some large stones I created a sort of dam, diverting the water via a different route. Totally mesmerised I watched the water trickle down it's new path which to me represented a new life, freedom, escape from the past. It was my private world of hope away from all my hurt. Often I sat by my stream, feeling safe, watching my water flow my way.

Sadly away from my steam the peace vanished, I became increasingly tormented as more of the past came back each day. It was all too confusing and slowly began to drive me mad.

On one exceptionally bad day, whilst washing up, I could hear all the other workers laughing loudly during their break in the staff room. When I went to collect my tea the laughing got louder, like giant drums beating inside my head. Looking at these carefree people enjoying each others company I felt threatened and ran from the canteen. I sat in the yard outside but the laughing got noisier than ever. I imagined they were laughing about me, ridiculing the silent weirdo dishwasher. A horrible storm had started to brew inside my head, getting worse all afternoon.

That evening, when I visited my stream, I was horrified to find all the stones had been moved with the water flowing back the old way. I went berserk, smashing the stones to the ground. 'Fucking bastards,' I screamed. 'Those cunts followed me here and stole my river !' The stream was several miles from the hotel but as the wind rose it carried the laughing again. I watched the trees blowing in the wind, even the leaves were laughing at me !

I had been betrayed, cheated once again.

Crying my eyes out I ran back to the village, buying two bottles of brandy in the local store.

Back in the hotel I got drunk and in a fit wrecked my bedroom, even destroying my precious radio. I went absolutely berserk and going downstairs to the kitchen began pulling dishes off the shelves, smashing them onto the floor. In the middle of all the bedlam someone dragged me back to my room and put me to bed where, with the laughing still going round in my head, I passed out.

Early the following morning I was woken by the manager. He was concerned about what had happened and asked why I'd been so upset. This compassionate man had the ability to look deeper than the apparent surface. 'I don't know what happened,' I replied, 'but I'm going back to London.' Inspite of the events of the previous evening he tried to persuade me to stay, saying London was a big town full of the wrong temptations. In tears I said, 'I can't stay now ! I have to go back.'

An hour later as I was getting into a taxi with my suitcases the young waitress came up to me. 'What a shame you're going', she said. 'I liked you. I was hoping you would ask me on one of your walks. I should have spoken to you but I couldn't. I was too shy. Too late now, I guess.........' She smiled. The cab drove off.

Twenty minutes later I was on a train to London. It felt good getting away from Ilkley, away from the people who saw me as a dishwasher. Away from the people who laughed at me. Away from the people who frightened me. This time it was all going to be so different.

As the train pulled out of the Yorkshire station I felt good.............. As the train arrived in London I felt terrible, frightened. I had no home, no job. It all seemed impossible. I was terrified. I didn't want to be a London dishwasher with new people laughing at me.

I needed things to seem better.

I needed to escape from having to face that I'd lost it all through drugs.

In order to escape.

I needed drugs.

Chapter 31

THE END OF THE LINE

Within an hour of returning to London I was on a massive dose of Dexedrine and all the good of the previous year was wiped out. After this long drug-free period confusion hit me worse than ever. I wanted the high but when it came it frightened me. Still desperately trying to cling on to reality I booked myself into a cheap hotel where, in a small top floor room, I nervously unpacked my suitcases. Trying to stay normal I hung my clothes up one by one and wanting to sleep like everybody else took a massive dose of sedatives. Like so many times before, with a huge amount of amphetamine still in my blood stream, the sleepers had the reverse effect. Instead of sleep came torment, but at least I wasn't alone. Sitting at the end of my bed was the Devil who smiled as he said, 'Welcome back !'

When it got to about 3 am, with no chance of going to sleep, I decided to wake up properly and took a handful of Dexedrine. Ten minutes later in the dark of night I left the hotel to aimlessly roam the streets. As dawn broke I wanted to return to my room but by now was so drugged I couldn't remember where the guest house was. Frantically I ran round Victoria, searching for the hotel and rushing about could hear the pills rattling in my pockets. By now I was in such a terrible state that every street looked the same and I was no longer sure which road I'd just been down. I never found that hotel again and lost everything.

Once more all I had left was the clothes I wore. Bewildered and very confused I went to an all-night cafe where all the other drug freaks with their eyes popping out seemed to greet me as I walked in. There, with the last of my money, I bought more cheap back-street amphetamine, the type that bends your mind even further. Within sixteen hours of arriving back in London I'd lost the lot, including my sanity. I was well and truly back in the twilight-zone.

The streets of London felt so lonely and desperate to find someone from my past I remembered Martin, the gay antique dealer from my Church Street days. The walk to Paddington took an hour and arriving there I found Martin chatting to someone outside his new shop. He was still addicted to drink, drugs and gambling and not suprisingly, his life-style had already cost him dearly. Although looking extravagant in his blue velvet suit he now had a jaded look about him. His once immaculately styled brown hair was unkempt. The banks had reclaimed his spacious premises long ago and he now traded from just a small lock-up shop further down the street. It was a long time since we had last seen each other and drugged out of my skull I greeted him, acting like I was the returning hero. Sadly I was unable to see that I was still the same pathetic addict that had left that street with Lanna all those years ago. Martin, already drunk at eleven in the morning, was glad to see someone from his own good old days. We talked about our high times and trying to recapture his own lost magic he suggested I started work for him. Martin, with his all day drinking, and me, stoned out of my head on pills, made the perfect combination. 'Start today,' he said, taking another swig from his bottle. The drug roller-coaster express was roaring its engines, waiting for us to board.

Although on the surface his business still looked quite grand there were none of the fine antiques that he used to trade in, just cheap imitations. In the street outside the shop was now a table piled with pots and pans selling for small change. The whole scene looked false. There was also something very strange about Martin himself. Same man, different song. Gone was the camp arrogance that had made him so successful and now, like his shop, he was just a facade pretending all was well. He was a chronic drinker and whilst not appearing drunk his eyes had a losing look. We addicts all get this look as our lights fuse one by one. As our addictions inevitably destroy our material world at first we try to camouflage our losses, desperately trying to hide what we've done to ourselves.

Martin had three small dogs, two white poodles and a Jack Russell. Watching him that day was like a video repeat of my own life back at Tottenham with Snoopy and the rats. Even his dogs looked beaten, as if they knew their master, who once dealt in priceless works of art, was now a drunken rag and bone man. Six eyes to cut out one day, I thought, thinking back to Snoopy's death. Martin had been on amphetamine and booze for years. From living in an elegant home in London's Abbey Road he had already come quite a long way down the same destructive route as myself. Today, tomorrow, the drug-drink game always finishes the same way.

Sadly, Martin's play was nearly over.

At his invitation that night I stayed with him at the 'American', a small private hotel in Gloucester Place, where he seemed to be living. In the room was one very large bed and stripping off naked he lay back,

317

saying, 'Let's forget our troubles for an hour and have sex.' He had always known I wasn't gay and it upset me to think that here was just another bastard trying to cash in on my situation. I was very hurt. With no sex available Martin drank on and soon passed out, leaving me wide awake all night with three sad dogs under our bed.

The next morning Martin had his usual breakfast in bed, three large brandies, which enabled him to function enough to get dressed. A few drinks later we caught a taxi to his shop for another deranged day.

Returning to the hotel that evening fresh, problems were waiting to greet us. The management insisted Martin paid his bill, refusing him further credit. Martin ranted and raved but eventually we left, taking a cab to his late mother's flat in an exclusive St. John's Wood block. When we arrived an ageing, effeminate man, obviously renting the apartment, opened the door and let us in. Immediately Martin started to argue with the tenant, demanding money. Using me as his strong-arm minder we evicted this not so happy gentleman there and then at eleven in the evening.

Now we moved in and on a heavy dose of sleepers I soon passed out in one of the bedrooms. It was Saturday night and I slept until late Sunday afternoon. When I woke I found Martin totally out for the count and after taking a handful of amphetamine I began to rummage round the flat. What the fuck was going on? There was dog shit, rubbish, dirty clothes and empty booze bottles everywhere. The kitchen was filthy and the toilet stunk. Each room had a mattress on the floor with clothes strewn everywhere. The wilton carpets had gone, leaving only bare floor-boards. I was speechless. Was I looking at the same exclusive flat where we used to visit his late mother? Was this where she had lived, polishing her beautiful antique furniture every day? I started to get frightened, thinking I was being transported back in some time machine to my old flat in West Green Road with the rats. What was Martin doing in Tottenham? I ran outside, relieved to find myself still in the Abbey Road. His filthy hovel finished at his front door. Outside in the communal hall everything was still as immaculate as always with royal blue stair carpet and golden mirrors on the walls.

Martin was breathing heavily in his sleep. I sat at the end of his bed and looking at him began to cry. How had Martin, once one of London's top players, come down to this filth? Oh fuck, ! I cried, what have we done to ourselves? Two playboy princes who once had it all were now broken rejects, paying the price. My sobbing woke him. 'Don't cry, lets buy some drink !' he said. After fumbling about he found seven pounds. 'Is this all the fucking money we've got between us ?' I shouted. 'Seven poxy pounds from all the fortunes we stole?'

There was a long silence as we stared at each other.

Momentarily regaining the camp confidence of old he demanded, 'Do as you're told and get the booze.' An hour later I returned with seven pounds worth of biscuits and other sweet food, the type amphetamine addicts crave for, and slung it all over his bed. 'Where's the fucking booze?' he screamed. 'Bollocks to you !' I shouted as we started hurling abuse at each other. Being the stronger physically I began to threaten him, demanding money to buy drugs with. I went wild and wanted to punish him. In a blind fury I walked out with several expensive leather jackets left over from his money days. These I sold ten minutes later in the nearby gambling club at 21 Abbey Road and soon my pockets were bulging once more with cheap drugs.

Hyperactive I was back to roaming the streets for days on end. My addiction now was worse than ever, I was powerless. The drugs were totally in control. Possessed I just couldn't stop swallowing pills. Martins sex demands had triggered off all the buried pain dating back twenty years. Even when I was blotto the heartache now got through. It hurt bad. Was life paying me back for all the cheating I had done?

That night I finished up in Clapton, a poor part of London, and stumbling onto a bomb site I came across a group of hard-core meths drinkers sitting by their bonfire. They asked me for money and giving them some I was welcomed like royalty. An old lady with a creased face handed me a bottle, saying, 'We love you. Drink this !' She was already very drunk. 'What's your name, little boy?' 'Stephen,' I replied. 'Mine's Mary,' she said, putting her arms round me. By the warm fire I felt like a child again as she held me close. 'Come here, let me be your mother. I had a little boy like you once.' Looking in her face as the meths lit up my belly I could see my mother in her eyes. 'Mummy, give me another sip,' I pleaded. 'Not too much, my little boy,' she replied, holding onto the bottle. 'Mummy, tell me a story,' I cried. The others started to laugh. 'Mother, you're pissed as usual and so is your new baby boy !' 'Shut up, you cunts,' she screamed, 'Fuck off ! He's my baby and he's sad !'

They stood up and walked away, leaving us on our own.

The fire was going out.

'How do you want the story to finish?' she asked.

'It's not the story that counts, it's how it ends that's important.'

She looked at me, screwed up her eyes and swallowed the last of the meths, gripping me tighter. As the flames got smaller her grip started to hurt but I was drifting off. The fire went out. Flickering, it re-lit for a moment, then darkness. Hours later I regained consciousness but couldn't open her hand locked around my wrist. Eventually, like prizing open a vice, I freed myself.

Her eyes stared upwards. She was dead.

I ran and just kept running until I was miles away. When I saw a policeman I rushed up to him, shouting, 'Quick, Mary just died. Went to heaven !' 'So did Jesus, now just keep it quiet and behave,' he replied, walking off.

Over the next few weeks, living in London's Salvation Army shelter at Victoria, I experienced a new tired low, a had enough of it all type low.

Was I nearing the end of my twenty year horror ride? Things were slowing down in my head and in a rare moment of sanity I went to see my mother and brother Paul for the first time in years.

Chapter 32

LOVE CALLS TO SAVE ME

My mother and brother were very relieved to find I was still alive but kept their distance. Alas, my behaviour on drugs was still so outrageous they were too frightened to let me live with them. It would have been impossible for my mum, now an elderly woman, to cope with the daily dramas. In one last do-or-die effort she found me a room and paid one months advance rent in the hope it would lead to something. The bedsit included breakfast supplied by the landlords, an Indian couple, who lived in the adjoining semi. All the tenants ate this morning meal together with them in their family kitchen. On the day I moved in my mother gave me a child's cardboard suitcase, about the size of a shoe box, which she had found years ago in the loft of our family house. It was full of documents and she'd kept them over the years, just in case they were of value. At this stage I was too drugged to be interested and pushed the little brown case under my bed. Could keep pills in there, I thought. Two days later my mother phoned and told me that unless I stopped moving around all night I would be thrown out of the lodgings. The other tenants had complained about the noise I made in the early hours. As usual I couldn't sleep with large quantities of amphetamine keeping me awake for days on end.

Meanwhile back in the familiar streets of London I began to look at buildings, thinking to myself - was it in that house I hid cash? It was impossible to work it out, I still couldn't piece the past together. Anyhow, for the moment I was more interested in getting drugs. I started shoplifting again and with the proceeds bought more back-street pills, a huge quantity, which I stored under my bed. Not wanting to lose the security of the room I now had to find a drug that would guarantee I slept at night. With that in mind went to see Dr. Lando. There he was, still dishing out his pills in Harley Street and without looking up asked as he'd always done, 'Well what's the problem?' I walked over to the lights and turning them off said, 'This is me going to sleep. I must pass out within minutes. I trust you understand, doc.' 'Put the light on and sit down,' he said, writing out a prescription for a hundred of the strongest barbiturates yet invented. 'Don't take more than two or you will be asleep forever.' he warned. 'Are you sure I will sleep?' I asked as I paid him. 'Very sure,' he smiled.

Leaving Harley Street I went to visit Louisa and Laura, my ex-wife's younger sisters who had lived for many years in the fashionable Kings Road, Chelsea. The drugged-up hero who'd rescued the three young children from Malta had occasionally begged them for drug-money throughout his tramp years. Those little girls in white ankle socks were now very attractive young ladies, enjoying the jet-set life of London. On the times I did find them I was in such a state and behaved so badly they were too frightened to let me in and would just throw money down to me from their window. Passers-by looked on in bewilderment as a scruffy tramp called out, 'Louisa, Laura ! I need money,' at which a beautiful woman appeared at the window, shouting, 'Hold on. I'm looking for my purse.' This left the onlookers even more puzzled.

Little did I know that it was this particular October day which was to alter my entire life. Laura was in on her own and waving down to me dropped a

323

few pounds from the window. She had long given up trying to help me any further. What was the point when all the doctors and so many others had failed to stop my life-time addiction. Like Louisa, she merely gave me something, patted me like a sick dog and sent me back to roam the streets.

After twenty years on speed I was now just like a chemically fuelled machine, unable to function without drugs, a totally lost cause. I picked up the coins and walked down the King's Road to go into the 'Chelsea Potter' - not for a drink but merely to use the toilet for water to swallow my pills. The bar was just opening with only one or two customers at the counter. Why the following happened I will never know but after taking my tablets I stopped to have a beer. This was very unusual because to an addict like myself a beer does nothing, and besides, any money I had always went on drugs.

As I paid for my drink I looked up and saw a beautiful young girl with golden brown hair and blue eyes smiling at me. I was stunned. Where had she appeared from? Surely she wasn't smiling at a gypsy like me. I turned to look round but there was no-one behind me, just the silent juke box. Puzzled, convinced I was imagining things, I sipped my beer and looked at her again. She was still smiling. What did I see? Was this life walking back to me? I stood there for an eternity, trying to say something. Speechless, I looked into her eyes. How could this girl be looking at a hobo like me? Again I turned round but still there was no-one.

Too withdrawn to accept this invitation back to life I just stared. I was falling in love. Not with an ageing nanny and her Robin Hood stories. Not with a

Maltese film star image. Not with the instant karma of drugs. I was falling in love with this young girl. I wanted to speak but I couldn't. I just stared at her for an eternity. She just looked back into my eyes as if she already knew the whole story.

I went back to the toilet to take more pills for courage, feeling more frightened than I'd ever been of all the gangsters and killers put together. I was in love. Going back to the bar I wondered if this Casablanca stranger would be gone, leaving Sam too drugged up to ever play it again - she was still waiting !

With my heart pounding I said, 'Hello, can I buy you a drink? I'm only a temporary embarrassment. Please, say yes.' She accepted and this broken man, destroyed by a life-time of drug addiction, proudly led her over to the table by the juke box.

We talked and laughed. It was the first time I'd laughed in ten years. She told me her name was Hannelore. She came from Bavaria, Germany, and was here on a week's vacation. Choosing songs together we sat there as if the rest of the world had ceased to exist. 'I once lived like a king. Lost it all,' I sobbed, shaking my head. We sat for a few moments, looking at each other, then, wiping my eyes I bought two more beers, putting the last of the money in the juke box. 'You choose the last two songs. You're my guest, the nicest guest I ever had,' I smiled.

This was my moment of dignity.

I was paying for my date, picking up the tab like in the old days.

We listened to more songs and after finishing our drinks I walked with her to Sloane Square tube station where we said goodbye. On parting I asked her to ring me at my mother's so perhaps we could meet one last time before she flew back. A new softer bell was ringing inside my head. Her eyes had said it all.

Back at my bedsit I took four of the light-switch sleepers, putting myself out for two solid days. Waking up after laying in the same position for probably twenty hours I had stiffness in my bones and that day it took many amphetamine tablets to get me off the bed. I was not alone in that room. There was a movie of hope on show inside my head. Watching it with me were more celebrities than at any Hollywood movie premiere - Elvis, Marilyn, Jimmy Hendrix, Brian Jones. They were all so happy for me as we all took our pills together.

A day or so later Hannelore phoned my mother, leaving the name of her hotel and a time for us to meet that Sunday morning. Sadly when the day came I'd been on a three-day drug binge and arrived in a terrible state. I had no money and suggested we took a walk in the nearby Hyde Park.

Savaged by the latest drug binge I couldn't walk for long and after a few minutes we had to sit down on a bench. Suddenly I began to feel ill thinking I was about to pass out. Not wanting Hannelore to see me collapse I explained I had to leave soon. Before parting I wanted just a few last precious moments together and asked a woman sitting on the bench opposite for some bread to feed the birds.

We walked a little further into the park where we sat down to feed our own sparrows. When all the bread had gone I said goodbye. Hannelore looked bewildered as I walked away. We'd only been together for twenty short minutes. I waited, then turning to wave found my princess had already left. She'd vanished through the park gate to join the other tourists enjoying the sights of

London. Returning to the bench I took some barbiturates and watched as the birds ate the last of our crumbs. It was late that night when I woke. They were locking the park and like a sick dog I made my way back to my little room.

We were unlikely to ever see each other again but I had a vision. Someone, somewhere knew my name, remembered me, remembered our birds in the park. I was no longer alone. I knew someone - someone knew me.

Although still hopelessly addicted I was now more at peace than ever before in my life. Somehow everything around me looked better. Had this entire book already been written in the scrolls of life? Inside my head the wild horses were peacefully grazing as I began to reduce the amount of drugs I took. I even started joining the other tenants for breakfast. The mystery man from the small front room was up and about, telling everyone of his German girlfriend and the birds they had fed together. Under some kind of magic spell I began to behave quite normally to the delight of my mother and the landlords. During the day, instead of roaming the drug districts, I went for long walks in the park. I now slept every night.

Several weeks later my mother arranged for two doctors and a social worker to talk with me at her flat. The meeting was a miracle in itself because by now every psychiatric hospital in London had given up on me. She had pleaded with them to give me one last try as an in-patient. The doctors quizzed me for over an hour and eventually agreed to take me back to the hospital in their car. As we left my mother's flat the postman handed me a letter with a German postmark on it. 'I knew it would come,' I smiled.

Life in the hospital turned out a new experience. Secretly, without the staff knowing, I still took drugs but only four pills a day. Compared with the previous handfuls this was a spit in the ocean. The four pills allowed me, a long term amphetamine addict, to communicate as against suffering the complete isolation always brought on by instant withdrawal. I'm not a doctor and have mixed feelings about controlled withdrawal of drugs as against cold turkey, especially in the early days. A long term addict like me needs slow, ongoing treatment over a considerable period. I couldn't be treated, cured and released in the usual eight weeks. One senior male nurse who believed in on-going rehabilitation always said, 'You can look happy, we won't send you home.' Sadly his views were not shared by the female head nurse shortly to give me the kiss of death.

I read the letter from Hannelore all day, every day, showing it to every patient and nurse that crossed my path, always saying, 'Careful with the photograph.' The entire hospital went through the compulsory viewing ritual every time they saw me. Taking so few uppers, even with the mild hospital sedatives, I slept every night. Sometimes in bed I began to think about all the institutions I had been in. Doreen, Fatso, Do Die, Roger the postman.... where were they all now? This is my last dance back to normality, I thought. I must tread with care.

As time passed I got a job as a sweeper with a local firm whilst still living in the hospital, paying a small sum for my keep. Carefully taking my four pills a day I never exceeded the dose, fearing if I did not sleep I'd be thrown out in the street. At work I was given three brooms and instructed by the foreman which broom to use where. I hated the work but aided by the drugs kept on sweeping. One day I suggested a better way of doing the job but the supervisor replied, 'No thinking in here, mate, just sweeping.' The continued control of drugs, regular food and sleep were showing their effects - I not only looked better but could think clearer than I had done for a long time. I was clawing my way back to normality but didn't like what I was being introduced to. Looking at my fellow workers, many of whom had been in the same job for twenty years, I often felt that I was swapping one type of imprisonment for another.

I wrote back to Hannelore, boldly suggesting we met for Christmas and she could either come to my flat or I would go to Germany. My flat? What flat? I was living in the upstairs ward of a psychiatric hospital. Thank God she replied, suggesting I came to Germany. I was over the moon, happier than ever before in my life. As I swept by every worker at his lathe had to stop work, read her letter and hear about my Christmas trip.

It wasn't drugs making my head spin now, it was a young German girl. After years of living on skid row and sleeping in toilet cubicles I was preparing to leave on a winter vacation in the mountains of Bavaria !

At breakfast one morning I met two alarm engineers who worked for a major security company. They were installing a fire alarm in the hospital. I appeared quite normal to the outside world now and one of them remarked, 'You don't seem so ill mate. Nothing mad about you.' Over the weeks we got quite friendly and I began to brag about past escapades I was remembering again, including various robberies from the early years. At first they took my tales with a pinch of salt until I mentioned the name of a robber the head engineer knew well. He asked me several questions about this character and satisfied with the answers winked at me. This man drove a much bigger car than his colleague and often secretly had sex with a female patient in a cupboard. He was a wild one.

As I came out of work one day I found him waiting outside in his car. Taking me for a drive he told me about a big country estate in Virginia Water which I shall refer to as 'County Hall'. He'd recently installed an alarm system at the premises for his firm and knew that a million pounds in cash was hidden in the bedroom wall-safe. The owner of this mansion was himself a well-known criminal character. The engineer explained in detail how access could be gained by cutting a hole into the roof, bypassing the alarm system. Upstairs only the windows were wired up. Hearing about the millions I became excited and thought that even if I couldn't open the safe I could drag the whole thing out through the roof. Not exactly the vaults of Lloyd's in Baker Street, I mused, but it would surely finance my new love life. He went on to tell me that the mansion was set in secluded grounds. With this set up the safe could be transported on a trailer behind a scrambler bike to the perimeter fence, then loaded into a waiting van. If problems arose I would unlock the trailer and with the police arriving down the main drive my escape would be easy through the wooded area where no car could chase me.

Oh boy ! Here I was, an ex street vagrant, having breakfast in a psychiatric ward putting together the finer points on a million-pound-robbery before leaving for my overseas winter vacation ! I was right back to where Gentleman George had left me so many years ago. The alarm engineer wanted twenty percent in return for all the details to which I agreed. As he dropped me off he gave me a contact number. The robbery at 'County Hall' was on. Thank God at this stage I wasn't on mega quantities of amphetamine or I would have attempted the job that afternoon by local bus. Thinking far more rationally I was able to consider the consequences and having found love didn't want a long prison sentence. Whatever I did or didn't do - it would all have to wait till after Christmas.

A week later it was vacation time and I felt very excited, having saved all my wages to buy my air ticket. The night before leaving I proudly reported to the head nurse that I would be away for five days over the Christmas period, visiting my German girlfriend. I expected her to be pleased but it was the exact opposite. I was devastated and couldn't believe my ears as this nurse curtly replied, 'If you go to Germany you will be discharged from this hospital.' Without consulting the staff who saw me every day she made this private and egotistical decision. Her ultimatum meant if I left for my five days made in heaven I would lose my safe bed when I returned. No longer would I have regular meals, a local job and nurses to talk to at night. 'Well,' she said 'What are you going to do?'

My answer was, 'Go fuck yourself. I'm going !'

Without batting an eye-lid she calmly replied,

'When you leave in the morning you are out for good.' Nice woman, caring nurse.

The Spanish hospital cook woke me early the next day with lots of sandwiches for my trip. She kissed me on the cheek, wishing me luck, and with all the other kitchen staff waving I left for a small village outside Munich dressed in my new charity shop overcoat.

I was about to experience the happiest five days any human being ever had here on planet earth.

Chapter 33

CHRISTMAS IN WONDERLAND

Try to picture the scene. Here I was, a man hopelessly addicted to amphetamine all his life who had lived the last ten years on the edge of reality. After a decade either in the gutter or locked asylums I was now having breakfast on Lufthansa flying to Germany. With my drugs seemingly under control, a million pound robbery on ice and a beautiful woman waiting for me I felt fucking marvellous, to say the least. It was like a fairy story but, excited as I was, I also felt very nervous. I was in love but there was a problem. Hannelore was the first person I'd spoken to for many years. Re-entering real life was very scary. Would we hold hands or even kiss? Would I take my clothes off and get sexually excited, make love to her? Was I clean? Did I smell? This was all a long way from the street benches and the living dead of Newcastle. What do normal people talk about outside institutions? Who talks? Perhaps I would have to listen and give my opinion. Fuck, it felt like I was becoming a doctor myself now. I'd only been with this girl for twenty short minutes in the park, feeding our birds, but the impact she'd made on my life was monumental. For the first time I had found real love.

Even addicts can fall in love.

I must keep cool, I mustn't blow this one, I thought as the plane landed at Frankfurt airport. I should have flown to Munich but in my stoned excitement had come to Frankfurt by mistake, discovering I now had a four hour train ride ahead of me. At least I was in the right country, which for me was one hell of an improvement.

The Christmas scene that unfolded on the journey was as if Santa Claus was opening the pages of a real-life picture book outside the carriage windows. With thick snow falling over the German countryside we passed little villages lit up like candles. Through the windows I could see the twinkling lights of Christmas trees. Here were normal families who gave each other presents. They belonged. Belonging to anybody was something I hadn't done for a long time.

Had I ever?

Missing the right train connection twice the journey took forever and I was beginning to feel the drug come-down. Determined not to blow it I resisted an extra pill, opting instead for a small swig from the brandy I'd bought as a gift for Hannelore's parents. Carefully removing the wrapper I took one swig and topped the bottle with water so her mum and dad would still have their present. Finally the train arrived at the local station from where I took a twenty minute bus ride to Hannelore's tiny village. Getting off the bus I telephoned her house as arranged and was told to wait by the phone box. It was snowing heavy again.

Five minutes later Hannelore's younger sister arrived on foot and greeting me in broken English said, 'You must be Stephen let me carry your bag. Follow me.' Walking through the fresh snow it felt like time

333

had stopped. The streets were deserted and turning round I saw our footprints behind us in the snow. It was as if the torment of the previous twenty years was vanishing.

The world I was apprehensively entering into was one where normal people lived and died without drugs.

Within minutes we came to a very big house, a mansion in my eyes. Her sister told me that Hannelore was driving home from another town and would be back in an hour's time. In the enormous lounge I was introduced to her parents, a typical Bavarian couple. I gave them the slightly diluted brandy which they put up on a high shelf. 'Strange place to put it,' I thought. 'If they don't drink it, I will.' Like a child I sat there mesmerised by this strange scene. A huge Christmas tree with real candles stood in the corner. Underneath the tree were presents of all shapes and sizes. I was sitting at the end of the rainbow in a pot of family love.

So this was where this young girl I'd left in the park had come from. This was her world - so far away from psychiatric wards, prison cells and park benches. For me to be part of their Christmas was a kind of magic. Again feeling the edge of the amphetamine wearing off I went to the toilet to swallow half of a mild sleeping pill to calm down. Feeling better I sat back on the sofa to drink a beer and at my request the little sister played Mozart on the family piano. Listening to the music I felt like it had been written just for me in Salzburg two hundred years ago. Two beers later, cautiously refusing the third, I felt hazy and momentarily closed my eyes. As I dropped off I reflected over the past..... Dr. Newam, the gay psychiatrist and my first pill. Gentleman George and the jewel robberies. The gangsters, the killers, the asylums, the prisons.

Was I asleep, dreaming?

Was I drunk on a street bench?

Was I about to wake up in a desolate mission with all those lonely faces?

I could feel myself drifting when ....

Someone was by my side, holding my hand.

'You were asleep. You looked so peaceful, like a little boy.' I heard Hannelore's soft voice as she kissed my forehead, saying, 'Happy Christmas, Stephen. Welcome to Germany, welcome to my family.' I felt so safe, those eyes said it all over again. The birds from Hyde park were back, eating whole loafs of bread this time. We chatted with her parents for a while but by now it was quite late and standing up I said goodnight to the family. As we left the room Hannelore's mother remarked, 'You were asleep, in another world.' 'I was. For a long time,' I replied. 'For over twenty years.'

Upstairs Hannelore showed me to my bedroom, a cosy room with wooden eaves. She smiled, asking whether she should stay or leave. 'Stay,' I replied, 'I love you. Let's get married.' 'That's a bit sudden,' she laughed. I started again, 'I love you. Stay with me forever. I'll buy you a castle, cover you in diamonds.' I went on and on, undeterred. 'I don't need any castles. I live here and diamonds would look silly on me. I'm happy just to be with you. Silly boy.' Holding each other we lay down on the bed - two people from totally different worlds. Alone at last we made love, falling even more in love with each other. Later, forgetting to take my sleeping pills, I fell asleep with her still by my side.

I woke early the next morning. It was Christmas day and looking out of the window everything in the garden was white, the big trees were dripping with snow. This was no dream. I was awake in a real-life happy story and what was more, I was the leading player in it !

I wanted to take my morning amphetamine but was too scared to do so in the bedroom in case my sleeping beauty woke up. Silently I crept into the toilet and took two. When I returned I stared at this intelligent twenty-four-year-old girl from a good family, wondering what she saw in a gypsy like me. Sleeping there in her yellow pyjamas she looked like a sunflower. I woke her with a kiss, saying, 'Marry me, I've got a big earner coming up, we can have everything, County Hall, a million pounds.' I rambled on and on. 'What hall? A million pounds? I don't understand, you speak to quickly,' she replied, a bit perplexed. 'Marry you? We've only known each other for eight hours and most of those we were asleep. Can I have till after breakfast to consider it, Mr. Englishman?' She got up, leading me to the bathroom where she poured a hot bath and went downstairs to make coffee.

I was now the happiest person in God's universe. Hot morning bath, beautiful girl, this was a miracle. I was alive again. Laying back in the hot suds I closed my eyes when suddenly a nightmare vision struck me.

Was all this a dream?

When does the horror movie begin again, like it always did?

Was I back with the gold mirrors of gay doctor Newam's bathroom where the drug roller-coaster ride began all those years ago? Panicking I jumped out of the bath and dripping water all over the floor opened the bathroom cabinet, expecting to find drugs in rows of pill-bottles. To my relief there were only toothbrushes and shaving cream - this was a normal family home.

'What are you looking for?' I turned to find Hannelore standing behind me naked. She locked the door and we made love. Her mum's Bavarian breakfast could wait. I was getting all I wanted on the bathroom floor.

Later we went downstairs and meeting the whole family around the table I felt very uneasy. For the next few days I had to become a normal person. I'd played a few parts before, but normality was a new one. I didn't know the lines and even today I'm not so sure of the script. I just improvise. Very anxious I held Hannelore's hand under the table so tight that for a while she couldn't eat. Sensing my nerves she whispered to me not to be afraid so I let go and we ate the home-made muesli and rolls.

That morning we visited a lake nearby. The weather was ice cold and walking round we watched families skate together on the frozen ice. Children, mums and dads all laughing with each other, not at me anymore. Seeing the kids play I wondered where this fairy story would lead to. Perhaps one day........? I was one of life's players again, very nervous but back off the substitutes bench. I didn't need to score last minute goals that morning, I was more than happy to be in the team.

What words can describe the following days? We visited ancient castles, walked in the woods, saw the street markets, ate wonderful meals, heard church bells ring. The magic went on and on.

Alone with Hannelore I felt safe but one evening, when we visited a friend's house for drinks I became very uneasy. I was introduced to about ten young people all of whom were friendly and seemed to speak good English. Full of drugs it would have been so different. I could have impressed them with stories of London. Full of drugs I would have been the hero, suggesting we all went out on the town or had a wild party. Full of drugs I would have been Mr. Clever Dick - but without my life-long crutches of heavy doses of speed I felt so exposed, so fragile. I prayed the evening would pass quickly so we could leave and be on our own again. Whenever people asked me how I was or how I liked Germany I tailored my answers to what I thought they wanted to hear. For me it was like I was on trial, needing their approval for even knowing Hannelore.

On the day before I was due to return to London Hannelore took me to Munich. After seeing all the sights and a winter walk in the English Garden we had a meal in a traditional Bavarian Gasthouse. It looked very expensive but Hannelore insisted I ate venison. A beautiful meal arrived. I couldn't take it anymore and started to cry. 'Why are you crying?' she asked, reaching across the table to take my hand. 'Because this is all a wonderful dream but I know its going to end tomorrow.' 'Why, it doesn't have to end. We can see each other again,' she said. 'Come back with me tomorrow,' I pleaded. 'We can find somewhere to live.' 'How can I just come to England with you? I can't. I've got a job and besides, we have to live somewhere, we can't sleep on a park bench !'

She'd made her point without realising it. I couldn't reply.

'You go back first and I will follow in a month or so after you've set everything up', she finally suggested.

Of course she knew nothing of my past, taking only the fantasy present.

I wanted to tell her I was on drugs and that I lived in a psychiatric ward but the words wouldn't come out. For the rest of the meal I sat in silence, unable to face the daunting reality that tomorrow I would be on my way back to the empty streets of London. Could I ever hope to see her again? I had nothing, no money, no home, no friends and no hope of giving up drugs. I was still addicted.

Early the next morning she drove me to the local railway station from where I caught the train to Frankfurt.

As the train pulled away I leaned out the window, waving and crying long after Hannelore was out of sight.

Chapter 34

A LITTLE KILLER STRIKES WITH BIG BLOWS

At first I was okay sitting on the Frankfurt train but the further I got away from Hannelore the more alone I felt. How would I find a home for us to live in? Come to that, where would I sleep that night now the bed and the security of the hospital were gone? Since I'd arrived with very little cash Hannelore had paid for the fairy-tale entertainment over the Christmas period. Now I'd tasted life I wanted to be a big shot again not a bloody factory sweeper.

If my bed had been available at Barnet Hospital I believe I would have returned that day to tell the Spanish kitchen girls all about my Christmas. It would have given me perhaps just a little time. Time to do what? To carry out the robbery, get away with it. Live with Hannelore happy ever after in a sunshine villa? To get caught and serve ten years in jail? Would Hannelore have waited for my release? Maybe I would have come to my senses and not done the robbery at all. Maybe I would have got a better job and saved up for a small flat. Off mega doses of amphetamine all these options would have been available but now there was nowhere to go. The storm between my ears was brewing with a vengeance as my fear and confusion grew. I couldn't face this frightening uncertainty. I needed an answer, a way to make myself into the winner of old, to recapture the glory-days. I had to find this answer and quick !

Looking in my bag the answer was staring me in the face - a bottle of amphetamine tablets. Still hopelessly addicted I swallowed half the pills in the bottle. Twenty minutes later as the drugs took over all my problems were instantly solved. A multitude of brilliant ideas, each one better than the last, rushed in and out of my head. As the evil madness re-exploded I looked up and sitting in the carriage opposite me was the Devil, back from his winter vacation, 'Welcome back.' he smiled. Engulfed in lunatic bliss I was no longer able to just sit down and rushed around in the corridor, shouting incoherent rubbish at the top of my voice which frightened my fellow passengers. The worst five day mayhem of my entire life had begun. It ended close to death.

At Frankfurt airport I acted so mad that it was a marvel I was even allowed to board the plane. With the last of my money I bought a bottle of whisky from the duty-free shop which fuelled the drugs even more, like throwing petrol over a coal fire. After the plane took off the combined atom bomb of whisky and pills exploded as I began to write the first of numerous love-letters to Hannelore. As the passion in me built up I persuaded the hostess to let me accompany a young child who was visiting the pilot to see the controls. I drove the cockpit crew mad, asking them to fly via Munich, 'Just for an hour so I can see Hannelore.' I begged the pilot. 'Ring her on the radio I'll pay, I've got millions stashed away !' My monologue went on and on. At first the pilots were amused and laughed but soon it started to get out of hand and I was escorted back to my seat by two stewards. One of them stayed with me for the remainder of the flight. The crew and all the passengers were more than relieved to get rid of me when we landed at Heathrow.

With all my money gone I went straight back to Soho, London's red light district, where it had all started over twenty years ago. I was on my final tightrope crossing, courting the inevitable disaster, but this time all the safety nets had long gone. Still high as a kite I went to one of my old haunts, a gay pub, where I begged for money. My story made the drink-merry customers laugh and I raised almost thirty pounds. With my new-found cash I went to Leicester Square, buying more cheap pills and with these chemicals roaring through my brain it was back to roaming the streets.

Going round those familiar haunts my drugged mind became so confused I believed I was back in 1960 ! I was looking for clubs in buildings that had long been pulled down to make way for new office blocks. Twice I went into the same pub within an hour, each time asking for the 'Two I's Cafe' where Tommy Steele had once performed. 'I fucking told you before, it went over twenty years ago. Fuck off and go home !' said the irate barman.

Home? I had no home.

Outside the pub I watched an old tramp slumped in a shop doorway, an older version of me. Was I looking at myself in twenty years time?

With my drugged mind out of control it was too late, there was no stopping my head now travelling at the speed of light. The goal-posts in my brain hadn't been moved, they were burning as my frenzy continued throughout the night.

The next morning I sat on a bench and totally disorientated my thoughts spun round. Shall I go to Newcastle, Phoenix House, West Green Road? I couldn't work out where I was or which year I was living in. Feeding the volcanic drug lava inside me on the hour I was on collision course with something dark, something bad. This was my final kamikaze nose-dive to a disaster. A fate predestined to happen to me since I was fourteen years old.

Deranged I spent most of that day going in and out of banks all over London, insisting I had opened an account sometime in the last twenty years in one name or another. 'Eric Shepherd, John Kimble, I must be here under some name !' I screamed. 'I want my money to bring Hannelore over !' 'No Sir, not in any of those names,' came back the replies. The ironic thing was that lots of money was found but not till many more years were to pass.

I was desperate, believing that if I didn't find the money within a few days I would lose Hannelore forever. It's got to be the robbery at County Hall, I decided. The fact that I had no scrambler bike, van or tools to cut the roof made no odds to my drug-soaked senses as I rode the trains without paying the fare to Virginia Water. After looking round the exclusive tree-lined streets for a while I came across an enormous property. I believed I had found County Hall. Whether it was or not made little difference to this lunatic, now into his third drug day.

The property backed onto a wood from where I climbed into the large grounds. Suddenly I heard barking and only just climbed back over the wall as a large Doberman took a bite at my leg. His teeth tore my trousers but thinking, I'll kill the dog when I return, I took more pills and went to the village in search of a motor bike. In a supermarket car park I found what I was looking for. With no keys or possible means of starting it I climbed on. Promptly the bike fell over, pinning me to the ground and only with great difficulty did I manage to free myself and run away.

Even more mixed up now I returned to Central London, spending the night looking for more people and places I'd left behind a decade ago.

On day five without sleep I returned to Barnet hospital, looking for John, my room mate from the psychiatric ward. John, whose breakdown had been caused by his wife leaving him, had also been discharged but I found him sleeping in his car at the rear of the hospital. John was fond of me and now I persuaded him to finance a hotel room where we could both live for the time being. This I thought, would give me time to find a flat so Hannelore could come over. Later that day we booked into a small hotel in Highgate where we were given a large room at the very top, up two long flights of stairs.

John lent me ten pounds and leaving him in the bedroom I went out again, looking for various characters with whom I'd committed crimes with years before. I went to South London where every pub I visited now looked the same. Even the people inside looked the same. Exactly where I'll never know but I had a bad argument with someone and ran away from one pub, taking a minicab back to Highgate. Outside our hotel I got into another row, this time with the driver, because I didn't have enough money to pay his fare. While we shouted at each other a large car with blacked out windows pulled up opposite. I couldn't see inside and getting frightened ran into the hotel. It was now about 10 pm.

I double-locked the bedroom door, feeling very strange. Something evil was hanging over me. The cloud was about to burst. The hammer was about to fall. I took a handful of sedatives and as the dizziness swept over me I began talking for what seemed like hours to the ever attentive John.

I rambled on and on about Halliwick, the first drug, Gentleman George, jewel robberies, rich gay stockbrokers, big houses, my night-club, the Krays, Malta, six white horses, Polish tramps, rock cakes, Lanna, a burning bed, hidden cars, Clara, fights with Little Legs, Mary the dead wino, smelly socks in Newcastle, giant policeman worms, black horses, Snoopy and the rats, monsters with long noses, suicide, little streams on the moors, stabbing Violet, my father's last words, hosed down like a leper, Scotland Yard, Martin, wriggling fish, terror with Tessa, meeting Hannelore.

Throughout those drug years I had got away with it all and beaten life's odds. I only stopped talking when I noticed John had fallen asleep and finally began drifting off myself.

Suddenly - A short dark person is screaming at me. His face is right in front of me. He shouts, 'I'll kill the cunt, let me kill him !' I can sense others but half unconscious on barbiturates all is foggy. He's crazed, drunk, foaming at the mouth. He's pulling me up. I am falling down a long flight of stairs. Pain. More pain. I'm at the bottom. Everything is spinning. There's shouting at the top of the stairs. The voice is getting closer. Someone is standing over me, hitting me with a baseball bat. I know his face.

It's ....

Bang ! Lights flash inside my head. He has hit me again.

I see the bat coming down. More flashes. Pain, excruciating pain.

I desperately try to cover up but still the blows ·rain down on me.

Then it all goes black.

It finally happened.

I caught my first glimpse of consciousness in a strange bed several days later. I had no recollection of what had happened, just visions of a baseball bat and the world exploding. So many times before I had woken up in hospitals after overdosing - but this time it was different. I was in pain, I was hurting all over. I couldn't move, my body felt paralysed and one of my eyes was shut. With the open eye I could see bars on the bed, like on a child's cot. I was alive but where was I? It all went black again, as if I was falling through to the centre of the earth.

Sometime later I felt the pain return. I still couldn't see anything but sensed there were people in the room. I heard someone say, 'You've been hurt badly. I'll get the nurse.' Soon I could see a blurred face. 'Keep still, the doctors are coming,' she said and it all went blank again, nothing. The next few days just blended into each other as I regained and lost consciousness.

For so many years I had ignored life's final demands and got away with the bill. Now a part of me had been permanently disconnected. Several days later I opened my eyes to see my brother Paul standing at my bedside. 'Please tell Hannelore I love her. I need her,' I pleaded, still unable to move. Promising he would and patting my hand Paul left so the nurses would allow my elderly mother to come in.

Leaning over me she cried with her tears falling onto my battered face. This was the first and only time I ever saw her cry. My mother, the woman whose love I had always craved for, had finally arrived. She had come to see her addicted little boy, beaten and badly hurt. Now an old woman, she burst open with all the motherly love she'd never shown before. Bending over the bed she kissed my face. I was paralysed and couldn't feel her lips. I had lost all the feeling in my body but what the fuck, I'd found my mum !

The drug withdrawal coupled with my horrific injuries was like cold turkey at the gates of hell. One morning when I was convinced I was about to die, an enormous bunch of flowers arrived. The nurse read out the card.

'I will always love you, Hannelore.'

Over the days that followed I merely lay on my back unable to move and watched the petals drop one by one as the flowers, like me, slowly died. I will never know what medical investigations took place at the

347

Whittington because at the time of writing this book they claim to have no record of me ever being in that hospital. I believe in view of what was to follow they destroyed the records.

A short time later, unable to walk, with blood seeping out of my deaf ear, double vision and the pain in my head getting worse every day I was told to leave. I have always maintained I was discharged because I took the beating under a self-induced drug overdose. The stigma of being a drug addict nearly cost me my life.

My mother collected me, protesting that I was too ill to leave. It was preposterous, but what could an old woman do? Put up a shotgun and say, 'Keep my son there and operate or I'll shoot !' Later it was found that if I hadn't received a lengthy operation, closing the badly fractured skull and ear, otogenous meningitis or an abscess of the brain would have resulted in my certain death.

I was very ill and back at my mother's flat lay down on her bed. That's where I stayed, too weak to move. All I did was write up to four letters a day to Germany. The days passed but I was getting worse, my vision was now so bad I couldn't see enough to write anymore. One day I remembered I still had two weeks wages owing to me from the sweeping job and persuaded my mum to collect it, which she did. A day or so later while my mother was out shopping I took a taxi to Dr. Lando's surgery. I was hardly able to walk but inspite of my obvious injuries he gave me the usual prescription for a large quantity of amphetamine without looking up.

I didn't take any of the drugs and returned to my mother's where I hid them. This was, ironically, the only time in my entire life when I wasn't looking for the high, just the strength to see Hannelore one last time before I died. Over the previous week I had lied to her on the phone, saying I was much better and we now had a place to live. Believing me she had agreed to come over and was due to arrive that Saturday with the boat train.

Somewhere to live? It was a local bed and breakfast hotel. With the last of the money I'd paid for a few days in advance, that was our lot.

Unbeknown to Hannelore all I had to offer was one horrific list of injuries and a pocket full of drugs.

I rested until early Saturday morning. With the train due in four hours time I swallowed the first handful of amphetamine pills. An hour later I'd gone totally mad. Instead of having an emergency operation I was charging back to drug island like a raging bull.

Chapter 35

HORROR TRIP TO HOLYHEAD

I was a desperately sick man waiting to meet Hannelore that morning and as time was to prove, the Whittington Hospital had discharged someone urgently in need of a life-saving operation. It was only the amphetamine that made me strong and mad enough to even attempt to walk, let alone travel to Victoria Railway Station. I loved Hannelore and couldn't live without her but nor could I live without drugs. To give up amphetamine for the rest of my life was like asking me to stop breathing.

That morning, continually falling over I was in danger of dying from a brain haemorrhage. At first I waited by the ticket collector for the train to arrive. Then, unable to keep standing I sat on the cold station floor with my back propped against a pillar. I must have looked like a drunk vagrant to the policeman who came over to move me on. 'I'm just waiting for Hannelore,' I pleaded. 'We're all waiting for her,' he laughed, telling me again to leave the station. Fortunately while we argued the train had arrived and looking up I suddenly saw Hannelore standing over me.

There was a look of horror and disbelief on her face when she found me slumped to the ground, beaten half to death. The left side of my face was lifeless, totally paralysed, and I still looked somehow green and yellow from the extensive bruising. What greeted her that Saturday morning was so different from the well-behaved man she'd waved goodbye to in Germany several weeks earlier. Worse than all my injuries was my behaviour. She was now meeting a lunatic whose brain was floating in a sea of drugs. Unable to believe her eyes and uncertain of what to do she helped me into the station buffet. Here we sat down, two people from different worlds who, having fallen in love, were now leading players in a real-life horror movie.

Before my beating, I'd been the good-looking mystery man from the big city, so different from the normal humdrum village boys Hannelore had grown up with. I was her ticket to leave behind the drabness of local life that bored her so much. Our only common denominator was that we loved each other.

But love with an addict can only end in disaster.

The worst ten days of Hannelore's life were about to begin. She'd given up her job to come to England for a new life. Now it was dawning on her that the man she'd fallen in love with was not only half dead but also a hopeless drug addict - one spaced out Humpty Dumpty that all the King's doctors could never put together again !

Sitting in the station cafe totally bewildered this young girl now alone in a foreign country heard the first of my deranged ramblings. 'Did you bring the car?' I asked someone who'd just got off a train. 'We need it for the County Hall robbery, I'm too unsteady for the scrambler bike.' My drug-soaked mind was in another world altogether to that of my young companion on that cold winter morning. 'You must lay down, you're very ill. You must see a doctor,' she kept saying. She began to cry as she handed me a single red rose. Taking the flower I imagined myself in a coffin down a deep hole looking up at her dressed in black.

I was in great pain and with considerable difficulty we made the hour-long journey back to North London. From Finchley station, hardly able to walk upright, with the red rose gripped between my teeth, I helped her drag two heavy suitcases a few blocks to our hotel.

Chumleigh Lodge was a small, immaculately clean boarding house with about ten rooms. Our nicely furnished room was at the back on the ground floor. This private hotel was run like a well-oiled machine by an elderly couple who soon became rather concerned about their new guests. Once inside I collapsed on the bed, not to leave that room again for several days. To remain calm I took a sedative every hour, keeping myself in a drunken-type stupor throughout the day. Whenever I woke, Hannelore, who mostly sat reading or writing at the table, came over to hold my hand. She wanted to get medical help but only became more confused when I showed her my hospital card. I had an appointment in a month's time. 'They've told me there's nothing more they can do,' I insisted. Hannelore went out to buy food a couple of times. Apart from that, for the next week we only saw the outside world through the large window overlooking the busy car park. Strangers in their cars would come and go but in our room time stood still. My mother and brother couldn't or wouldn't help me any further and now, apart from Hannelore, I was on my own. The beating had left me a brain-dead zombie and of course, the drugs only worsened everything.

Hannelore's money was running out and soon I realised that unless we were to live together on the park benches she'd be forced to return to Germany. We didn't have long left together and both knew it. Towards the end of the first week Hannelore left me for a few hours, returning with an open-dated rail ticket to Germany. 'I must go home,' she stated firmly, 'but first I'll get you into a hospital.' Her words sounded to me like the final goodbye.

Unable to accept the inevitable I took one more mega dose of amphetamine to get the strength to beg, borrow or steal enough money to buy time to repair my broken head. I just had to keep her with me !

As the amphetamine high arrived I managed to pull myself up off the bed. Going into drug overdrive I announced we were going to Central London to get the money I once hid there. 'Look,' I cried, showing her documents from my missing millions bag, 'I know there's money somewhere.' Hannelore just tagged along totally bewildered, too confused to know what was going on. First we visited the block of flats at Marble Arch where I'd lived in my hey-days. We couldn't get in but standing outside in the street I began remembering more of the past and the cash I'd hidden. All day I dragged Hannelore along to various places looking for money but, alas, we found nothing.

Now there was not a penny left even to eat with. We wandered the streets for hours. Late that night we arrived amongst the neon lights of the sleazy clubs looking for Moses, the Jamaican who'd been my minder years before. With only one paid night left at the hotel I had to find someone like him or we no longer had a bed to sleep in. I cried in the street as we unsuccessfully called at one dive after another, eventually to be told that Moses was in prison. By now it was morning and exhausted we took the early train back to our hotel. On the journey Hannelore whispered in a dejected voice that she would stay for the one last night but then return to Germany.

Back at the hotel the other guests were just getting up as Hannelore, pale and tired, having been awake all night, collapsed on the bed. She soon fell asleep. The sun was shining through the large window and as she lay there I could picture her by the lake in Germany away from the evil clutches of drug island. She slept all day as I lay by her side spaced out on amphetamine.

During the early evening she woke up very distraught and cried, 'Why won't your family help us? Haven't you got anyone that cares enough?' She was very upset and getting nowhere went back to sleep. As I lay awake listening to her breathing, the pain in my head got worse as it came on in waves. Much later I got up to sit at the writing table. The hotel information under the glass read, 'All rooms must be vacated by 10 am.' I looked at the wall clock. It was 4 am in the morning.

I felt like I was on death row with six hours to live.

Now, more desperate than ever, I decided to do a smash and grab robbery. Taking more pills, I left the room to go looking for a jeweller's shop. Twenty minutes later, not exactly in the best of shapes, I threw a brick at a window in the high street nearby. I was so weak it wasn't a proper throw, more a drop, with me falling to the ground alongside my brick. I hadn't even cracked the glass and crawled away in tears to rest in a nearby bus shelter. Sitting there with my mind spinning out of control I suddenly remembered Violet, my old nanny who had lived only a mile or so away. She will help for sure ! I told myself, setting off for her flat. She probably would have, had she not been dead for many years. At 6 am I stumbled against her door. The new occupants were furious and threatened to call the police if I ever called again, saying I'd been there a couple of years before.

I eventually arrived back at the hotel where Hannelore was still asleep. Taking more amphetamine to consider my next move I came up with by far the most insane plan yet, highlighting the true horror of my amphetamine abuse. With no money whatsoever I decided to take Hannelore to Cork in Southern Ireland. The purpose of the trip? To recommit the robbery which had gone wrong with Gentleman George when I was fourteen years old.

I woke the sleeping girl with a pack of lies. I told her that everything was okay and I'd just phoned friends who were waiting for us in Ireland with boat tickets. 'They'll help find a hospital, too,' I cried. Hannelore had grave doubts about the story but her love for me made her want to believe it was all true. Two hours later, with us both in a terrible state, we boarded the train at Euston Station. On the journey towards the Irish Channel the amphetamine so entwined fact and fiction that I actually started to believe my story. Friends, waiting in Ireland? What fucking friends? My only friends over the last twenty-five years had been little yellow round ones with Dexedrine stamped on their backs.

With no tickets we were put off the train many times. On each occasion we merely sat around in another cold waiting room to get on the next passing train. The usual four-hour trip took all day and it was late that night when we arrived, hungry and tired, at Holyhead ferry terminal. It had been two days since we'd last eaten. Drugged beyond belief I half expected Gentleman George to welcome us as we walked up the ships gangway with all the other passengers. Alas my dreams of a new Irish life vanished abruptly as the ship's officer stated coldly, 'No tickets, no boat ride.' Inspite of my promises that friends were waiting in Cork with money he simply refused to let us on board, repeating, 'No tickets, no ride.'

Seeing the hopelessness of everything I began to lapse into a child-like insanity, screaming, 'They won't let us on the boat !' like a little boy would shout at his mother. Walking down the pier Hannelore quietly sobbed her heart out, now realising that the friends in Ireland story was never true and we were now in an even worse mess.

As we were standing there like two earthquake victims at the dockside a plain-clothes police inspector came up to us. He was quite friendly and asked us to accompany him to a nearby police station. I pleaded with him to talk with me alone. Asking Hannelore to wait on a seat outside he took me into his office. Inside I begged him to leave her out of it, explaining that she came from a respectable family in Germany. Quizzing me as to what we were both doing in Holyhead with no money I told him the whole sad story, omitting the part about the intended crime. He looked puzzled and asked me for my name and date of birth. After checking he came back, telling me there were three warrants out for my arrest. Nothing serious, just non-court appearances, but it was enough to arrest me and keep me in custody.

'Oh fuck no,' he said, 'I didn't need this one.' It was strange to feel his hand on my shoulder as he said, 'What a bloody mess. You two truly love each other. Get her to Dover and get yourself into a hospital - and stop taking those bloody drugs.' Stuffing five pounds in my pocket he smiled, 'Here, get something to eat and now fuck off out of here, I haven't seen you.'

The next train for London didn't leave till the following morning and with the station waiting room locked we began to roam the streets near the beach. Hannelore followed me round, forever begging me to sit down and rest. We came across a rowing boat and totally deranged I tried to pull it out into the sea, screaming, 'We'll row to Ireland. Get in !' Hannelore, cracking up herself now, began to call out for her mother, 'Mama, Mama, save me !' Thank God I was unable to even move the boat and with Hannelore refusing to help, my rowing boat departure was cancelled.

A while later I found an empty bottle which gave me the brilliant idea to send a message across the ocean. Opening the missing millions case I took out a document and stuffed it into the bottle. With the waves soaking my feet I threw the bottle into the sea, shouting, 'They'll know it's me and send help over for us !' Hannelore was now on her knees, praying out loud.

An hour later the station buffet opened. Hannelore was starving and became furious when she realised I'd lost the policeman's five pounds. It was probably in the bottle, floating out to sea along with our chance of breakfast. Demented and in tears I went back to the beach on my own to search for the bottle. A while later Hannelore found me and miraculously got us on the early morning train to London.

On the four hour journey back my behaviour got worse and I threw all my spare clothes out of the train window. Ticket inspectors came round but seeing the state I was in they got frightened, thinking - easier to let London deal with it - and left us alone. When we arrived at Euston the staff there almost helped us through the barrier, anything to save them getting involved in a tragedy.

By now we both were very upset and couldn't make up our minds where we would leave each other to say our final goodbye. Wanting to delay the inevitable we sat for ages on the benches outside the station. We didn't speak but eventually travelled to Victoria for Hannelore to catch the boat-train back to Germany.

The last train of the day had already gone and with the next one leaving the following morning we now desperately needed somewhere to sleep. In those days the British Airways terminal building was behind the station and in there we slumped onto a seat out of the cold night air. At first we were undisturbed and Hannelore rested her head on my lap. After a little while a security guard spoke with us, explaining we had to leave because he was locking the terminal. I pleaded with him and somehow he agreed to let Hannelore sleep there till morning, providing I left the building. I begged Hannelore to forgive me for bringing her to London and promised I would return at 6 am to say goodbye. 'I loved you. Here, you keep the millions,' I sobbed, giving her the battered attaché case. The security officer looked inside the bag, checking for a bomb. Satisfied he let the case stay and I staggered out.

Out in the street I thought of Alen. However much I'd hurt him, he would surely help. His home was only about three miles away but the streets now looked so strange. I'd walked those roads for years picking up cigarette butts and knew every crack in the pavement, but now with my vision impaired the buildings looked so much higher. It was like they reached the sky. I stumbled around for hours trying to find Alen but finished up completely lost, unable to even find my way back to Victoria. I couldn't walk on and crawled into a shop doorway to lay down. Sixteen years later I discovered that I was on the corner of Exhibition Road and Thurloe Street, only half a mile from Alen. Daylight was breaking and laying there I could feel myself about to pass out never to see Hannelore again.

Had I ever seen her?

Did she even exist?

Had it all been just a drunken skid row dream?

Suddenly I heard a voice. 'Come over here.' I stared and slowly recognised the Cigarette Queen, an old woman who had slept rough for many years in this place. Many taxi drivers knew her and regularly brought her packets of cigarettes or hot drinks in plastic cups.

In my Robin Hood help the poor days I, too, had stopped my car to give her money. She remembered me and when I myself became a tramp had always befriended me. A portly woman she wore many skirts on top of each other, like a character in a Dicken's novel. There was always cigarettes stuffed down her knickers. That night she gave me some brandy which seemed to help. As I lay next to her I heard the sad story that had led her to the streets. Working for Harrods as a young twenty-year-old virgin she began a love affair with her supervisor, a man of forty, with whom she had sex in the store room. He was the love of her life and she believed he loved her, too. She became pregnant. Thinking of marriage she decided to tell him the good news over their usual after work drink. As the store closed that afternoon a woman and two children arrived to surprise him. 'Daddy, daddy,' the children shouted as he picked them up. She watched in tears as he walked away with them. An abortion, heartbreak and drink followed, leading to a life of loneliness on the streets.

For a few moments she gazed into space then, suddenly, she stood up and standing over me said, 'Go back to your love, back to where you belong. I can see it. Only good will come, it's written for you in the scrolls.'

A taxi driver called with tea. 'Reg, this kids lost, take him to Victoria,' she said. He did without speaking. Even as I thanked him he remained silent.

At the terminal I could see Hannelore inside and tapped on the window. She came over and as we spoke through the glass the same guard allowed me in. I begged Hannelore to let me come to Dover to say goodbye there, promising I would not make a scene and get myself into a local hospital afterwards. Reluctantly she agreed. To at least stay awake till Dover I took the last of the amphetamine pills. Now there were no more uppers.

We hardly spoke on the train, just sat holding hands. Remembering the Cigarette Queens words of a new life I thought she meant with God, in Heaven. I closed my eyes, thinking, Hannelore will bury me somewhere. It was strange, but I was at peace.

My races had been run. I was ready.

Arriving at Dover I took a deep breath. Don't cry, not now, I thought. Men don't cry. They hold their heads high and wave the boat off into the horizon. I owed this to her and this was how I wanted her to remember me.

'Catch your dreams,' the Cigarette Queen had said but now my dream was leaving ! The boat was about to sail with the crew shouting, 'Quick, get on !'

Hannelore, holding her ticket, rushed up the gangway.

With one last breath I followed and pushed past the sailor, falling down on the deck of the boat.

'Where's your ticket ?' shouted the sailor taken by surprise. 'Here's one,' I said, snatching Hannelore's ticket out of her hand. 'The other's in here somewhere,' and with that I emptied Hannelore's suitcase all over the floor. 'It's in here somewhere,' I screamed, rummaging through her clothes to stall for time. By then it was too late, the hatch was up and with hundreds of passengers on board they were not about to stop the ferry sailing just to put off one non-payer !

Time proved that this boat trip saved my life.

On my own in Dover I would have died.

Hannelore gave them her German address after which the crew took no more notice of us. On seeing the coast of Belgium come into view I got frightened, expecting arrest, and took my missing millions bag on deck to empty it overboard. All those years of crime were put to rest at the bottom of the ocean.

As the ferry docked at Ostend, with only destiny holding us together, we walked off without being challenged. Neither of us had any conception of what would happen next or why I had come to Belgium in the first place. Hannelore hadn't contemplated taking this human wreck home to her parents. Shell-shocked she was now ready for an asylum herself.

Here I was at the end of a five day drug binge with no sleep.

Crippled by horrific injuries I had no place to go.

Hannelore said something to me but I couldn't hear her as I began to cry uncontrollably. Several people tried to help but nobody could stop me crying. I was beaten.

I had taken all life's self-inflicted blows on my path to nowhere.

I was hurting so bad, not just physically but emotionally.

Full of anger I kept shouting,

'Fuck those bastards, lousy cunts, every one of them !'

I had thrown my coat away and putting my freezing hands deep into my trouser pockets felt the last four pills - light switch barbiturates. This was my escape from life that hurt me so much ! Unable to swallow the tablets whole I chewed them as we climbed aboard a stationary train to get out of the bitter cold. Soon I felt the white clouds of sleep arrive over me like a tidal wave. Like a baby I curled up and passed out aboard a Russian bound express.

Chapter 36

LONG AND WINDING ROAD

The train was slowly pulling out of Ostend station on route to Siberia as I opened my eyes. Still groggy from the barbiturates I saw the outline of other passengers and heard them talking in a foreign language. Someone had tied the empty missing millions bag round me with string.

I jumped from the train like in a scene from a wartime movie and tumbling on my back finished up in the middle of the platform, unable to move. I'd hit my head again and my nose was bleeding. When I eventually sat up I found a note pinned to my chest which read, 'I loved you but had to go home.'

Hannelore had just completed a survival course that trained commandos would have failed. With practically no sleep or food for the last four days she was mentally and physically at the end of her endurance. In self-preservation she had been forced to jump off the helter-skelter in order to stay alive.

Travellers stepped over me in disbelief as I sat there, dirty, half paralysed and smothered in blood. Hannelore, my ticket back to humanity, had gone. I was alone again, but this time in a strange Belgian town with my head and heart smashed to pieces. As people hurried past me I could see seagulls flying above, looking like vultures waiting to eat me. Through one eye I could see the blurred outline of shops across a street. I tried to stand up but couldn't and instead, like a dog, crawled out of the station on all fours. It was snowing heavy and wading through the slush on my hands and knees with the attaché case tied to my waist, I looked something like a St. Bernard dog.

To escape the snow I sheltered in a shop doorway as a beer lorry was being unloaded in front of me. Where the strength came from only God knows but when the two men were out of sight I stole an entire crate of beer and dragged it round the corner. A few yards further down I found the entrance to a small underground car park. I slid down on top of the beer crate like on a toboggan. Down there I was at least out of the freezing snow. I broke the first few beers open and gulped them down. The alcohol fuelled the drugs in my system and inspite of my injuries I soon felt great. I was king again.

For the next two hours everything in that damp Belgian car park was just wonderful.

Some time later I passed out, waking up again just as dawn was breaking. Laying on my back, cold and stiff, I was unable to move at first, it was as if rigor mortis had already set in. Even moving my head caused everything to spin round, like I was being shaken upside down by a giant. I could do no more than lay there but breaking open the last of the beers I began to pour the contents into my empty stomach. Adding to my pitiful condition I cut my lip on a broken bottleneck, now swallowing blood and beer mixed. Slowly the alcohol fired me up and drunk I decided to follow Hannelore to Munich. Shortly after I was sitting in the warmth of a train on route to southern Germany, at least I hoped it was going that way.

The problem with travelling like this on German trains is that the ticket inspectors are far stricter than their English counterparts. No ticket, off you go ! Is the strictly obeyed rule. The only good thing was they waited for the train to stop before they threw me out each time. They don't listen to sob stories, especially in a foreign language. I was put off at every bloody stop and with the journey taking forever I got weaker and more dehydrated as time went on. At each station, too weak to go in search of food and drink, I just sat around to get on the next train south.

With typical German efficiency the railway police eventually rang ahead with warnings of a foreign gypsy making his way across the country on a freebie. My rail travel finished in Koblenz where I was confronted by a stern official in a big hat and long coat. 'You vill come vith me,' he said, leading me to a large green car. I was taken to the local police station and locked into a cell for about five hours,

There, as if by miracle, I found about ten marks in coins all neatly piled on top of each other. At last the door opened and an interrogation began which made the English police seem like kindergarten teachers. The police were furious and warned me of the severe punishment for cheating the national railway system. They made it sound like the death penalty. What they didn't want, however, was the aggravation of arresting me and all the lengthy paper work involved in returning me to the park benches of England. The boss man in his big hat now spoke, 'Go anyvhere you vant, by ship, car or plane but not, I repeat, not by train. Is zat clear or shall I repeat it?' He looked rather annoyed. I wanted to reply, 'Heil Hitler' but thought better of it. Instead I nodded and left quietly, walking out into the snow covered streets of Koblenz.

With the help of a passer-by I used the coins to phone Hannelore's home. Too upset to speak she put me on to her father who was by now aware of all the facts regarding his daughter's English nightmare. He spoke to me at length in German. I didn't understand a word of it but there was concern and compassion in his voice. He kept saying my name, as if wishing me well and forgiving me. I could picture him in his warm lounge with the piano playing and the lights of the Christmas tree. When my money ran out I left the phone box to find the winter snow falling heavier than ever.

I must not give up, I told myself and began to sing, 'Maybe it's because I'm a Londoner.' My singing seemed to spur me on as I trudged towards the autobahn. Petrified of the railway police and having no conception of the distance from Koblenz to Munich, over four hundred kilometres, I set off to hitch-hike there. On that cold night the few cars that went by probably never even me, because, covered in white, I looked like a human snowman. Realising that nobody would ever stop I decided to walk instead. Half dead, needing an urgent operation and on one of the worst drug withdrawals of all time, I was asking quite a lot of myself. About a kilometre down the motorway I fell over into a ditch and sunk beneath a snowdrift. I couldn't get out and lay there for ages on my back with snow falling on my face. Hell was supposed to be hot, I thought. Eventually I scrambled out of that ditch but lost one of my shoes in the process. I was so cold, my body was numb. Walking with just one shoe I got off the motorway and back into Koblenz. I had been in the snow for hours. I found myself once again back near the railway station where, as if I was being guided, I found a dry cellar. Inside I collapsed but it was impossible to sleep on the ground, the cold from the stone floor penetrated my entire body. I untied my missing millions case to use it as a pillow and prepared to die.

I began to cry and laugh at the same time as I spoke with God.

I wasn't stoned or drunk. I was remarkably calm and very sane now. I needed help and with the rest of Koblenz still asleep God was the only one awake to listen to me. 'Oh my God,' I cried. 'You and only you can help me now. Only you can give me the power to stop taking drugs !'

At last I had conceded defeat, admitting my horrendous addiction and how unmanageable it all had been since I was a child.

With everything in my life destroyed I was one very sick addict, praying for the first time to be rescued. I handed my will and destiny over to my maker and lay back, feeling an immense sense of relief as God came to me in that basement. He didn't come in with a flash of light surrounded by angels. He was just there alongside me, that's all.

One tired, battle-weary addict at the end of a twenty year nightmare, I forced myself to my knees and in the pitch black asked again and again for his help.

He did help.

I never took drugs again in my life.

Chapter 37

IN FROM THE COLD

I still had a long way to go if I was to stay alive. At the far end of the basement I found a large commercial dustbin and to escape the cold floor I climbed inside amongst the refuge. Falling asleep in there I had a vivid dream about Hannelore and her father. They were beckoning me through a large wooden door into a garden bright with sunshine.

Suddenly an earthquake woke me with a start. Everything was upside down and I was falling to the middle of the earth with all the rubbish. The bin with me inside was being emptied into a dustcart. I screamed and pushing my head out from under the rubbish only just escaped the closing teeth of the cruncher. The dustmen, more stunned than me, just stood there speechless with their mouths wide open.

'Just having a rest,' I said in English, tumbling out of the dustcart. I staggered to the nearby station where I saw a stationary train and climbed on board, hoping it was going the right way. Nobody will get me off this one, I promised myself, locking myself inside the small toilet. Soon I'd fallen asleep on the floor, completely blocking the door which prevented it from being opened. Periodically I woke up, hearing foreign voices shouting outside, but I just kept silent and continued my journey, praying we were going south. Many miles later I stood up and through a scratch in the painted-out window could see we were in Stuttgart - heading in the right direction. I counted a few more stations and then jumped off the train. I just kept stumbling along until I was in the safety of the street. It was very cold and with only one shoe I was in a terrible state but I kept moving, afraid the railway police would arrest me. As I walked further away I realised I was in Augsburg, the exact station I had wanted. God was guiding me.

Hannelore's village was still ten miles away and with no chance of travelling on the buses without money I had to walk there. Progress was slow and half walking, half crawling it took forever. Nobody came to help me. That's our society. We couldn't give a fuck.

A mile or so away I came to a toilet and with my shoeless foot very swollen it became a welcome shelter. I drank gallons of water from the tap and revitalised carried on my final walk to freedom. On route I passed a shopping centre and walked into a supermarket helping myself to a bottle of wine. Half the staff watched me stealing it but they were too afraid to come near me. To lose a bottle of cheap wine was far less hassle than challenging a deranged lunatic.

Outside I sat on a wall and drank it practically in one go. The wine gave me strength and I walked on crying loudly but with my head held high.

I was walking all over the road with cars having to swerve to miss me. As if by miracle one of those cars stopped and the driver got out. It was Christine, Hannelore's sister, returning from her college. She took what little was left of me to the family home. Standing in their garden I refused to go into the house, too ashamed of what I had put Hannelore through. When Hanne came out I held her and cried every tear I ever had.

Hannelore's mother, in a state of shock, telephoned her husband who came home from work immediately. Finding me still standing in his garden looking like death he put his arm round me and took me inside. There I was given hot soup and put to bed. If he had turned me away I would have died. I will always owe my life to this man. It had taken all those long and winding roads to get me to his Bavarian door, but that's how it was written in the scrolls.

God had brought me home at last.

I had been released from drug island.

Chapter 38

HAPPY EVER AFTER

Early the next morning a doctor examined me and I was taken immediately to Gro§hadern Hospital in Munich where I underwent an emergency operation a few hours later. The ten-hour micro surgery saved my life.

The surgeons removed broken pieces of skull and inserted a plate to hold my broken head together. My inner ear was smashed beyond repair and as a result I completely lost the hearing in it. During the long operation they managed to rejoin the facial nerve which, over the next five years, grew to about sixty percent of its original strength. It means today I smile with a crooked smile, but after such a crooked life any smile is a miracle. The vision in my eye remains impaired but has improved over the years. These injuries and subsequent operation prove that being discharged from the Whittington in the condition I was in was a total disgrace.

Hannelore made the two-hour journey each day to visit me. It was her love that was my main medicine. I was very weak and outside of that hospital had nothing.

But Hanne loved me and that was enough.

I had a reason to live.

Some considerable time later, when I was finally discharged, Hannelore found a small flat and worked to support us both. The next twelve months were the hardest of my entire life - not so much recovering from my injuries but learning to live in a normal world without drugs. Overcoming the psychological damage of my lifelong addiction was harder than anything I'd ever done. Meeting people was the worst, simply horrendous. The only time I felt safe was when I was alone with Hanne.

For the next few years I woke every night hearing Snoopy, my starving dog, crying and would wake Hannelore, asking, 'Will I be going back to the park benches?' She would reassure me saying, 'The monsters are gone. There's no more gutters in your life. This time you're going to make it.' With her arms round me I'd go back to sleep.

Many mornings, imagining I was back in the Salvation Army Mission, I woke up looking for the rows of old men.

Nobody, especially Hannelore's relatives, thought we'd make it together. As a recovering addict I was very hard to live with and for Hannelore, an independent young woman, it was a very trying time. My mind was still a long way from being normal and after about six months, in a fit of jealously, I smashed up our entire flat threatening to kill myself. The ambulance crew put me in a straight-jacket and I was taken off to a German lock-up asylum. Hanne was very distressed but when she visited me a few days later it was obvious I regretted what had happened. She forgave me, saying, 'At least you didn't take any drugs !

Please get better. I still love you and we will make a new start when you come out.'

A while later they released me and with firm promises not to smash up this one we moved into a new flat.

It was March now, fifteen months since the beating and during the day while Hanne was out working I went on long walks. I watched spring burst open with all its wonder. I had no responsibilities, no work, no worries. All I had to do was get up and live through each day but just doing this was one uphill struggle.

But struggle I did without drugs. I was getting better but inspite of my progress the insane thought of how easy life would become with those magical pills returned regularly. For a long time my life remained a constant battle and it was to take many more years before those crazy ideas went for good.

When Hannelore became pregnant we were both very pleased and shortly after got married in Augsburg. I was very proud. Sadly, six months into her pregnancy Hanne lost the child, a little girl who today would have been fifteen years old. We were devastated. After visiting Hannelore in hospital I sat alone on a park bench and cried and cried. For the first time ever I dealt with pain without drugs. I sat there for hours before I eventually got up to go home. As I did I noticed an old tramp asleep on the bench opposite - he was home.

Early the next year I took a job of sorts with an import-export firm in Munich. There were no wages, it was a profit sharing deal and considering my train fares it actually cost us money. But this didn't matter, it was helping to rebuild my fragile self-respect.

Through this job I was thrown back into the tiger's mouth when the boss asked me to go to London to negotiate with an English cigarette manufacturer to supply their brand directly to Turkey. Feeling very apprehensive I flew to England alone. The negotiations failed - but here I was in London with money in my pockets and Dr. Landos drug factory only a phone call away.

I was riddled with insecurity and still half believed the magical pills would take me from a bit player back to a main contender. I desperately craved for the crutches I'd known all my life and inspite of the ruination they'd caused they were like an old friend, hard to live without. It was all too much of a temptation and soon I found myself standing outside in Harley Street. Moments later, reasoning I'll take these pills carefully and Hanne need never know, I was cashing a prescription for three hundred tablets. Shaking with nerves I ran to a sandwich bar nearby. It was the same place I had gone to all those years ago after each doctor's visit to wash down the pills before returning to Snoopy and the rats.

In the cafe I sat in a trance, unsure of what to do and began to cry. The owner recognised me and asked what was wrong. It was late and the place was closing as he sat down to hear my story. When he had heard enough he said, 'Listen carefully son,' and went on to tell me about his own daughter Francesca who had died the previous year of a heroin overdose. As he spoke his wife began to sob behind the counter. With tears in his eyes he put his hands on my shoulders and said, 'Throw away your drugs and go back to your woman.' He gritted his teeth. 'Claw your way back to life inch by fucking inch, day by fucking day. Throw that evil shit away, it killed Francesca and very nearly killed you !'

What he said made me think and for the last time the penny dropped. I realised there was no easy way back and threw three hundred pills down the cafe toilet. As I left the man kissed me, smiled and said, 'Now fuck off and be happy !'

On the plane back to Munich I cried. I had finally rid myself of that evil bastard, Mr. Drug, who had imprisoned me for twenty-six years.

Thank God almighty, I was free at last !

Meeting me at the airport Hannelore asked, 'What's wrong? Have you been crying?' 'I had a bad fight in London,' I replied. 'Who with?' she said. 'Not a physical fight, another kind of fight,' I replied.

'Who won?' she asked. 'I'll tell you later,' I said and left it at that.

The following day down at the lakeside I picked a handful of daisies. Throwing them up in the air I shouted,

'Who won ?

Who fucking won ?

I did.'

Nine months later we returned to live in England, driving there in our small second-hand car. Catching the ferry at Ostend I got very emotional, remembering my last horrendous stay at that Belgian seaside port.

Back in London we found a small flat in Haverstock Hill and both got simple jobs. Like the cafe owner had said, I clawed my way back inch by inch, day by day. Fuck, it was so hard but I had someone special alongside me. With a love like that no mountain was too high.

After two years back in England I met my daughters Tessa and Antonia both now beautiful young women. They came down to London by train and I met them at Euston Station, of all places. Here were those precious children I had said goodbye to all those years ago. We were all a bit overcome and sat down for a while on the benches in front of the station. Opposite us was a tramp, sleeping off his hangover. 'Look at that poor bugger,' said Tessa, unaware of what had happened to her dad. 'You should always be grateful. That could have been you,' she continued.

Could? I thought was, for so long !

The tramp turned towards us and looking into his eyes I saw just a stranger, a lonely old man.

Today I see both girls regularly and we have become very close.

As time passed, thinking clearer, I looked for some of the buried money.

We found some, not exactly millions, but enough.

Through all my years in the gutter it had remained hidden, perhaps kept for a better day.

There were no more robberies or gangsters, there didn't need to be.

Like drugs, crime was history.

I became involved in numerous businesses and invested in property until UK prices slumped. We bought a luxury villa in Spain where we lived for a while. Once sitting by our swimming pool I thought back to Kenneth and the old men of Newcastle singing Hallelujah with God each afternoon.

It all seemed like a dream, but sadly it wasn't. Those were the days of my life.

Four years ago my mother died and as we buried her I threw a note into her grave which read, 'Goodbye mum, I'm glad you lived to see me off drugs and shared the joy of watching the boys grow up.'

I pray mums and dads of other suffering addicts can experience the same joy.

Life over the last sixteen years has not always been easy but I never took drugs. Somehow I coped. I still get very nervous at times, especially round railway stations or when I see tramps. It all becomes so real again.

Two years ago we sold our remaining properties in England. With our sons Oliver and Julian, now eleven and ten years old, we returned to live in a small village in Southern Germany near where Hannelore was born. She is back with her family where she always belonged before her fateful visit to London.

Now I lead a very quiet life and watch our boys play football for the village team every weekend. Standing there with our two dogs Micky and Molly I look a real Joe Regular, average kind of guy.

An ordinary, everyday guy is exactly what I've become and I'm happier like this than ever before.

Sometimes other parents ask me what I'm doing in Germany.

'Just writing a book,' I reply. 'What about?' they want to know.

Perhaps one day I will have the courage to tell them -

'The book is about a man who was cursed with a lifetime addiction to drugs.

A man who lost his mind.

And that man was me.'

Watching the village children go to school I pray that none of them are headed for the same roller-coaster hell-ride I took.

Sadly, in our instant karma world some kids are.

Thank you for reading my story.

EPILOGUE APRIL 2009

It is thirty years since Little Legs beat me half to death. From that horror I hope lessons are learned to help us understand young people today. What distinguishes addicts from the normal kids building successful lives? Getting caught for the major crimes I was involved in doesn't bother me. It's too long ago. The only person who wanted me dead died with bullets in his head. Only his ghost can get me now and I don't believe in ghosts. How much of the buried cash did I find? Was I involved in other major crimes since 1980? Does any of this matter? No!

What matters to me is that before I die we win the biggest war mankind ever fought. The war against drugs.

Drugs finance terrorism, corruption in major companies and police forces. It even influences the outcome of elections. Presidents and prime ministers are knowingly or unknowingly put in power on election campaigns funded by laundered drug money.

Street addicts kill for drugs. Teenage stabbings are now common news. Executive bankers defraud for drugs while government ministers turn a blind eye for drugs. High level boardroom and ministerial decisions are made under the influence of drugs or under blackmail threats from criminals laundering money. Drugs and the corruption they bring are eroding civilized society across the globe. Unless something radical is done, I predict that 20 years from now armed gangs, outnumbering the police, will roam the streets killing for a fix. Global warming won't destroy the world. Global addiction will first.

Introduce the death penalty for drug dealers. Whether caught selling hash worth £5 or £5 million pounds of cocaine the penalty should be death. Parents whose kids have died from overdoses won't argue with this.

In 1963 the Train Robbers who were caught got thirty years and other long sentences were handed out for robberies that followed. By the end of that decade criminals turned to drug dealing. It was more profitable with less chance of being caught. Drugs are sold like pyramid selling from the Mexican cartels to the main importers right down to small-time teenage street dealers.

If kids today saw that the hanging was enforced without exception for any dealer caught there would be no more drug dealers. If drug barons like the Mexican, El Chapo Guzman, worth now £1billioin are caught they're soon replaced. There's always a line of ruthless criminals ready and waiting to take the throne. But close the market-place with capital punishment and overnight a kilo of heroin or cocaine is worthless. Drug cartels will become history.

Alcohol is already a huge problem. Weekends resemble a battle zone as our young mix booze with drugs doing things they otherwise would not. Car crashes, fights, sometimes deaths fill both the hospitals and magistrate courts the following week. Unplanned pregnancies, dramatically interrupting the lives of teenage mothers, are the result of another wild night. This is not exaggeration. Ask your local police chief. The swinging sixties came back to haunt us. Morals have not just got worse! They've vanished.

Recently I converted to Islam and found an inner peace for the first time ever. Many associate Muslims with terrorism but nothing could be further than the truth. The people I pray with in the Regents Park Mosque are decent upright people. The Qur'an is not a religious history book. It's a guide to leading a decent worthwhile life. Muslim women's dress is toned down not over-advertising their body shapes. They still look beautiful but in a pure way. Islamic customs reduce temptation and family breakdown ending in divorce and confused children. During my Islamic Sunday School, I asked the Imam (our teacher) if Allah would approve of me robbing the bank of England's £73 billion gold stash in the vaults beneath Threadneedle St. "Definitely not!" was his sharp reply. What if I gave it all away to the starving in Zimbabwe? "Still no," he firmly replied.

I smiled that day walking back through Regents Park thinking of the research done to win a bet as to whether such a naughty thing could actually be done. It could! In 1925 Herbert Baker re-building the Bank of England found decay in parts of the original underground stonework. These areas were filled with soil, then sealed leaving small rooms under the main foundation. 'How yer gonna get into a fucking room under six foot of concrete foundation?'' laughed one of my fellow cockney diners, thinking he'd won the bet. "I know," laughed another retired gentleman now in his late seventies. "He's gonna ask if can excavate inside the gold vaults for bleedin fossils.'' When the drunken laughter stopped I continued to win the bet. In the early 18th century the sewer tunnels from the main sewerage between London Bridge Finsbury Circus had four sub sewers: two in Princes Street, one in Threadneedle St and the last in Lothbury. Off one is a tunnel leading to the empty soil-filled rooms.

Microtunneling technology developed by the Japanese in 1970 was not available to the Baker Street robbers digging team. Yes vast areas under the Old Lady gold vaults are accessible. The old men around me honoured their debt and paid for my meal. One toasted me. ''Arry the kid's right. It's fucking do-able. Fucking laptop gold bullion robbery.'' That old bastard still sees me as kid, I smiled, I'm 65 years old now and a granddad! Our annual reunion dinner was over and my old mates went back to their gardening. One's collecting stamps! Fuck why did we all have to get old?

With all the reminiscing excitement gone, I felt flat for a few days but then at the Kilburn Mosque I met another man who said when you die you alone meet God on his own: no jury, no majority vote. ''So the robbery's okay if I feed all the starving?'' I almost pleaded. Smiling he replied, ''Ask God when you meet him. Don't get caught and give all the money away. That will give you a better chance with Allah.'' He laughed leaving the Mosque.

I always believed everything's pre-destined. Islam believes our lives are written in Allah's scrolls before we were born. Everything we do down to the exact time we will die is already decided. Would I consider robbing any gold vault? My answer is twofold. Firstly it's illegal. Secondly £73 billion is a lot of money and would feed a lot of people. As I write and you read our own books are too early for publication. God's the author and only he knows how each story ends. Don't take drugs. Don't hurt anybody. And whatever you do, make sure you've got God's advance approval. God is the boss of bosses, the Godfather over all Godfathers. He really is the main man. God is the creator of each and every one of us and his decision is final.

Aged 13 about to take my
first amphetamine pill.

Aged 23 with Camilla.

Aged 43 with my sons
Oliver and Julian.

Aged 63 happy to still be
alive.